ADVANCE PRAISE FOR *IF YOU WANT THE RAINBOW, WELCOME THE RAIN*

"Perhaps at the deepest core of all true healing is the experience of grace that tells us, 'You are not alone.' AnnE O'Neil's deeply honest, deeply courageous, and deeply human sharing of her own journey offers an experience of loving companionship to those on their own journey from loss and grief to renewed life and joy, and to anyone who seeks to support others on that path."

—Rev. Diane Berke, Founder & Spiritual Director
One Spirit Learning Alliance/One Spirit Interfaith Seminary

"Ann O'Neil is a healer of the first order and in this moving and engaging memoir she shares what she has learned about how to move from grief—and *through* grief—to joy. Her honesty is compelling and her journey offers many lessons. I could not stop reading this book."

Sally Helgesen, author, *The Female Advantage, The Female Vision*

"Osho said 'Courage is a love affair with the unknown.'" This book is courageous, human, insightful, and truly inspiring, as is Ms. O'Neil. It will help many readers immensely."

Kimberly Hughes, Psychotherapist / Healer /
Spiritual Counselor, www.sacredselfliving.net

"A memoir of heartbreaking losses frozen in time by addiction. With admirable honesty, O'Neil recounts her journey from family dysfunction and alcoholism to a life of spiritual exploration and understanding. O'Neil offers some wonderful insights on ways to move through grief."

Susan Richards, author of *The New York Times* best seller,
Chosen By A Horse.

IF YOU WANT THE RAINBOW, WELCOME THE RAIN

A Memoir of Grief and Recovery

Jacqui —
May life always bring abundant
rainbows — and just enough rain.
Thanks for being a beautiful rainbow
AnnE O'Neil   in my life.

Blessings galore,

BALBOA
PRESS

A DIVISION OF HAY HOUSE

Balboa Press books may be ordered through booksellers or by contacting:

Balboa Press
A Division of Hay House
1663 Liberty Drive
Bloomington, IN 47403
www.balboapress.com
1-(877) 407-4847

Because of the dynamic nature of the Internet, any web addresses or links contained in
this book may have changed since publication and may no longer be valid. The views
expressed in this work are solely those of the author and do not necessarily reflect the
views of the publisher, and the publisher hereby disclaims any responsibility for them.

The author of this book does not dispense medical advice or prescribe the use of any
technique as a form of treatment for physical, emotional, or medical problems without the
advice of a physician, either directly or indirectly. The intent of the author is only to offer
information of a general nature to help you in your quest for emotional and spiritual well-
being. In the event you use any of the information in this book for yourself, which is your
constitutional right, the author and the publisher assume no responsibility for your actions.

Any people depicted in stock imagery provided by Thinkstock are models,
and such images are being used for illustrative purposes only.
Certain stock imagery © Thinkstock.

ISBN: 978-1-4525-7470-7 (sc)
ISBN: 978-1-4525-7471-4 (e)

Printed in the United States of America.

Balboa Press rev. date: 6/18/2013

Dedications / Acknowledgements

My heart.
The water.
Hear the steady pulse of each.
Feel their pounding, the turbulence, the rush—

Waxing and waning into a gentle flow, a rambling.
See the glint of the sun on each drop of water and
Know it is the soul of each person
who has ever touched my heart.

- AnnE O'Neil

Borrowing from the poem I wrote years ago, I would like to dedicate this book to "each person who has ever touched my heart." That of course means it is primarily dedicated to my beloved late husband, Brendan DiBuono. Thank you for everything—for helping me to become who I am today, for making this book possible in so many ways, for making my life possible in so many ways.

It also means this book is dedicated to every person mentioned or referred to in the upcoming pages: my family, Brendan's family, my friends, my teachers, my clients, my fellow students in Seminary and healing classes, the Inspired! community, the thousands of people I have sat with in the rooms of recovery, the many I have met in my spiritual journey...I love you all and thank you for how you contributed to my healing, because you all have.

I would also like to thank all the people who walked the journey of writing this book with me, the writing teachers and editors who provided insight and expertise as this story took shape. I could not have done it without you.

You will all always live in my heart.

CHAPTER 1

I knew I had found a hiding place where I wouldn't be found. My thin 6-year-old body was well hidden by the corn, standing almost twice as tall as I was. Wiping the sweat from my white blonde bangs, I settled into my safe place. The heavy humidity and circling flies threatened to push me out into the world, but I was not about to let that happen. Standing way back in the cornfield (or at least, what felt like it was way back in the cornfield), I finally could taste the moment when I was going to be able to touch home base and yell "free" without being caught. Shortly after I heard the seeker shout "ready or not," I heard other yells from our game of hide-and-seek. One of my older brothers yelled "safe" as he tagged the back porch. Way at the other end of the large backyard that flowed into the cornfields, I heard the seeker yell "gotcha" when he had found a hider. Could I make it? I wondered. It was an open run to home base and my rival seemed far, far away. Yes, perhaps I was going to be safe at last.

The next yell I heard definitely did not fit in the game. It didn't fit anywhere in my life. I'd never heard anything like it. It was the scream of my Aunt Veronica on the side porch. "Robbie's dead," she howled, repeating the phrase a few times, "Robbie's dead," with sobs and wails in between.

An absolute stillness hung over the whole area, making the air even heavier. I couldn't breathe. It felt like the time I had the wind knocked out of me when I fell off the rope swing at the cottage.

Slowly, everyone gathered in the yard to join the rest of the family members, ranging in age from Grandma Karpen at 72 to my youngest cousin at 3. A few straggling hide-and-go-seekers who had been far away were the last to complete the circle, totally stunned as they neared the group.

Between the tears and shock the story came out. Robbie, my 4-year-old cousin and number one playmate, had drowned at their home on Lake Oakland in Michigan, less than one mile from our house. One of his older brothers had been watching him but had run in the house to get the phone, telling Robbie to stay out of the lake. When my older cousin returned just a few minutes later, he found his brother's little body face down in the water.

Even though we had just gotten out to South Dakota two days earlier for the weeklong summer vacation we took to visit Grandma every year, my parents decided we would pack up the white station wagon and matching storage trailer and go home in the morning. At least Grandma Karpen was coming with us; that made me happy.

I didn't really understand what was happening. I kind of knew what death was. My grandpa had died a few years earlier when I was 2, but I didn't really know him. I was told Robbie had gone to heaven, which meant very little to me. I had heard of heaven because we were being raised as devout Catholics complete with Sunday mass and parochial school, but I didn't know what it meant. "What do people do up there? Do they still look like themselves? Is it like our life down here? Will he still be hogging the sandbox toys?" All these questions filled my mind.

But I knew I couldn't ask anything. Mom only cared about her sister and how sad she was. There was no room for me—my feelings or my confusion. As we walked into the funeral parlor for the wake, Mom kneeled down to speak to me. Her words were ones I carried with me for decades to come. She whispered, "This is really hard for your Auntie Loris so I want you to be especially good today." I got the message. I was not to cry, I was not to say anything. I was to sit like a good little girl in my fanciest dress and black patent leather shoes. I was to go up to the casket with my mother and kneel in front of the small body of my cousin in his little blue suit and tie, and I was to be the perfect little doll—contained and controlled.

At the graveyard, I watched as the wooden box my friend had been closed into was lowered into the ground. I remembered the big fight Robbie and I had over the toys in the sandbox and wondered if that was why he died. That thought made me very fidgety, so my mom gave me a stern look and grabbed my hand. I bit my lip to remind myself of the rules: Don't cry. Be quiet. Behave.

My life changed that day. For one thing, these rules became a huge part of how I lived my life. At a more mundane level, I took swimming lessons I probably never would have taken had he not drowned. The summer after he died all five of us O'Neil kids were at a community beach by 8:00 every Saturday morning. It was never discussed this had anything to do with Robbie, but Mom was adamant that my oldest brother and my sister would take lifesaving classes. The irony was that those classes were held in the same lake Robbie drowned in.

The most important change was that my playmate was gone. My counterpart in the Schmidt family—the cousins who were so close they were practically an extension of our own family—was no longer. Robbie had been their fifth child, just as I was in my family. My older three brothers and sister still had their Schmidt cousins—but not me. So at first I was happy to hear when Uncle Burt and Auntie Loris decided to take in a foster child about my age. I hoped it would make them happy—plus I didn't like having to stay with Mom and Dolores as all the other kids paired off to play. But the reality of my new playmate was not what I hoped. The first foster kid was a mean dark-haired boy with a crew cut. After he left, the Schmidts took in mischievous blonde twins Tim and Tam. They were all about my age. They all played with Robbie's toys and slept in Robbie's room. *But they weren't Robbie.* Couldn't anyone see that?

I wondered if I died if some other little girl would sit at my place at the dinner table.

Today I sometimes wonder if my feelings about death, about grieving, and about the connection between those of us on earth and those in the spirit world would have been radically different if I had been in the kitchen instead of the cornfield that hot August day that Robbie drowned. Over twenty years after his death, my sister shared with me a story about what was going on indoors as we were out playing. Since she was all of 11, she had joined the women inside who were making potato salad and slicing tomatoes and onions for the burgers.

A few minutes before the phone rang with the news about Robbie, Grandma Karpen had been standing at the kitchen sink, peeling potatoes, when suddenly she put down the paring knife and looked out the window, saying, "Check the children. Something's wrong."

This story still can bring tears to my eyes. It reminds me of the wisdom and spirit of my grandmother. It reminds me of the strength of our connection to those we love. It gives me comfort that the Spirit world is nearby and accessible to us. Not that I would have recognized any of this as a 6-year-old…but one never knows.

CHAPTER 2

Even before Robbie's death, the lessons of not feeling and not asking questions were already well underway in my family. It was something I learned very early on.

I can see myself as a toddler, still wobbly on my feet and sporting rolls upon rolls of chub on my arms and legs. Like many kids that age, Mom was what felt safe to me—so I stayed as close to her as I could. Usually this was OK, often even welcomed by her, since she was somewhat possessive of her baby, appropriately called "Baby Ann."

This one day she didn't want me around. She spent a lot of time in the bathroom. She even went into her bedroom to put on a new dress because she got blood on her first one. I didn't know where the blood came from because she didn't have a scratch or cut—but there was a lot of it. There was so much that Mom sent Peggy next door to the neighbors to get help. As soon as Mrs. Rapaski came in the back door and saw Mom, she headed for the phone mounted on the wall on the front porch. Her first call was to an ambulance. Her second was to Dad at work to tell him Mom was being taken to the hospital. Dad's work number was on a card tucked into the phone but no one ever called him there. If we needed to talk to him, we knew the phone would ring at 4:30 right when he was getting ready to leave his office, him doing the daily check-in as to whether we needed milk. It had to be bad for Mom to let Mrs. Rapaski make that call.

I remember my sister and me standing at the edge of the car-length gravel driveway holding hands as the paramedics loaded up Mom and took her away. Instead of the safety of my mother, who was now lying in the back of a loud, shrieking car unlike anything I'd ever seen before, my 7-year-old "big sister" was the one there to protect. But she couldn't; she was just a child herself. There was no explanation offered to us of what was happening to Mom. Where they were taking her, I didn't know. When she would be back, I didn't know. Why she was bleeding, no clue as to that either.

I also didn't understand why Aunt Helen showed up later that day. We never saw her during the week…and she never spent the night with us like she was doing now. By the time Dad got home that night, my sister and I were already tucked into the fold-out bed in the living room and my brothers were fast asleep on the front porch. Not being able to sleep, I listened to Dad and his sister saying that Mom had lost a baby, that she had been about fourteen weeks pregnant, unbeknownst to everyone—including her. Of course that meant nothing to me at the time. What baby? I never saw one. I'm not even sure that it registered in my kid brain for many years afterwards.

Only two things registered in my kid brain at that time. The most important one was that Mom was not around. She had been sick and bleeding and she was gone and I didn't know where. At that time, children were not allowed in hospitals to visit their parents, so several days went by before I saw my mother. Dad came home at night and told us he had seen her, but that was about it. That somehow had to be enough to placate the worry of this pudgy 2-year-old—but it wasn't. It just couldn't be.

CHAPTER 3

Fifth grade was the happiest year of my young life. Having finally settled into the public school after years of being shuffled back and forth between it and Catholic school, I looked forward to each and every day. My teachers truly enjoyed children, something I hadn't experienced at St. Michael's. I got to do a lot of fun stuff like pottery and basketball. I wore jeans to school most of the time, instead of skirts. The kids at Jayno were nicer, more fun and more approachable than those I knew at St. Michael's. I knew what it was to have friends, not just classmates.

The highlight of the year was my slumber party. I finally got to have one! A few weeks before school was out, eight of my best girlfriends walked home with me. I led the way in my very cool new purple hot pants with the orange flowered suspenders and matching orange shirt. That night we ordered pizza, then pulled out our sleeping bags in the family room—which was off-limits to everyone else in the family. We stayed up until midnight, giggling and watching TV, until finally my parents told me we had to go to sleep. I had never been happier than I was that day.

People around me were happy too. Dolores (aka Auntie Loris) was healing from Robbie's death, keeping busy with her kids' sports and sometimes helping Burt out at the store. Mom went back to refresher training for nursing and was now working at St. Joseph's Hospital two days a week. She too was more positive than I'd ever seen her and was enjoying having her own income and a life outside the confines of motherhood, which had been the defining force in her life for almost seventeen years.

By the time I started junior high two years later, this world had changed. A growing dark cloud had entered our home. Mom started having convulsions. At first these happened every few months, then became more frequent as time went on. These convulsions would sometimes land her in the hospital for a day or two; longer as they came more often. Fortunately, I only witnessed one of these episodes. In the middle of the night just three years after my blissful slumber party, I heard Dad's panicked yell "Anita, Anita" from their bedroom directly above mine. I ran up there to see what was going on. Mom's body was twitching furiously, foamy saliva was creeping out the sides of her mouth, her eyes were rolling backward, and her face was purple and blotchy. Dad quickly sent me out of the room to call the paramedics from the beige wall-mounted phone in the dining room. Once again, Mom was being loaded into an ambulance and whisked away without me understanding what was going on.

All this meant a lot of doctor appointments for Mom. There were many theories thrown out as to what her diagnosis might be—epilepsy and multiple sclerosis were thought to be the most likely—but these were eliminated through testing and new symptoms coming forth. Despite the doctors not knowing what was causing Mom's symptoms, she was put on a growing number of pills to address her growing number of symptoms—Valium and Prednisone were her two mainstays for years, with others being added to and taken off the list on a regular basis. Since she was increasingly confused, whether by the illness or the medication, she laid out her pills every week in a large pill box, with another soon added to handle the overflow. In my mind, I can still see her sitting at the kitchen table every Saturday afternoon surrounded by her pill jars, carefully filling the boxes with her medications.

Despite all this, Mom continued working whenever she could. When her illness or the resultant confusion got worse, she would take a leave of absence for a few months but return as quickly as she could. She was on one of those leaves of absence the summer that I was between ninth and tenth grades.

That summer Dad asked my older sister to come home from college to handle the house and take care of Mom. Peggy had already accepted a job at an amusement park a little over two hours from home, largely to get away from the growing stress in our family. However, being the dutiful daughter, she cancelled her plans. At the time, I never would have been considered able to handle such a job, especially since I had very successfully avoided cooking, cleaning, and all other household tasks. Instead, I spent the summer babysitting full-time for the adorable little 4-year-old girl down the street. Without realizing it, I too had my way of getting away from the family drama—and, for me, it worked. Even though I was home every night and weekend, my sister had to share with me this story as an illustration of how completely out of it Mom was that summer.

Mom had never been an immaculate housekeeper, but with her illness it got even worse. Often she started chores and then either get distracted or needed a nap and left whatever unfinished. As a result, clean laundry sat on the family room sofa, the vacuum cleaner would sit in the middle of the living room, and piles of magazines were scattered on the floor. Peggy's job was made all the more difficult by needing to clean up after Mom's "cleaning" but rarely did she face an objection from Mom when she started on a task. The only exception this particular summer was when it came to cleaning the kitchen floor. Every time Peggy would get out a bucket and detergent to get the grime off the white (now yellowing) linoleum floor, Mom would get really upset and almost cry, saying "I can do that. What do you think I am...a complete invalid?" To appease Mom, Peggy would then back down from her cleaning task. The task never got completed then because Mom was so emotionally upset she would put away the bucket and detergent, thinking the floor had already been cleaned. This went on for almost three months, with the kitchen floor getting filthier all the time. Come mid-August, shortly before Peggy was to go back to school, she came home from her morning shift cooking at a local diner to find Mom in the kitchen on her hands and knees scrubbing away. She was rambling about how disgusting the floor was, ranting about how it was allowed to get that way, appalled that she was on her third bucket of water already and it was still filthy. Peggy described it as though Mom had just come out of a three-month blackout.

I witnessed Mom in a blackout one very early spring Saturday afternoon while I was in eleventh grade. It remains one of the most fearful moments of my life.

Mom was working days at this time and had just gotten home, having car-pooled with Mrs. Noble across the street who was an OB/GYN nurse at the same hospital. Dad was out for his weekend 20-mile run as he was now running marathons, a huge change from the obese, heavy-drinking smoker he had been the first ten years of my life. I was scheduled to work at five that afternoon, having just recently started a part-time sales job in the women's department of Hughes & Hatcher's, a local clothing store. After giving Mom a quick greeting as she walked in, I headed for the bathroom to get ready for work. On my way back down the short staircase into the living room, I saw Mom on the floor. Initially I didn't think anything of it because she often napped on the floor. Then I noticed the heavy bronze lamp next to her had been knocked over. Her glasses also still sat on her face, but they were now askew. Dressed in my long slate blue robe with the white satin piping and with my wet hair wrapped in a towel, I nudged Mom to try to get her to come to. After a few seemingly endless moments, she weakly propped herself on her side. With a totally perplexed look on her face, she asked, "Who are you?" I stammered that I was "Ann, your daughter," but that answer was met with an equally befuddled look.

As soon as I registered what was happening, I flew out the front door and across the street to the Noble's house, knowing Mrs. Noble had also just gotten home from work and I had no idea when Dad would be back. Banging on their screen door, still in robe with towel wrapped around my head, Mrs. Noble peered from the kitchen.

"What's wrong?" she asked.

"It's Mom," I replied with a quiver in my voice. "She doesn't even know me."

Before I could finish that sentence, Sally was crossing the street to our house. I trailed behind, describing what I had seen and sharing the hypothesis that she must have had another one of her convulsions. Once again, as another adult tended to Mom, I was told to call the paramedics whose number by that time was kept tucked in the top of the phone for easy access.

Just minutes after the paramedics arrived, Dad got home and joined us in the living room, drenched in sweat and wearing his matching red and white nylon running outfit. The paramedics tended to Mom on the cream-colored carpet with the big floral bouquets as Mrs. Noble and I stood off to the side. It was clear Mom needed to go to the hospital, the very one she had worked in less than two hours earlier as an Intensive Care nurse. She was still wearing the uniform. Dad went upstairs to hop in the shower to rinse off his sweat and get changed as the paramedics loaded Mom in the ambulance. He then joined them in the back to accompany Mom on the twenty-minute trip. I was to go pick him up at the hospital later. I called in to work that I would not be in that afternoon as my mom was being admitted (again) to the hospital. By this time, I was the only child left at home so a lot of these tasks were falling my way at the tender age of 16. After getting dressed, finding something to eat, and calling to tell my Aunt Dolores that her sister was taken to the hospital, I got ready for my only high school visit to Mom while she was in St. Joe's.

Back around Jefferson, South Dakota, where I had heard the words "Robbie's dead," another cousin my age was also dying. My cousin, Kim, a twin who had been born severely retarded and with cerebral palsy, was diagnosed with leukemia at the age of 15. During our summer visits for two years, Kim was bald, emaciated, and subdued. Her twin sister, Kay, also retarded, alternated between being subdued like her sister, and more boisterous than ever.

Having grown up with them, I was severely challenged by their limitations. Since they were just a few months older than I, I was expected to play with them. Just as I was shunned by the older kids who wanted nothing to do with me (the little pest), I found myself shunning Kim and Kay. Norma, their mother, understood this, although I think it saddened her. My mother was not nearly as gracious in her understanding. I was expected to play with them and be their friend.

Kim's death got me out of this unwanted contract, so I was a little relieved. I know that sounds awful, but it was true. At that time, I so did not yet understand or acknowledge the value of each and every human life. It had been an inconvenience to have the reality of mental illness in my face when I so desperately wanted everything to be OK.

CHAPTER 4

I was so relieved and excited when I finally got to go away to college; I was intensely ready to be out of the house I had known as home all my life. I had had enough of Mom's illness; I wanted to escape the reality that had stared me in the face every day for the last seven years....*now*! I especially wanted to escape seeing Mom's face every day, ever more showing both the ravages of the disease and the increased confusion of how to live life. Never a person big on social protocol, Mom had always been known to do things like join a game of jump rope while on playground duty or sweetly hold a man friend's hand in the bleachers of a basketball game after his father's death. Now her mental state moved even further from the center as the disease took its effect, and even more so the medications. Her physical appearance also reflected this. Mom was once a beautiful woman who, while normally not anywhere close to high maintenance, could clean up rather well when she chose to. Now she was bone-thin, gaunt, bloated around her belly and knees, with purple blotches on her arms and legs. This look was accented by a bad perm, big glasses, and her ever-present dead front tooth. It hurts me to say she was a mother I was ashamed of.

Even though I now had some physical distance from Mom's illness, its effect on me was clear. Being away from home, I got a little more honest with myself—and myself *only*—as to what was going on within me. The cheesy adolescent poetry I had written for years, still filled with hope throughout high school, took a turn. In freshman year, on a windy, gray, bleak day, I wrote:

A Solitary Life

Outside the wind howls
And I think of life.
It's a lonely existence.

You meet people.
You even love people.
But it makes no difference.

You're still alone.
Still a single solitary soul
Mingling with others just to survive.

You might try to be different.
You might spend your life living with and loving others.
It makes no difference; you'll die alone.

That poem was written on a particularly dark, heavy day; there were many days in college when life was good, fun, interesting. Yet of all the many, many days at college I remember, there is only one that has had an unwavering impact on my life. It was another spring Saturday, this one during my senior year of college. I had just gotten back from a run when the phone rang in my single dorm room in Wonders Hall. As I picked up the phone, I realized it was my mom on the other end of the line, crying. When I asked her what was wrong, she answered, "They finally know what is wrong with me. I have lupus. I have about five years to live." She continued to sob a little while longer, over my questions of

"When did you find this out? How do they know? How do they know how long?", then promptly ended the conversation with an "I've got to go."

I didn't know what to do with this bombshell that had just been dropped on me. Numb, I sat on the single bed with the geometric rainbow bedspread. My mind just kept repeating the questions I had asked Mom over and over again. "How do they know it's lupus? How do they know how long she'll live?" As my brain spun out of control, I lay down—crying, confused. I called Mom back about five times, but the phone just rang and rang. I called my best friend, Serena, who had been my suitemate until just weeks before when she had graduated a term early. She was out. I called my sister, now also at Michigan State in grad school. Her phone also rang and rang. The loneliness was crushing. Finally, after most of the afternoon dragged by with me caught in a mental blankness, trying to get a little studying done but afraid to leave my room lest I would miss a call (pre-answering machine days), I got through to Mom again, who was completely dismissive of our last conversation. "Oh," she said, as I started to ask the questions again. "I was wrong. I spoke to my doctor again. I misunderstood. I do have lupus, but with medication they can control it. I'll be fine." While I think even then I knew what she was telling me wasn't true and didn't even make sense, I wanted it to be true so badly, I was willing to believe it.

Upon graduation, I moved home, went back to the summer job I had held the previous two years, and continued my hunt for the right advertising position that would launch my career—and, hopefully, provide me some sense of meaning and security. A tall task for a job, but I didn't know where else to find those things, or how to develop them for myself. My search focused almost exclusively on the Detroit area, home for most of my life. Largely this was a response to Mom's statement, said with more than a little self-pity, "Why do all my kids leave me?" Given what she was going through, as well as what Dad had to deal with as her caregiver, a big sense of obligation kept me rooted to the area. After painful, frustrating, depressing months, I landed a promising entry-level traffic coordinator job with D'Arcy MacManus Masius, one of the larger and more prestigious agencies around. I moved out of the house and into an apartment with a friend of mine just a few months later.

Shortly after that, my Aunt Alice succumbed to her lung cancer. A lifelong smoker, she had been battling the disease for almost a year. Near the end, I had visited her in the apartment she shared with her 38-year-old daughter, Colleen, who was also my godmother. Lying in a hospital bed in their living room, she frequently asked for the oxygen to be turned off so she could have a cigarette. I was disgusted and appalled, yet this was a death that most definitely affected me. It affected me much more than the death of my uncle a few years earlier; even more than the death of Kim, someone my very own age.

Alice's death shook me for many reasons. She was the mother of my godfather and godmother, both who had been very generous and kind to me throughout my life. I also felt for my dad who had had his kid brother die of a brain tumor just a few years earlier. This second loss of a sibling left him with a heaviness I had not seen in my father in years. Yet the biggest reason this death impacted me so was something much more personal. The thing that gnawed at me under my awareness was that it would probably not be too long before it was my mother who was being buried. It was increasingly appearing that the five-year prediction I had been told of while in college was probably not too far off after all.

CHAPTER 5

Despite my mom's illness, my parents travelled a lot, having the freedom to do so since Dad had retired from his second job by then. Most of their trips were throughout the US in the home-on-wheels RV Dad had bought. The summer after Alice's death, they ventured on a trans-Atlantic cruise to England. For Father's Day, I bought Dad a beautiful travel journal for this special trip. They left on the two-month voyage shortly thereafter.

Even though I had seen them upon their return, I was taken aback by how badly Mom was doing when I saw her in late October 1986. I had driven to the home of my oldest brother, Tim, and his wife, Sue, for a joint celebration for Mom and Tim, he having been born on her birthday. Mom was worse than I had ever seen her. She had been declining since they returned from their European vacation. I suspect she hadn't been as up for that big of a jaunt as they had hoped. Not that I think it mattered; worse case it might have expedited the inevitable ever so slightly.

As we sat in the family room eating cake and ice cream and looking out the window at the dying leaves in their shades of crimson and gold, as beautiful as they were, the conversation turned to Mom's health. It was Tim who brought it up.

"So when's Mom going to the doctor again?" he asked Dad.

"Thursday" was the reply.

"Do you think they'll put her in the hospital?" Tim inquired.

"I suspect. It does look like she needs some fluid drained," Dad responded, referring to her enormously bloated joints. Mom said nothing as she played with Travis, her precious 4-year-old grandson with the beautiful blue eyes and sweet grin.

I just took it all in as I alternated between eavesdropping on the conversation and joining Mom and Travis on the floor with the Legos.

As we were all getting ready to head out the door, Sue suggested we all have our picture taken together. She snapped the shot of Mom, Dad, Tim holding Travis, and me, none of us knowing that would be the last picture ever taken of Mom.

The following Thursday while at work, I found out the result of Mom's doctor's appointment. The entire Cadillac account group, to which I had very recently been promoted to account executive, had just descended en masse from the boardroom where we had been in a three-hour meeting with the clients. As I was entering my office with a list of fifteen things that needed to be followed up on, Dot Mason, one of the secretaries for the group, handed me a stack of pink message slips, also saying, "Your dad called. They are taking your mom into the hospital."

I kind of groaned. "We figured this was going to happen. I'll go see her after work before I go to class," I said as I took the slip from her. Even though Dot was my assistant, she couldn't fully hide her dismay at my flippant reaction. After all, she was only about ten years younger than my mother and had daughters with whom she was very close. What she didn't know was the full story on how typical Mom's hospital visits had become. What I didn't know was how atypical this visit was to be.

When I got to the hospital just shortly after five that afternoon, I found Mom's room on the usual floor. As I stepped inside, I noticed a nurse administering an IV. I assumed it was a pain medication, as Mom was writhing in pain while Dad worriedly looked on. Hoping my visit would calm her somewhat, Dad moved aside so I could step up to the metal bedrails holding her thrashing body in the bed. All Mom was saying repeatedly was, "Jesus, Mary, and Joseph," a phrase she had often used throughout life whenever she was overwhelmed and frustrated. This time it had a distinct pleading tone to it.

I grasped Mom's hand. "He's with you. Jesus is here with you," I said, ignoring the complete lack of faith in my own life. Having lost whatever connection to Spirit I seemed to have had as a child, I didn't necessarily believe what I was saying, nor did I necessarily not believe it. Personally, I didn't give it any thought at that time in my life. I was just trying to offer my mother some peace and some hope.

When the response, "I don't think He is" came out of the lips of my devout Catholic mother, I began to understand the level of her pain. She gripped my hand more tightly than I would have imagined possible and continued to twist and twist. It was as though she was trying to press the pain out of her body so each contortion was necessary as the pain spasms moved from joint to joint.

After several minutes, the undulating movements stopped and mostly peaceful sleep overtook her body as the medication kicked in. Her doctor came by for a conversation with Dad.

"We're thinking of transferring her to the ICU. She's in bad shape and needs more care than she'll get on this floor," he explained.

"If you think that's best," Dad said.

Shortly after the doctor left, Dad turned to me. "Don't you have class tonight?" he asked.

"I'll blow it off," I replied.

"You shouldn't do that. This is important to your future, you know," he replied, dismissing the importance of what was going on at that moment.

19

"It will be fine. I just had the midterm last week. I can get notes from a friend," I retorted.

Knowing it would take at least an hour before they were ready to make the actual transfer, Dad and I took turns going to the cafeteria to grab dinner so one of us would be at Mom's side in the event she woke up. She didn't. As darkness set in, they rolled her bed upstairs to the ICU, a ward where Mom had spent thousands of hours over several years as a nurse, but one where she had never been a patient until this moment. Quite a few of the staff still remembered her from those days and came by to connect. It was clear to everyone she was definitely ready for Intensive Care. The doctor confirmed this by telling us the next day would be critical. She might live a while longer if she got through that twenty-four hours, but he was not confident that was going to happen.

Shortly after they settled her in, I left for the evening for the fifteen-minute drive up Woodward Avenue to the adorable pre-war apartment I had moved into a year earlier, lined with windows and accented with dark mahogany wood in every room but the kitchen. Both these features gave me a sense of comfort, never more needed than now. I walked into the living room with the new blue sofa and the hand-me-down round living room table, the very table responsible for the two very faded scars on my face as I attempted to toddle past it in the early walking days. As I dropped onto the couch, numb, exhausted, confused, I realized it was only 8:30. On a normal Thursday evening, I would be sitting in managerial accounting as my classmates currently were. Instead I cracked open the cold Signature beer I had bought on my way home and turned on the TV to veg out. It never occurred to me to call a friend or any of my siblings.

The next morning, although I had decided I was going to spend the day at the hospital rather than my office, I got up at my usual 6:30. I knew it was likely to be a long, stressful day so I wanted to get in my morning aerobics class. I pulled into the gym parking lot, already emblazoned by the neon "Vic Tanny" sign, as the light of day was starting to break. I was just in time for the 7 a.m. class. Pulling off my sweats to reveal the bright blue tank leotard and black leggings, I assumed my usual place in the second row. As soon as the warm-up song started, I could breathe. As the songs increased in tempo, my breath deepened and the sweat started to drip. By the time we were into the into the peak song, "You Drop the Bomb on Me," I was entirely lost in the beat and the movement. It allowed me to give some release to the anxiety that otherwise percolated just under my skin, but could be admitted to no one. Absolutely no one.

After class, I headed straight down to the locker room, treating myself to a few extra moments in the steamy shower. Standing in front of my locker, I dried off, then donned the freshly cleaned rose-colored silk shirt and the perfectly fitting black Bill Blass wool pants I had selected for the day. (It is not what I would wear today for such a long, trying day.)

Since I had no idea how bad Mom was when I left work the previous day, I had not told anyone I wouldn't be in. Since the list of things to follow up on from the previous day's client meeting was long and in process, I stopped by the office en route to the hospital long enough to turn things over to my boss, Tim. Just as I was walking onto the floor a few minutes after nine, he came up to me, "Oh, there you are. Can you...?"

"I'm not staying," I replied. "They took my mom into intensive care last night. They're not sure she's going to last the day."

"Oh," he gasped. "OK. I'll get Keith to follow up on these things." Even with the worry about Mom, that statement annoyed the shit out of me. Keith was my fellow account executive and my rival. He had almost two years seniority on me, so he got all the plum assignments. With this round of work, I had just started to really delve into the bigger jobs. I hated that I was going to lose whatever authority I was starting to gain, but at that moment there was nothing I could do about it. I gave Tim a quick update and handed him the notes from my desk before heading to the other D'Arcy building to tell my closest work friends what was going on. After a five-minute chat with Peggy and Karen, I headed out the door—never having even sat down.

Fifteen minutes later my father gave me the same greeting as my boss had, "Oh, there you are" as I walked into the ICU visitors room. When I asked why he wasn't in Mom's room, he explained that she was in surgery having a tracheotomy put in—that she needed to be put on a respirator if she had any chance of lasting the day. I never asked Dad, that day or ever, why Mom was put on a respirator when her living will stated she didn't want any artificial means to keep her alive. I don't think I thought of it right then, but it's a question that has plagued me for the years since.

CHAPTER 6

T hat day began a long seven-and-a-half weeks. Dad and I sat in the ICU waiting room until that afternoon when Mom was back in her room after the tracheotomy. While sitting there, I asked Dad, "Did you talk to Peggy?" His reply was a simple "No".

My next inquiry was, "What about any of the boys?"

Again, he answered a simple "No", to which I replied, "Not even Tim?" Dad started getting a little defensive, and stated, "There's nothing to tell. We don't know what's going on and they all have their own lives to live. It makes no sense for them to worry or think about coming home now."

I argued back, "They have a right to know if their mother may be about to die. If they choose not to come home, that's their decision—but it's not yours to make for them by not even telling them what's going on." Continuing my very unusual diatribe against my father, I then added, "If you don't call them, I'm going to." That was enough to get Dad to deal each of their numbers, one by one, from the visitors' room pay phone, telling them how precarious Mom's situation was.

No day in my life has ticked by more slowly than that one. Twelve straight hours were spent mostly between Mom's room in ICU, where she now lay hooked up to a respirator, and the ICU visitors' waiting room ten steps away, with an occasional trip to

23

the cafeteria for sustenance. I had not spent twelve straight hours in a hospital since I was discharged as a newborn.

The day passed by with Mom mostly unconscious as they worked to find a medication routine that kept her comfortable. Her sister Dolores came to visit and stayed a few hours, trying to make sense of what was happening to her younger sister. My older brother Tim came by in the evening after getting off work. Other than that, it was Dad and me hanging out, occasional chats with her physician for updates, and waiting. The doctor stood by his statement that if she made it through the day, she'd have a chance but that he still wasn't sure she was going to make it through the day. My breath was almost as shallow as Mom's, now supplied by a respirator, as the day went on. But, as nighttime rolled around, it appeared the medications had started to stabilize her condition, and her body had adapted to the respirator. She was starting to release fluids that had built up, so the bloating was also subsiding. She looked to be in the clear for that moment.

As nighttime set in on that late October Friday evening, I left for home, relieved Mom had made it through the critical day but also knowing in my gut it still didn't mean she would live much longer. I thought about stopping for a drink at Bennigan's as I drove by, figuring that someone I knew would still be there since that was our office's usual after-work watering hole. Then I realized I would have to explain my day and what was going on—in my life, my head, my heart. I couldn't do that. I didn't even know myself, so I thought it best to retreat to the safety of home. I did.

Over the next several weeks, with one or two exceptions, I was at Mom's bedside every day. Most days it was after work so I could spend a couple of hours. On class nights, I had to sneak my visit in on my lunch break; fortunately the hospital was only ten minutes from my work. Between all this, I continued to work between forty and fifty hours a week, work out, attend and study for my two MBA classes (the hardest I'd had so far) and keep my social life going. All the activity kept me busy, busy, busy—and therefore kept me from having any real feelings about what was going on.

Yet there were a few particularly heartbreaking things I could not ignore. As the weeks ticked by, it was becoming increasingly clear to me why Mom had signed a living will. With the respirator, she couldn't speak or eat, and was receiving her nutrition through a feeding tube. Although she never communicated this, her eyes pleaded that she wanted to go, she wanted to be released from the trap of her illness-plagued body.

There was very little she did communicate during her entire time in Intensive Care. It took too much effort. Dad had bought her one of those brightly colored toddler boards with the alphabet on it for the times she wanted to spell out what she was trying to say. Usually, it sat on the window sill of the off-white 12' x 14' room, overlooking a four-story concrete parking lot. Mom only motioned for it once, as far as I know, as if she urgently wanted to convey something to us. It was at the end of my lunch hour, and I had just said to her, "Well, I guess I'd better get going. I'm going to grab a sandwich downstairs and go back to work." With the mention of sandwich, Mom's eyes got huge and hopeful. I said sympathetically and with a bit of a chuckle, "You want a sandwich, don't you?" To this, she nodded her head more vigorously than I had seen her do anything this entire hospital stay. She then started motioning with her hands that there was something more to that statement too. When it became clear Dad and I weren't going to figure out what it was, she pointed at the board. Shaking slightly, she took the board in her hands and started to point, "B"—"E"—"Another E?" I guessed. She nodded. I laughed. "A beer!" I exclaimed. "You want a sandwich and a beer!" to which she once again nodded vigorously. I kissed her forehead, grabbed her hand, and said, "Awww, Mom, you know you can't have a sandwich and a beer" and walked out the door with my eyes welling up. How I wish today I would have had to courage to do whatever it took to fulfill that simple—yet not—wish for her.

As October turned into November and November marched on, not much had changed. There was occasional talk of moving Mom from Intensive Care, a sign that progress was being made, but that discussion would fall by the wayside quickly as her condition slipped again. A few weeks into her hospital stay, all my siblings, led by my sister Peggy, decided it was time for a visit. Joe flew in from Florida where he was in the Air Force, Dennis came up from Louisiana where he was a deep-sea diver on oil rigs, and Peggy flew in from Boston where she was heading up accounting for a direct marketing firm. Tim also made the hour jaunt to be with the family every day our siblings were in town. A lot of time was spent in those few days by Mom's bedside, but my fondest memories were with us kids all hanging out in the cafeteria, sharing memories and laughing uncontrollably, even at the morose situation we all shared.

Growing up, we had spent a lot of time together but still didn't have the strong bond—that deep emotional connection—that siblings often enjoy. All five of us had kept up a bit of a wall. The boys' wall took the form of attention to their sports. Peggy's and mine was an emotional wall to steel ourselves against the cruel, hurtful "teasing" our brothers dished out. For at least those few days we had a common bond that transcended everything, even though we had not spent time together in nearly a decade.

The reunion of all the O'Neil kids came and went. Then Thanksgiving came and went. Dad and I were invited to Dolores's for the holiday. After a few hours with Mom early in the day, we headed over to Waterford for a turkey feast with the Schmidts, now another generation deep. Shortly after dinner, we headed back to the hospital; this time with Dolores to wish Mom a happy thanksgiving. As her condition was once again declining, I wondered if she would see Christmas.

The weekend after Thanksgiving, after Mom had been in Intensive Care for over a month, her 92-year-old mother decided she needed to brave the onset of winter and make the seven hundred mile journey from the sticks of Jefferson to the suburbs of Detroit to see her daughter for what was almost certainly going to be one last time. At that point, I had not seen Grandma Karpen for just over two years and was surprised to see that she had gotten even smaller. Grandma now stood, slightly stooped over, at barely five foot tall, looking frail for the first time ever. She shuffled down the hospital hall in her tan wool winter coat holding tightly to Dolores's arm.

The weekend Grandma visited was Mom's best in her entire stay. She was often animated and present, a different person than the woman who had been lying in that ICU bed for over the last month. I hoped this was indication of another turning point, yet one more shot at hope. That was not the case. It was merely the will of a 63-year-old woman wanting a connection with her mom—wanting the validation she felt had been withheld from her many times throughout her life. Whether this was true for Mom or not, I like to think that her sprightliness that weekend showed she accepted her mother's love and forgave her for the hurts she carried.

Time seemed to expand that weekend given how packed my days were. I spent more time than usual at the hospital so I could be with both Mom and Grandma. Sunday breakfast, Dad stayed at Mom's side while the rest of us engaged in a decades-long tradition associated with Grandma Karpen visits. Whether we were in her hometown or ours, our one restaurant meal was always Sunday breakfast. Grandma, an otherwise very thrifty woman, would be dressed in her Sunday best and treat the whole gang of us. For this meal, fifteen Schmidts and O'Neils gathered at the Howard

Johnson's just up the road from the hospital. It felt remarkably familiar, taking me back through lots of childhood memories, but also very strange since neither of my parents was there.

The evening before the family breakfast, I had a date, something I was not doing a lot of in those few months. Knowing I needed a treat with everything going on in my life, I had gotten tickets to see *Little Shop of Horrors* at the Birmingham Theatre. I mentioned this to my friend and classmate, Judy, who asked me who I was taking; I said I had not yet figured that out. Having started toying with the idea of fixing me up with her boss at IBM, H. Jefferson Rae (known as Jeff), she convinced me this would be an easy, low-pressure way to meet him. I agreed she could mention that I was looking for someone to join me for the play and give him my number. Early in that week, I received the call confirming that he would love to join me.

That Saturday evening, after a day at the hospital, I received a knock on my door. Dressed in a monochromatic off-white outfit—sweater dress, hose, and low pumps—I opened the door to find an equally well-dressed counterpart. Jeff had on a blue blazer, gray sweater vest and pants, white shirt and tie under his gray wool coat. His blue eyes twinkled as he held out his hand and gently smiled. "Hi. I'm Jeff Rae." He spoke with a pronounced remnant of a Texan accent. I welcomed him in, got my coat, and we headed off to dinner and the theatre. Jeff had made reservations at 220 Merrill Street, most definitely one of the finer restaurants in town; one I would normally only go to during business lunches or for drinks after work. We had a nice, easy conversation over dinner, despite the inclusion of the topic of dying parents. As I let him in on what was going on with Mom, Jeff shared with me that his father had died several years earlier. We hit it off quite well, accented by definite sexual chemistry as well. When he dropped me off at the end of the evening, despite the other circumstances of my life, I was floating.

Jeff was so what I was looking for in my life at that time. At 31, he was already enjoying a good deal of career success as a marketing manager with IBM in the Detroit office. He owned a beautiful older home in upscale Grosse Point Parke; rarely had I seen a home decorated more perfectly and maintained more immaculately. Granted he was divorced but it didn't seem to be an issue as I didn't have the sense of any resentments being harbored; they "just weren't meant for each other after all" was the explanation I had been given of the divorce. The picture was perfect.

Over the next week, I now fit Jeff into the mix of my life's activities. We spoke daily, with me informing him that Mom's uptick during Grandma's visit most definitely seemed temporary. With both of us having events we needed to attend that upcoming weekend, we decided to get together for brunch the following Sunday, December 14. Shortly after noon that early winter gray day, we hopped into his blue upscale sporty hatchback and headed south to Fox 'n Hounds, another of the area's finer dining establishments, for brunch. After enjoyable conversation, a scrumptious brunch, and a few mimosas, we were back in my apartment, settling onto the couch when the phone rang.

"Where have you been?" my father asked.

"I went out to brunch with a friend," I responded.

"Well, your mother's not doing well. Not doing well at all," Dad replied.

"How bad is she?" I asked, not really wanting to know. I wouldn't have wanted to know under any conditions, but I most definitely did not want a romantic afternoon interrupted.

"I'd get here as soon as you can," was the reply I got.

"OK," I said as we both hung up the phone, not even saying good-bye.

Having interpreted the conversation correctly, Jeff gave me a hug and said, "I guess you'd better get down there. Let me drive you." After very little dissension on my part, I agreed, even though it would leave me at the hospital without my car. It was something I was not going to worry about at this point. We once again headed for his car to travel south on Woodward Avenue. I was still dressed in the black silk shirt and raspberry pants that had been intended for my date, not to witness my mother's death.

As we drove, Jeff grasped my hand between shifts. He tried to comfort me, saying, "I understand exactly what you're going through. It will be hard but you will get through this. I am here, whatever you need." I sat hopeful this would be true, that someone could help me begin to make sense of all of this—of my mother's death, even of my own life.

As we reached the hospital, I joked to him, "I'll bet this is the most unusual second date you've ever had in your life." He chuckled, then gave me a hug and kiss as I got out the door to head upstairs to that all-too-familiar room.

By the time I got there, Dad was frantic, although he was trying to hide it. Watching my parents go through all the years of Mom's illness, especially the last few, made me question my lifelong assumption that my parents would have been better off divorced than to live in what had appeared to me to be a loveless marriage. Throughout my life, Mom had bad-mouthed Dad badly, even to us kids. I thought of the time in high school where I finally had stood up to her about this. As she and I sat on the front porch that day, she had eluded to me that Dad was less than a satisfactory lover. I tilted my head at her and said, "I don't want to hear this. He's my father—and I do love him." Tears welled up in her eyes and she said, with a quivering voice, "I know. I'm sorry. It's just—" and let the sentence drop. She did get remarkably better with keeping her comments to herself after that. Today, on the day her life was to come to an end, I wondered how she felt about the man with whom she had shared over half her life.

Even though Mom was not conscious when I walked into her room just after 3 p.m., her body twitched and shifted slightly, I assume trying to find some comfort. Her breathing, even through the respirator, was labored. Dad, understandably agitated and therefore speaking rapidly, walked me through the decline that had started the previous Monday, but increased significantly over the last twenty-four hours. Not thinking about the fact I had seen her just the day before and most of the days of that week, he outlined each and every day, almost as if he needed to convince himself that it was really happening, that she really was in the end stage of her life, and there was no longer any way to deny it. Dad ended his monologue by telling me he had gotten in touch with Tim, who was on his way, and Dolores, who was also on her way, although from Cincinnati where she and Burt had been visiting their oldest son, Mike, and his family. Now there was nothing to do but wait.

When Dad stepped out to go to the bathroom, I whispered in Mom's unresponsive ear that I had met someone that seemed very special and that I was hopeful about. She did not stir, at that statement or any other statement made that day. She just slipped deeper and deeper into a grayness that matched the grayness outside. Tim and Sue showed up a little over an hour later, having dropped their son, Travis, off with Sue's family. Sue was now quite large at seven months pregnant with a grandson Mom would never see. They assumed a place around Mom's bed to join us in the deathwatch. Shortly after five, Dolores and Burt arrived, Dolores worried they would not get there in time to say good-bye. They did, even though it was a good-bye to which Mom couldn't and didn't respond. For the next hour, we all just stood around Mom's bed, watching the respirator moving more and more slowly as whatever life remained escaped from Mom. Dad stood immediately to her left, next to the respirator he had had installed over seven weeks earlier, I was next to him, with Dolores on my left. Tim and Sue stood at the foot of the bed; Burt stood in front of the window on Mom's right, looking as though he would rather be anywhere in the world but there.

To me, each moment by moment shift was imperceptible, so I was surprised when, just after six that night, Dolores grabbed my arm and said, "Go get the nurse." Dutifully, I did as I was told and marched out to the nurse's station, and quietly explained that a nurse was needed. The nurse followed me back into the room as we witnessed that one last strained up and down of the respirator before it—and Mom—came to rest. I realized in that moment how much will was required to die over the power of a respirator. Also witnessing that last breath, the nurse whispered, "I'll get a doctor to pronounce" then she stepped out of the room.

Dolores turned to hug me just as Dad broke down, his body convulsing as he stood over Mom's body, not touching her but instead bathing her in his tears. My aunt then physically turned my body around and said, "Go hug your dad. Your dad needs you." I held him for a few moments as he quickly composed himself, wiping his tears and professing that he was fine. Tim shifted uncomfortably back and forth on his feet as Sue leaned against him trying to comfort him. Burt just looked onto the whole scene.

Less than one hour after Mom's last breath, we were headed out the front door of the hospital, Dad absentmindedly yet fondly holding the small bag of Mom's personal belongings. Normally a man who not only understood but relished in having complex plans, he was completely befuddled when I explained to him that a friend had dropped me off at the hospital, so he was going to have to drive me home. At home, I picked up my car and an overnight bag, pausing long enough to call Jeff to tell him that Mom had indeed passed on at 6:14 p.m., before heading out to dad's for the night.

Jeff sweetly said, "I am so sorry. Have you figured out when the funeral will be? I will be there for you."

I replied, "Mom was very clear that she wants no service and Dad intends to respect those wishes. There will not be one." His stunned silence was the first of many strong reactions I got to that statement—some of confusion, some of horror, and many just not knowing what to say.

CHAPTER 7

Other than the tears Dad shed by her bedside, I don't know of any other tears wept for Mom until my own came a week later. I am sure there were some, but without a service where people could gather, those tears were shed in private.

I don't know when or why Mom came to the decision she wanted no acknowledgement of her death. It never made sense to me, especially since church and Catholic ritual had been so important to Mom through most of her life. I did speculate about her choice in a memorial I finally wrote for Mom fifteen years after her death. I wrote with great sorrow, "I suspect she did not feel worthy of it." Whatever her rationale was, it was a wish Dad would honor fully—to the point of even getting upset when her sister, Norma, placed an obituary in a paper back in her hometown of Jefferson.

The morning after Mom died, Dad and I went to the funeral home near their apartment to identify her body before cremation. In a brief awkward conversation with the funeral director, Dad confirmed to him there would be no wake, no service, no mass. Dad would pick up the cremated remains once available; that was the only task required of the funeral home. Upon mention of her remains, I asked Dad what he planned to do with them, to which he just shrugged. Clearly he wasn't open to thinking about it or talking about it.

After our brief chat, we were shown to the back room, where Mom's body lay on a rough table-like structure, rigor mortis having set in, her skin almost purple. I experienced a very odd detachment to what I was viewing—the body of my deceased mother. Having only seen dead bodies that were appropriately primped and coiffed for wakes and funerals, I was surprised at the color of her skin, even mildly entertained that her nose was a more pronounced purple than the rest of her. I suppressed a half-chuckle, thinking about the jokes bantered about in our family about how big Mom's nose was. I wondered if that was forever how she would be remembered.

Dad and I spent less than five minutes identifying Mom's body. We then headed to Big Boy's for lunch, before returning to Dad's apartment. It was still early in the afternoon, and everything that needed to be done pertaining to Mom's death had been done. Dolores had called her sisters and brothers the night before. Dad had called Joe, Dennis, and Peggy before I got to his apartment that evening. They all confirmed they would be home in a little over a week for the holidays. Dad was planning to go visit Helen, his only remaining sister, a little later that day. I suggested to him that I go home to pick up clothes for a few days and stay with him. I was surprised by the intensity of his reaction.

"No!" he shouted. "I don't need anyone to be here. I'm fine."

Both startled and wounded by his angry response, I got a little choked up and found myself unable to say the words surfacing in my mind: "Maybe I do." Backing down, I got him to agree to come out my way for a few hours the next day. Then I left.

Having no ritual to honor Mom's passing was awkward. Since there was no service to come home for, all my siblings decided instead they would visit for Christmas ten days later. Outside the family, so many people—friends, coworkers, even clients—were asking about the services. When I told them there were none, I got a baffled "Oh, OK. How are you doing?" I doubt anyone was even surprised when I answered with a dismissive, "I'm fine. This has gone on for so long and at least now Mom is not in pain." I had no sense where she was, but at least I knew the pain she had known in her human life for so long was over.

Internally, I was confused. Very confused. I had just spent almost two months going daily to visit Mom in Intensive Care, the capstone of a fifteen-year illness, and all that was over. There were no more hospital trips. The check-ins with Dad became a lot less frequent and more stilted because there were no longer medical updates. All we had to talk about were feelings, and that was not a welcome topic.

I took a week off work as my boss told me I should in our phone conversation. He asked me if that was enough time; I was baffled as to how I could possibly fill the emptiness of even seven days, but of course I never said that. Classes were over, and my finals were waived for me because of Mom's death. I couldn't understand how work and school could acknowledge this as such a significant event in life, but my family—most notably my father, in support of Mom's wishes—did not. My closest friends kept tabs on me as I would allow, which wasn't much. My friend, Kris, whose mother had died while she was in college, called to check in frequently. The group of work friends with whom I shared a quarterly girl's night out and many lunches in between, probably managed to get into my heart the most with their cards and flowers, but, even to them, I kept repeating, "Really, I'm OK."

I managed to keep up a strong front for a few days, secretly enjoying the attention but reeling in confusion. With Christmas now less than ten days away, I decided one way I could fill time was to finish my Christmas cards. That Thursday evening, not even one hundred hours after Mom took her last breath, I sat down at my dining table, another hand-me-down from my parents' home, and got out the cards I had bought and started sorting them. Most of them were boxes of cards I had bought; one lone card stood out from the sets. It was the Christmas card I had bought for Mom the weekend Grandma was there—the weekend where there seemed to be hope, just one week before she died. It was one of those mushy Hallmark cards talking about how important a mother is, acknowledging how much a mother—my mother—affected my life. As I read the card, tears streamed forth with such force my whole body was shaking, snot was running out of my nose, and my breath was heaving.

I had no idea where to take all this. I couldn't take it to anyone in my family. I felt weird taking it to any of the friends I'd just been telling how fine I was. I finally decided to call Jeff. After all, as he drove me to the hospital the previous Sunday, he had said he'd be there for me whenever and however I needed him. As it was now 5:30, I figured I'd still be able to catch him at the office. I heard "Jeff Rae" in that cute accent, and the tears flowed again. I managed to sneak out the statement, "Hi. It's me. It's Ann." After spending a few moments regaining my composure, I explained what had happened with finding the Christmas card and what it brought forth. Jeff volunteered to come over that evening. He held me sweetly as I cried; we then made love for the first time that night.

Over the next few weeks, it was Jeff I turned to almost exclusively. Even when he went to Texas to visit his mother for Christmas, we spoke almost every day. This romance of grief lasted less than two months. We had some fabulous times, going to charity events and an elegant New Year's Eve dinner. It was a life I longed for but did not feel at all comfortable in. I'm not sure I could have felt comfortable then in any life, given how much emotion, confusion, and turmoil was being stuffed inside my body and psyche. All I knew was that, as much as I wanted a glamorous existence like the one Jeff lived, something about it most definitely didn't fit me.

Still the unprocessed grief and heartbreak I held over Mom's death was compounded when, shortly into January, Jeff told me he wanted to take a break from our relationship. "You're too needy," were the exact words he delivered. While that was entirely true, it was coming from a man who, just a month earlier on the day of my mom's death, had told me he'd be there "no matter what." Since he had been the only one I had turned to with my feelings about this huge loss in my life, once again I felt as though I was being told that it's not OK to feel. It's not OK to express my grief. I was being reminded once again of the lesson I had learned as that little girl in the black patent leather shoes at Robbie's funeral.

CHAPTER 8

I handled all of this exactly as I had been taught to deal with emotion. I ran. Only this time I literally ran. Eighteen months after Mom's death and one week after finishing my graduate degree, the U-Haul was loaded for Boston. I was going there with no job and knowing no one who lived there, leaving behind a very sweet—and very perplexed—boyfriend whom I had started dating several months earlier. I pieced together a life there for a year, then felt the pull of New York City. Justifying that it was the most logical career move, I landed a better job than I'd ever had and moved. A new decade—the 1990's—was just a few months away; I was hopeful for what the new decade, new city, and new job would bring.

Several months after living in NYC, on a night out with friends before leaving for Martha's Vineyard to celebrate my 29th birthday, I met a man. He was tall, charming, cute, professionally dressed—and drunk. It turned out his 29th birthday was just five days after mine; all that was enough for both of us to believe we had a future together. Within four months, I gave up my apartment and moved into his as a temporary transition to the apartment we would move into together. By Christmas we were engaged and planning a wedding for the following November, despite many warning signs this was not a healthy relationship.

One of those telltale signs was his response to the death of Grandma Karpen, a woman I loved and respected more than any other person on earth. She had been diagnosed with colon cancer right around the time I met Ed and was dead by the following January, just as we were beginning our plans for this big, elaborate wedding.

I was one of the few grandchildren that didn't go back for the funeral. Ed's logic was that we couldn't afford it; trying to keep peace in my relationship, I did not make the trip. I justified this in my mind by reminding myself I had seen her just over a year earlier in a Thanksgiving visit to her. Not attending her funeral is a decision I regret to this day as she was one of the most loving and blessed souls I have known. She had a remarkable talent for making everyone feel special, a gift I've seen in very few people.

As Grandma's estate was getting settled, my brothers and sister and I were told that what was to be Mom's inheritance was to be passed directly on to us. This took the form of approximately 1-1/2% of the family farm, which was quickly translated into just over $15,000 for each of us when my uncles, who worked the farm, decided to buy out the rest of the family. When Ed heard this, given that we had saved no money to pay for the big, elaborate, traditional wedding he wanted, his statement was "I guess it's a good thing your grandma died." I was heartbroken that the man I was to marry could have this take on the passing of my loving grandmother, especially since he himself had long been tortured by the death of his grandma on Thanksgiving years earlier.

That comment marked the beginning of the end of our relationship, although I didn't realize it at the time. The verbal abuse was growing worse and felt like it might be a precursor to physical abuse. After trying to have a conversation about the strained distance between us and getting shot down, I packed my bags and stayed with friends for about a month while we tried to talk things through. Finally, I accepted this relationship was one that was not meant to be. As I extricated myself from the life we had built together, I realized that not every loss that hurts comes through death. This pain was screwing with my life too. My focus at work was shaken. My confidence was shattered. It was becoming clear I did not know how to cope with life.

Just a few months after the death of my beloved grandma and while trying to find my footing after my broken engagement, I received another call that someone else I loved dearly had died a sudden death. My 45-year-old godmother, Colleen, was found dead at her home one morning after she hadn't shown up for work. I was told it was a heart attack. This time I did travel to attend the funeral, knowing how badly I felt that I had missed Grandma Karpen's and remembering how good Colleen had been to me over the years. It was also important for me to be present for Colleen's brother, Mike, who was my godfather. I suspected Colleen's death would be hard on him, not just because of the loss, but also because it left him with sole responsibility for their older sister, Patty, who was severely retarded and living in a home.

As we got to the funeral home, I was very surprised to see it was a closed casket funeral. Mike and our Aunt Helen supposedly had come to the conclusion it would be easier on Patty that way, which made sense to me. It did seem to help some as Patty was distraught and very anxious but she was not inconsolable. Colleen was buried next to her parents.

A few months after Colleen's death, Meg (my sister formerly known as Peggy), told me she thought Colleen's death may have been a suicide as opposed to the stated heart attack. The closed casket seemed very weird to her. She also reminded me that Colleen had been going through a tough time—her job wasn't going well and she was having problems in her relationship, a man we had never met and suspected was probably married. Besides that, Colleen had a tendency to drink way too much, as many in our family did.

For a long time I sat with the question of how Colleen died. I still don't know but when Mike did not answer some basic questions I had years later—like the date on which she passed—it began to feel to me like Meg may very well have been right. Another instance of not dealing with the truth or the pain of losing a loved one. Another "par for the course" with my family.

CHAPTER 9

I n my efforts to make sense of things, I began to seek out a simpler life. This shift included a move to Chicago where my sister lived. It would also allow me to be closer to Dad, who was settling back into the Detroit area after years of traveling, including a two-year stint in Villarica, Paraguay, as a Peace Corps volunteer.

Dad was willing to put down roots because, at the age of 69, he was in love and getting married. He was tying the knot to Pat, a woman he had known since elementary school. They had never been romantically involved until just over a year earlier when they started dating, but they had always had a strong pull to each other. Finally, over Labor Day weekend, they were to be wed at the chapel at Michigan State, my alma mater.

It was a lovely, casual wedding with only one glitch. As I turned around after walking up the steps of the altar to do a reading, I heard this audible gasp and the name "Anita." It was a good friend of my mother's, part of a couple who had been my parents' closest friends in their 20's and 30's. She had not seen me in decades and therefore was unaware of how dramatic my resemblance to my mother had grown to be. As jarring as it was for me to hear my mother's name uttered at the wedding of my father, I suspect it was more so for both him and Pat.

Dad and Pat headed off to Ireland for a long-dreamed of trip to start their life together. Both of them were active and healthy, so I was not surprised to see the photo of Dad kissing the Blarney Stone, despite the climb that required. My dad was a hearty soul—or so I thought.

After returning from their honeymoon then spending the holidays in Michigan with family, Dad and Pat had gone to Florida for the winter when Dad started having digestive problems. I first heard about this in February—with the dismissive statement that it was probably a bug of sorts. Next time we really heard about it was in early March, when things progressed rapidly over a one-week time period. I had gotten a call on Monday that Dad was in the hospital. Tuesday's news was they thought it might be cancer and that a biopsy was scheduled for Friday. Wednesday and Thursday brought the news that the doctors fully expected to find cancer. When I spoke with Dad that Thursday, I reminded him that Friday, the day of his biopsy, was March 17, St. Patrick's Day. My 100% Irish father looked like a leprechaun with formerly-red, now-white wavy hair, twinkly blue eyes, and a sweet, mischievous Irish grin. Grasping for hope, I reminded him he clearly had the luck of the Irish on his side. This gave him some momentary comfort, so much so that he insisted on wearing his lucky cap that morning before the surgery.

Unfortunately, that did not prove to be the case. While he was in surgery, I was at my part-time job at a Chicago hotel reservation service, absentmindedly taking reservations and just watching the clock for what, once again, felt like an eternity. The blessing that day was that I was working with my dear friend Irene, a very spiritual woman. Even though I did not then share Irene's faith or her path, her peace mitigated the rather spastic manner of Polly, the owner. It was a perspective I always appreciated around that office, but I was in definite need of that day.

Around 3:30 p.m. I finally got a call from my sister. The news was not good. They had taken seven biopsies from his liver, pancreas, kidney, and colon; six of them were riddled with cancer. I broke down in tears at the front reception desk of the office. Meg and I decided we would both leave work to meet up. Agreeing upon her favorite form of comfort, we decided to meet at Baker's Square for their awesome pies. I knew that later that night I would be indulging in my favorite form of comfort as the Chicago bars were sure to be hopping on St. Patty's Day.

Over the next couple days there was a phone chain going on between Pat in Florida and the five of us kids spread out between Michigan, Chicago, Louisiana, and California. It was decided that Meg would travel down to Florida first to help out, I would take the next shift, and Joe and Tim would take the final shift to drive the trailer home as Dad and Pat flew home. When I got to Florida, I was shocked by how my dad looked. The last time I had seen him was just three months earlier at Christmas, when I had given them an "Our First Christmas" ornament as a gift. At that time, Dad was still running five miles a day, trying to prod me to join him, which I would have none of. (Dad had succeeded in prodding me into my one and only 10k race while I was in college, so he was trying to keep his track record going.) On that holiday trip, we had also had a lively game of hearts with me nagging Dad when it was his turn, "C'mon, Bill, we don't have all day." In jest, Dad replied that I should be showing more respect than using his first name. I countered with the statement, "OK, asshole, just play the card." We all got a major chuckle out of that one.

Obviously there would not be a lot of levity on this trip. It was just my second night there, tucked into the uncomfortable narrow bed in the guest bedroom of the trailer, when I heard the commotion of Dad charging to the toilet to get sick. Instinctively, I headed to their bedroom to help, not realizing that Dad slept in the nude. There I was, a 33-year-old woman, watching my naked 69-year-old father puke bile, food, and other stomach contents into the toilet bowl. I ran out of the room to wet down a washcloth to apply to Dad's forehead, grateful for the escape, as he pulled on a sweat suit then came out to the couch after that particular bout subsided. It was the first one I had seen on my short trip, but I was informed by both Dad and Pat that it had become a commonplace occurrence, which I would come to learn firsthand over the next weeks and months as well.

The most dramatic example of Dad's nausea came a few weeks later in the hospital upon their return to Michigan. Dad was immediately checked into St. Joseph's, the very hospital Mom had died in just over eight years earlier. He was discharged after a few days, but was back in again for Easter Sunday. Meg and I were at his bedside, having arrived a few days earlier for a visit. The nurse had brought in an Easter tray for Dad, with the question as to whether he was feeling up for it. He ventured into the plate heartily, followed by its return all over the tray in front of him just as heartily. It most definitely toned down my appetite for the holiday meal Meg and I were invited to at, of course, Dolores's. Spending holidays there while a parent was in St. Joseph's dying was becoming de rigeur.

One thing I will always hold in my memory from the trip to Florida is a conversation Dad and I had while lolling in the kiddie pool on one of his better days. He explained to me how his estate was structured. Even before he went into the Peace Corps, he had divided all his monetary assets into five Merrill Lynch accounts. These were all set up as joint accounts with right of survivorship, one with each of Dad's offspring. In his infinite wisdom and sense of fairness and justice, he had looked at all of the money he had given any of us kids over the years, and calculated what would be the exact equal distribution after all previous disbursements were considered. He also figured in the fact that my oldest brother Tim, recently divorced, would be buying his condo. Needless to say, this exercise reminded Dad how often he had come to my financial rescue, ergo how poor my money management skills were. He made me promise him that I wouldn't be broke in a year.

Dad did have some chemo and radiation treatments. The doctors were very clear and honest that his cancer was terminal and that he didn't have long, but they did think the treatments might be palliative and may even give him a bit more time. There was one thing Dad was holding on to see. My brother Dennis was about to graduate from medical school. After a career as a deep sea diver / welder, including a potentially fatal case of the bends, Dennis had started college seven years earlier, in his late 20's, to become a nurse. In those years, he had married, gotten into medical school after three years of college, and become a Dad three times, with his wife, Vicki, again pregnant—with twins as we were to later find out.

Dad was so proud of Dennis he paid for the flights of all us kids to go to the graduation, as well as Pat and himself. We had all been together at the same time only once since Mom died—on a vacation to Martha's Vineyard right before Dad left for the Peace Corps. At that time, we certainly didn't know when and why we'd be together again—and what we'd be facing when we were.

As Dennis's graduation neared, it became increasingly clear Dad would not—could not—make the trip. Finally, two days before our departure it was decided that his sister Helen and her son Bill would take Dad and Pat's tickets. He spent that weekend in the hospital.

Despite Dad's absence and the pall it cast over the festivities, it was a weekend of celebration. Many photos were taken, with Meg assembling them into a hilarious story that poked fun at each of our vices. Video was shot, with a sweet tribute by Dennis to Vicki about how he couldn't have done it without her, followed by her laughing that she was going to keep a copy of that in case he ever thought of divorcing her and running off with some young thing. A beautiful hot Southern May afternoon was spent in Dennis and Vicki's pool, with my youngest niece, Claire, spitting up all over my face as I held her above me, and my 2-year-old nephew, David, taking a head-under-water dive into the pool, with me quickly grabbing him. It was as carefree a time as possible given what was going on hundreds of miles away.

Back home in Michigan, Dad's visits to the hospital were becoming more frequent—and the stays were becoming longer. He spent some time at home after the stay that prevented him from being at Dennis's graduation, but was back in the hospital quickly. With Father's Day right around the corner, Dennis and Vicki decided to make the schlep north with the three kids in tow before their move to Texas for residency. It was entertaining to watch Dad, as weak as he was, issue a stern warning to David for whatever acting out he was doing in the hospital room. It worked; David got in line. Dad was given a nice, very informal tribute on this, his last Father's Day. Four of his five kids were there; Joe, being in the Air Force, had limited leave time.

Meg and I headed back to Chicago the day after Father's Day, suspecting it wouldn't be long before we'd be returning to Michigan again. Dad's illness certainly made me grateful that I was in a position, both geographically and in terms of my flexible schedule, to spend quite a bit of time with him in those final months. Being closer to him had been a small part of my rationale for moving to Chicago; I had had no idea how important it was going to be.

That spring felt different to me. I was more in tune with the world. I looked at the blooming trees with a strange melancholy, recognizing it was the last time Dad would see this sight. I kept up with both my jobs as well as the increased number of association marketing plans that came my way from the agency I was contracting with. I was most definitely more affected by

Dad's condition than I had been with Mom's years earlier, but I still answered questions as to how Dad was with a strange detachment. I did let myself have an occasional cry, something I don't ever remember doing during Mom's illness—and only rarely after her death.

It was a late Saturday afternoon, June 24, when I stopped by Meg's apartment overlooking Lake Michigan after I had taken a stroll along the beach. Her doorman, Tony, greeted me as I stepped into the elevator on my way up to her "box with a view" as she called her apartment. As I stepped in her apartment, I got an "I'm glad you're here. I just got off the phone with Pat, and Dad's bad, really bad. We've got a flight in the morning." I just stood there, taking it all in, for once infinitely grateful for my older sister's tendency to take charge. I didn't want to have to think about anything.

Meg and I arrived at the hospital just before noon, June 25. Dad was in and out of it. He acknowledged our presence but didn't say much more. As the day dragged on, Tim came by for a visit, and we all decided we should call Dennis and Joe with an update. Joe decided to catch a red eye flight to Detroit. Dennis, in the middle of a move to Temple, Texas where he would be doing his residency, knew he had said his good-byes the week before.

As night settled in, Meg, Pat, and I took turns getting some rest in the visiting room. Finally, Meg and I convinced Pat to go home to get some real rest, promising we'd call her if there was any turn whatsoever. Given they only lived fifteen minutes away and she was exhausted, Pat agreed. As Meg and I stood by Dad's bed in the dark of the night, with the hall lights outside blazing away, I told Dad, "Go towards the light." I wasn't even sure where that came from, except that I had heard that people who have had near death experiences confirmed there being a white light into which they passed. This caused a loud chuckle from Meg, who translated this visually into seeing Dad get out of his bed (which he was in no shape to do) and head for the lights of the hallway. I took great umbrage at Meg's chuckle. I had just offered Dad the freedom and permission to leave this world, only to have it ridiculed, as it seemed so many of my statements and actions had been all my life by my older siblings.

Meg chose to take the first rest shift, and I would stay in Dad's room, keeping vigil. Since he was mostly sleeping, I was quite surprised when, about ten minutes after midnight, Dad sat straight up in bed and asked what time it was. When I told him it was shortly after twelve, he laid back with a sigh of relief. Thinking about it, I realized what he was reacting to. His wife, Pat, had had both of her previous husbands and her father die on the 25th—different months, but the same day nonetheless. This had been a bittersweet joke between them. He knew he had escaped "being just another one" and adding to the heaviness that day already carried for Pat. He could rest, and sleep the night away.

Come early morning, Dad asked about what time Joe was supposed to get there. Ever since we had told him Joe was on his way, Dad had been hanging on to see his middle-born, with whom he definitely shared a bit of a bond. First of all, Joe (Joseph William) was the closest thing Dad (William Joseph) had to a namesake. They both, too, had taken the brunt of Mom's disapproval more than most. Plus they both knew how to drink. Dad was once again years off it, but he definitely understood my brother's predilection.

Tim picked Joe up from the airport early that morning, and headed straight to the hospital. Pat had already arrived by the time they got there. With the room overflowing with visitors, Meg and I decided to take a break and go to Pat and Dad's condo for a shower. We had been there not quite an hour when all of a sudden Meg started rushing me. "Hurry up. We've got to go." Almost ready, I rushed to put on my sandals, breaking them in the process. I was tying on my sneakers instead, as my anxious sister gazed on.

Meg's sense that we needed to rush was explained as soon as we got to Dad's room. The priest was giving Dad last rites; he had just been pronounced dead. After all our hours keeping vigil, we were not there for Dad's last breath, so imagine our surprise / fright when Dad's eyes popped open, his body lurched forward, and a huge gasp of air left his body. The nurse, who was in the room at that time, explained that this was a common occurrence. I've since come to believe that is the moment when the spirit leaves the body, as there was a most definite chill in the room while that was happening.

After about fifteen minutes went by, I suggested all us kids go on ahead to Pat's to allow her some time, which garnered a loud "No" from Meg. She thought I was saying we should all go our own separate ways, which elicited a strong negative reaction. Apparently, I was not the only one bothered by the lack of family unity around Mom's death. Finally, she got what I was saying and we all left for Dad and Pat's apartment to join Tim's kids who were hanging out there. I'll never forget my shock and dismay when Tim walked in and very matter-of-factly said to his kids, 14, 11, and 5, "Grandpa's dead." They could react with nothing but an "oh." How else could you respond to a callous statement like that?

Plans started in earnest for a memorial mass at the nearby Catholic Church Dad and Pat had recently started attending. Dad had had his own separation from the church for a variety of reasons but had returned at Pat's nudging when they found a priest whom Dad could respect. Dad's test for the priest was asking his opinion of him and Pat moving in together a few months before their wedding. When the priest replied that it was the intent and commitment, not the formal sacrament, that mattered most, Dad signed on. The mass would be held at that church.

Initially when he was diagnosed, Dad had stated he wanted no service whatsoever, just as Mom. Aware of the damage done by Mom's lack of service, Meg and I worked hard to persuade him otherwise, with the backing of Pat as well. He finally agreed to a memorial mass, as long as it wasn't the traditional two or three days of wake before a burial, as his family had always observed. That was fine with me as I had always found wakes and long viewing periods to be uncomfortable. Dad also informed us of his desire to be cremated. That was something we could get behind.

Dad died on June 26; my birthday is June 29. When Meg and I arrived on the 25th, one of the few things Dad said was "I don't know if I can hang on four more days," without making any explanation as to what he meant by that. I responded with a "That's OK," a squeeze of his hand, and a kiss on his forehead. What I really wanted to say was "If you can't hang on five, then don't hang on four," although it may have been fitting had Dad transitioned out of this world on my birthday. Just a few years earlier, partially based on Dad always getting my birthday wrong, I had done the math and concluded I was probably a 35th birthday present for Dad, that in all likelihood I had been conceived on his birthday. There was a sweet irony to his leaving just before my 34th.

Dad's memorial was on the 30th, the day after I shared a birthday dinner with my siblings and Aunt Helen at the golf club near Tim's apartment. It was a beautiful, glorious, summer day. The sun was shining bright, the sky was blue with just a few wisps of cloud, and the temperature was definitely warm but not unbearable. The mass was lovely; traditional enough to appease Pat, yet nontraditional enough to appease Meg. The lunch afterwards was well-attended with people from relatives to old neighbors to old St. Michael's people to former co-workers of Dad, and even a few of my friends / former co-workers from

D'Arcy; I imagine even they were relieved this time there would actually be a service. Since none of my brothers or sister wanted to share a tribute to Dad, I, dressed in a long black tank sweater dress and black hat, spoke about him and all his accomplishments, his humor, his heart. We shared laughter over some of my father's running escapades. Sweet tears were shed when I talked about the service he had given in this world, both during the Peace Corps and earlier. My talk elicited many more memories and fond tributes to Dad in the hour or so that followed.

After the luncheon, my brothers and sister and I were off to dispose of Dad's ashes. Although I had never been told where Dad had taken Mom's ashes, Tim and Meg knew it was up in Lexington, Michigan on Lake Huron at a site he had worked on for the Army Corps of Engineers. It was a trip he often took Mom on, a place where she had found peace. He was now to join her in that peace. Pat opted to stay back with her daughter and family, but encouraged us to go ahead and distribute the ashes.

We took the one-and-a-half hour drive up in two cars, me with Tim in his muscle car, Joe, Dennis, and Meg in Meg's rental gold Ford Focus. Arriving simultaneously just before 4:00, we all headed down the L-shaped pier. Since it was late on a sunny Friday afternoon, quite a few people were hanging out on the pier and the beach around it, so we tried to find a discreet distribution point. About halfway down the lower half of the "L", there was a place with no one around and the rocks situated such that Tim and Dennis could climb almost down to the water to dump the ashes. They did so, unceremoniously, as none of us had any religious or even spiritual inclination at that time, at least not enough to share a prayer with our siblings. We did close the tribute with a simultaneous last look back as we were about to get off the pier, only to see for the first time "Stupid" with an arrow spray-painted on a rock directly across from where we had dumped Dad's ashes. We all cracked up, knowing that Dad was smiling down at us, appreciating the humor. We weren't sure whether Pat would also enjoy the irony, so it was years before I finally told her that story. Fortunately, she too got a chuckle out of it, mostly in appreciation of what would have been Dad's appreciation for it.

Upon my return to Chicago, I opened a posthumous birthday card from Dad and Pat, including Dad's signature and a short note scrawled to me. According to the postmark, it had been mailed the day Meg and I headed to Detroit. It was a strange feeling looking at that card, knowing that was the last thing my father would ever sign. I gently placed it on a table in my living room, but took it down after just a day. It was disconcerting.

It was an odd feeling having lost both my parents by this time. At least now I was living near my sister and had the comfort of reconnecting to my other siblings during Dad's illness, so I did not feel totally bereft of family, but close. Not only was I now part of the elder generation in my family, but my sister and I were not always in sync during our grieving. We were sweetly connected at a 4th of July picnic in Grant Park, when we were talking of Dad's patriotism and war service, but then not so much when, months down the road, Meg picked up the habit of singing "I'm getting nothing for Christmas, Mommy and Daddy are dead," changing the words from "Mommy and Daddy are mad." I understood she was using humor to deflect her pain, but it was not humor that I shared.

Dad's death offered me the opportunity to see that most of the world didn't handle death well either. My family had been so weird around Mom's death that it was impossible to see how others reacted. Now I could see that others were way out of their comfort zone too. My close friend Michelle, normally Miss Etiquette, dropped off the face of the earth, not acknowledging the news of my Dad's passing. My neighbor, Jamie, alternated between avoiding me and being very caring. Initially, I did not know what I would get at any time, then I finally realized I got the avoidance after particularly loud bouts of crying. It all helped me to understand that grief was confusing to a lot of people.

CHAPTER 10

There was definite evidence I was not effectively dealing with the pain in my life and in my psyche. I drank. I drank a lot.

In junior high I had snuck a couple of drinks out of my parents' liquor cabinet with my friend, Cathy, but it was nothing we did on a regular basis. The first time I got drunk was in the winter of my sophomore year in high school. A bunch of us from the debate club—including my friend Cathy from the earlier years—had gone tobogganing. It was a cold Michigan day with a fresh foot of snow on the ground, which had caused the cancellation of school that day. Despite the elements, eight of us—six girls and two guys—went outside to play at one of the local hills. Little did I know my life would change that very day.

Arriving at the park, we had agreed to gather in the parking lot before heading to the hill. There I discovered about half of the kids had brought flasks with different kinds of liquor. It was the leather flask containing sloe gin that won over my heart. I felt my body relax and open like it never had before as the sweet, syrupy liquid poured down my throat. I had drunk almost half of the pint flask before we finally ventured up the hill, me staggering, laughing, tumbling with a freedom I rarely had felt in my life.

Since most of my friends had already had drunken moments by this time, they were thoroughly entertained by my new discovery. They giggled at normally reserved me hamming it up as we pulled the sleds. Their eyes opened wide in surprise as my shy awkwardness around the boys fell away and I began fawning all over them. They also kept passing the flask to me to keep their entertainment fresh.

From that day on, I drank often throughout high school, pretty much every weekend as well as on a lot of other "special occasions." Fortunately and miraculously, there were no real incidences to speak of. No accidents or DUI's. No getting busted at school. Not even an impact on my magna cum laude grades. Still, by the time graduation rolled around, drinking had most definitely become a defining part of who I was. So much so that when, just three weeks after commencement ceremony, my friend Wanda threw a joint surprise birthday party for her boyfriend, Brent, and me, her joke gift to me was a baby bottle I was required to drink from, stating she thought it might slow down my ravenous drinking. Downstairs in her parents' finished basement, that bottle was refilled at least ten times that afternoon, as I chose beer and frosting over cake and ice cream. By the time the party was over, I called home to tell Mom I would be spending the night at Wanda's. What I didn't mention was that I was staggering, slurring, sick, and generally unable to function.

My high school drinking was largely fueled as an escape from Mom's illness and what was going on at home. Then it offered me fun, silliness, and the opportunity to really be a teenager; the complete opposite of the confused, isolated daughter playing nursemaid I was at home. So of course my drinking was voracious. I felt it was the only thing I could turn to for comfort. I had learned not to speak of sadness. I dared not let anyone know the confusion that was going on in my head and in my heart. Drinking was quickly becoming my best friend, my confidante, my solace.

Until the trouble started about a week before I was to leave for college. My drinking buddy, Cathy, decided to take me out to get me drunk before I left for Michigan State. She picked me up around seven that evening in her green Ford clunker and we headed for this club / bowling alley near the mall where we knew we could drink. Plus there was an added bonus for the ride there! She had bought these scrumptious chocolate candies, each filled with a shot of high-proof liqueur. By the time we got to the club, I was already feeling woozy from the effect of the eight or so candies I had eaten on the way. We then started pounding down mixed drinks, talking about our friendship over the years since 5th grade and what our new lives were going to bring. It was nonstop drinking and bullshitting until shortly after eleven, when we were cut off from any more drinks. So we decided it was time to hit the road and drive home. Unfortunately we had to stop along the way for Cathy to pull over so I could get sick. Not surprising, because I was drunker than I ever had been to that point, despite the practice I'd gotten over the previous two years. Who knows at what point on the drive home we caught the attention of the cops (she thinks it was when I got sick), but we were followed by the Waterford Police the whole way to my home, where they finally turned on the flashers and booked Cathy for drunk driving. For whatever reason, they were willing to let me go even though I had obviously been drinking underage.

As I stumbled in the front door of my home, I was torturing myself as to whether to wake my parents up and tell them what had happened or just go downstairs to my bedroom and the inevitable bed spins. I realized I had to own up to what had happened. Why I woke up Mom instead of Dad, I don't know. Granted, of the two of them, Mom did handle most things related to us kids—but in retrospect I probably would have gotten a lot more understanding from Dad. When I nudged Mom awake and told her what had happened, she looked at the Big Ben alarm clock next to her bed, now showing after midnight, and said scornfully, "We'll deal with it in the morning. Go to bed." I knew that was going to be trouble.

Shortly after seven the next morning, Mom was pounding on my bedroom door, matching the pounding going on in my head. My mouth was dry. My head ached. I was in no condition to face this—but I had to. I went up to the kitchen, where I told my mom what had happened, explaining that Cathy had just wanted to take me out before I went away to school. Wrapped in her white terrycloth robe, Mom gave me a look I had never seen before (one that had been reserved until now for my dad and my brother Joe), and said, "Well, I guess I'd better call her mom." After a brief conversation on the phone with Cathy's mom, she came back disgusted that her reaction had been "Great. Now I'm going to have to take a day off work to go bail her out." Mom then just went on with her day, maintaining a slightly milder version of that disgusted look for the next four days—although she would not speak to me or even look at me all that time. I pleaded and pleaded and pleaded for forgiveness; after all, I was to be moving away to school in less than a week. Finally, on the fourth day of her silence and the day before I was to go off to school, after another round of pleading on my part, my mom just looked me in the eye and said, "There's nothing you could possibly have done to hurt me more." Feeling like I had just been stabbed in the heart, tears started flowing down my face as I watched my mother turn and walk away. The topic was closed.

It was a quiet, tense day the next day as I moved into my dorm room on the seventh floor of Hubbard Hall at Michigan State. My mom was still angry, plus no doubt had other feelings going on about her baby moving away from home for the first time, but we had to make it look good. We had to make my new roommates, Holly and Jane, think we were the perfect all-American family. After all, we were well-practiced by then.

In many ways, my college drinking career reflected my high school drinking career. It was out of control from my first month there. I quickly became known as the girl on the dorm floor who would go to the bar any night of the week—regardless of whatever schoolwork I was supposed to be doing. I countered this with enough focus on my studies to be named to the dean's list every term but one in my four years at MSU. As much time was spent at fraternity parties as was spent in the library. My extracurricular activities included invitation-only academic competitions and free-for-all trash can parties. I desperately hid my internal pain and confusion and just as desperately built a polished exterior—a trim, well-dressed young woman who could pull off a know-it-all attitude without being too overbearing.

By the time senior year rolled around, I was on two fast tracks. I was one of the top students in Michigan State's advertising program—both in terms of grades and the experience I was acquiring. My alcohol consumption was also among the top in the school. Of my college drinking escapades—some funny, some treacherous, some heartbreaking, most routine—very few made it into my awareness as to how evident my drinking problem was, even years after I quit. This one did.

As we were revving up for the national advertising campaign competition I had won a place in, midterm exams also rolled around. It was winter term, and one of the midterms was crucial to me graduating on time. The professor's policy was that if a student didn't get at least a 2.5 on the midterm, he or she would fail the class. Between that test, the two other midterms I had that week, the paper that was due, and the mounting pressure of the campaign competition, my stress level was at an all-time high. Unfortunately, I had not known what the week's schedule was going to look like when I signed up months earlier to take the GMAT that week too, the entrance exam to get into grad school.

Fortunately, everything turned out fine. I did well on all my exams. The paper got turned in on time. I showed up for all the AAF meetings. The one thing that hadn't worked its way into my schedule was studying for the GMAT. So, my logic was that if I attempted to spend the Friday evening the night before the exam studying, all I would do was psyche myself out with what I didn't know. No, most definitely the smarter plan would be to go out that evening and relax, especially since my buddy Cameron and his housemates were having a party off campus. I would go there for a few hours, be home by midnight at the latest—maybe a little tipsy but definitely not drunk, and be in good shape for the exam the next day.

Not the way it happened. When I showed up at the Victorian house just two blocks off campus, now home to six college guys, the first thing I noticed was the trash can in the living room. SCORE! My favorite kind of party. Next thing I knew I was engrossed in a deep, intense conversation with Cam about his relationship with this tiny, ultra-preppy Texan sorority girl, the polar opposite to the charming but burned-out Cameron with the northeastern accent. Several hours passed quickly. My drink had been refilled—and consumed—at least a dozen times. By 1:30 in the morning, I realized I needed to be sitting in a 400-person auditorium in exactly six hours, ready to take the exam I was convinced was going to define my future. Oh shit!

Somehow I stumbled to my huge brown '76 Grandville, drove as many back roads as I could to avoid the cops, and managed to be tucked into my bed, spinning as it was, within the next half hour. When the alarm rang a mere four hours later, I pulled on a light green sweat suit (definitely not the height of fashion), brushed my teeth, threw on my glasses, which I rarely wore in those days, slipped into my boots, and slogged off into the cold darkness of campus on a winter morning, hoping beyond hope that no one would see me in such a condition.

The rest of the morning was a blur. I had a pounding headache. I needed water. My stomach was still doing flip-flops with all the grain alcohol I had consumed the night before. Totally unprepared, I had to borrow the requisite two freshly sharpened #2 pencils from one of the other test takers, no doubt someone who had been smart enough to stay in the night before. Still, miraculously, I did well enough on the exam to be admitted to the part-time evening program at The University of Michigan, one of the top business schools in the country. That allowed me to convince myself how clever it was of me to go out that night and not stress as to how I would do on the exam. Today I wonder what would have been possible had I actually studied.

A mere six weeks later, it was time for yet another "drunk to end all drunks." The ad campaign that we were so certain was absolutely the most brilliant entry in the national AAF competition, placed fourth. We were all devastated. The news was delivered on a blustery March day. There was only one solution. Those of us who hadn't travelled to the actual presentation decided we had to get together to examine every page of the plans book, every supporting thought as to why we were sure our campaign was so intelligent.

Intermingled in all our analysis was two things: the gossip and analysis of how the team itself had splintered and shots of Jose Cuervo chased by beer. At the end of the day, the winner was the Cuervo, so I uncharacteristically retired from an evening of partying before the last bell—already anebriated— and poured myself home to nurse my wounds. Yet the evening wasn't over as the phone rang every time I lay down. The first call was from my friend, Dorman, who serenaded me with "Jose Cuervo, you are a friend of mine" before his voice trailed off into nothingness. The next call I received just under a half hour later was from Bob, who wanted to know if I'd seen Dorman.

"I lost Dorman," he said, holding back a sob. I knew that stifled sob was more for the fact that we had lost, rather than that he had lost Dorman.

My blood alcohol count in summer was even higher than during the school year. For three summers, my job was as an usher at Pine Knob, an outdoor music theater. We busted everyone trying to bring alcohol into a concert, only to consume massive amounts ourselves in the parking lot after the show was over. It was there that I celebrated my 21st birthday on a humid over eighty degree night by working a Jimmy Buffett concert, with a party afterwards. To quench my thirst, I swilled two cold bottles of sweet bubbly cheap Asti Spumante in about a half-hour, followed by my own incessant rendition of Buffett's "Why Don't We Get Drunk and Screw." The night ended with a group of us staggering up one of the nearby ski slopes, deserted since it was summer. Halfway up the hill, I passed out and had to be carried back down. It was far from a glamorous beginning to my legal drinking years.

For several weeks towards the end of summer, when the after-hours parties were no longer welcomed in the parking lot by the venue's management, they shifted to my parents' home, who were usually on their road trips in the summer months. This became so status quo that the cops knew to drive by to see what was going on at the house. Cars were parked up and down the quarter-mile street I lived on, music blared in the front yard as an occasional line dance broke out, and my 8-year-old collie with the butchered bark that now took the form of a high-pitched yelp enthusiastically and loudly greeted all newcomers to the party. Often I would have a friend or two staying with me for weeks at a time, so the party turned into an all-day affair. After everyone left around one or two in the morning, we would crash for the night, get up in the morning to do something like "cabrewing" where we would take the remaining beers out in a boat for the day, only to stop drinking for an hour or two before getting cleaned up to go to work. So was spent three summers of my life.

I dismissed it all as normal college-age partying. Even at the party when I threw up in the waste bin right next to the keg, then decided it would be smart to refill my beer before standing back up fully, I thought I was OK. I thought I was in control. It was all "fun, fun, fun" on the outside, while the emptiness grew on the inside. My drunkenness kept me from caring about myself, from believing that I had any right to be treated well. If a guy I liked wanted to feel me up under the table no matter how many people were around, that was fine with me. Just as it was if I was led on, belittled, or used. That was all part of the territory of the life I was living.

I have been asked whether I drank to feel or not to feel. It's not that simple.

I drank for many reasons. I drank to escape that painful, lonely feeling that I didn't belong—anywhere. That no matter how I tried, I just didn't fit in. So I drank to connect—to forge a bond with another human being no matter how brief, how tenuous, how not based in reality it was.

I also drank because it was the only way I could keep up the show. With my drinking came bravado. I could live up to what the outside world expected of me...or at least look like I was. I could shut down (at least temporarily) that teeny, tiny, soft voice that kept reminding me this wasn't the real me, that I was a phony, that I was hurting people, that I was hurting my soul.

Since I drank to connect and fit in, the drinking around Mom's death was definitely drinking to not feel. After all, the people closest to me, my family, who were sharing the same experience, were basically saying, "Eyes straight ahead. Don't let this slow you down." So that drinking was to hide my shattered heart. It was to not let anyone know the pain and confusion I was experiencing.

By the time Dad died, I drank because that's what I did. It was a core part of how I lived my life—perhaps *the* core part. A former boss had nicknamed me a "maudlin drunk" by then, showing how common the bouts of over-the-top tears and drama were. That didn't mean I was truly feeling my feelings, but at least they were not entirely stuffed inside.

In sharing with a friend how unexpressed grief fed my drinking, he correctly noted not everyone who has ever squelched their feelings around grief drank it away. That is very true. I am an alcoholic. That is the difference.

Alcoholism is a genetic condition and, I believe, a hereditary one as well. Non-alcoholics may get some relaxation from a drink, but they do not feel the total transformation of who they are that an alcoholic experiences with that first ingestion of their magical elixir. On that wintry day on the toboggan run with my friends, I was able to leave behind the "tall, smart, nice girl" that every note in my yearbooks cited until then. The next yearbook was filled with reminiscences about how wild and fun and crazy I was. If drinking could do that for me, it certainly could protect me from those pesky feelings.

I also drank because that's what I knew. It was what I had witnessed others doing my entire life. I had indeed inherited the family legacy. In my early life, Dad had spent years drinking excessively as his family grew and his career progressed and he got farther and farther away from any true passions. He turned to cases of beer to squelch the emptiness of his marriage and the frustration of being a middle management cog at General Motors.

While incessantly bitching about Dad's drinking (oddly even for years after he quit), Mom chose a milder route—just a couple beers while cooking dinner to numb out but rarely get falling down drunk. She insisted she "never had more than two", which prompted my brother Joe to start teasing her about whether that was her second second or her third second. It was an appropriate question. Plus her drinking was supplemented by the handful of prescription drugs she took daily, many of which were pretty powerful on their own.

I had been raised by two people who used alcohol to check out of life and here I was, doing the same thing. It was the only way I knew how to live.

CHAPTER 11

Graduating from college and beginning my professional career only meant more seeking outside of myself for happiness and approval. I most definitely had ambition, yet I also had this growing emptiness that I needed to fill. Drinking alone was not doing it. My frenzied drunks no longer provided me that relief—that "Ah", that glow—it first did. Yet I still chased that feeling I had experienced while tobogganing on the hill, warmed and emboldened by the sloe gin.

Two years into my career, I was moved onto the Pontiac account, the largest and most prestigious account at the agency. There I found a group of people who were as hard driving as I was, both in work and in play. The group account supervisor, the highest level with which we had day-to-day dealings, had the motto, "If you're going to party with the owls, you just better be up bright and early with the roosters as well." For the most part, I managed to do this. Even the night our media planner took me out to a party in chic Birmingham and I tried cocaine for the first time ever and ended up in bed with the party host, I knew I'd better be early to work in the morning. It was easy to do since I was wired from the coke. I only needed to go home long enough to shower and change before driving to the office.

That night two vices surfaced; one that was blessedly stunted that very night, the other that would follow me as a dark secret for years to come. The stunted one was the use of cocaine. I loved it so much I knew, by some miracle, I had to stay away from it—and I did. Since I was keeping up appearances rather well, my career was flourishing—and that I was not going to jeopardize. After all, my external success was my badge, my reason for being, and the proof that I was worthwhile. The increasingly out-of-control drinking, OK, lots of people did that, but I was not going to let drugs get the best of me. So far it had been limited to very occasional pot smoking and some speed in college. That was where it was going to stop.

The other secret that emerged that evening was where my drinking took me in terms of my relationships with men. Having never learned how to date and get to know someone, my relationships were short-lived. One took the form of a series of bootie calls, long before that term was in vogue, when what I desperately wanted was a relationship with that man. Another was a fling with a college student, a boy who was not in a position to do anything to advance my place in life, so he was summarily dismissed. Underneath all of these truncated encounters was my terror that anyone would really know me, so either I ran or clung so tightly the man I was involved with would run. Sprinkled in between these relationships were a fair amount of one-night stands—most of which I hoped would grow into something more, some of which I didn't care.

How could I possibly know how to connect with someone else? It was not a skill I had learned or witnessed in my own family. I had also been told by my brothers how big, ugly, gross and unfeminine I was pretty much every day from sixth grade until they moved out of the house. One of them had gone so far as to tell me, "You are the only woman in the world that would have to file for bankruptcy if you went into the world's oldest profession." My mom's response to their nasty bantering was "They wouldn't pick on you if they didn't love you." In recent years, my brother Dennis and I have talked about how that phrase opened the door to abusive and neglectful relationships; it was a message that was inherently damaging.

Still I tried—desperately—to find the right man. I thought a relationship could both fill that void inside and prove to the world on the outside that I was acceptable, even lovable. Yet the need to not let anyone know how empty I was, how numb, how much I needed a drink to get through life, cut short the few relationships with sweet, cute, amazing, available men who were really into me.

I met the first of these men during a visit to Michigan State the spring after Mom died and Jeff had broken up with me. My friend, Chrissie, who I had worked summers with at the outdoor music theater, was in vet school and was planning a major blow-out party with her roommates after finals were over. It was just what I needed to heal from both Mom's death and the aborted relationship with Jeff.

It was a typical college party. The keg was the star of the party, sitting in the middle of the living room. Doors were wide open with a constant stream of people in and out in various states of inebriation. A group of us were just hanging out in the kitchen. That's where I caught Mike's eye, as I was perched on the kitchen counter, drinking many plastic cups filled with not-great beer. He came up to me with some funny statement, which turned into amusing banter for the rest of the evening. Unlike most of the men I was meeting around that time, he wasn't looking for an instant hook-up. At the end of the party, he went home, and I stayed behind to help Chrissie and her roommates do a cursory clean-up before we all crashed.

I saw Mike several times over the next couple months. I went up to Michigan State on a day he had to work and got a tour of the large animal facility and just hung out. It was fun, easy, comfortable, and playful. One beautiful evening, he called on the spur of the moment to say he was making the ninety-minute drive down with a picnic to take me to his favorite lake. I remember having the conscious thought, "This is great—but what happens when he really knows who I am?" as we started to delve into our history and our emotions more deeply. Shortly after that, I had my friends Kris and Pat over for dinner, along with Mike, for an evening of board games, food, and drinking. My friends thought he was terrific. That night, Mike stayed and we made love for the first time—and it really was making love, unlike most of my sexual escapades of those days. I immediately began pulling back as there was no way I was capable of the level of intimacy we were headed toward. I started finding fault with everything.

Our relationship only lasted a few more weeks. He came down for a dinner and theatre night with one of the media reps I worked with at the agency. I was mortified that he showed up in a short-sleeve dress shirt, understandable since it was the summer. I was even more mortified when, during dinner, he started telling a fairly graphic story about a rectal exam he performed on a horse. Our hosts didn't seem at all fazed by this; I wanted to crawl under the table. Shortly thereafter, I broke up with him, using the excuse that I just wouldn't have time to be in a relationship as I was going back to school full-time and would still be working part-time at D'Arcy. The truth was that I had absolutely no idea how to be available to another person. Hell, I had no idea how to be available to myself.

Around this time, I had a very brief foray into therapy—about six visits with a counselor who was recommended by a friend. I justified it was probably "acceptable" at that point since Mom had been dead less than a year, but that still didn't mean I was willing to explore my feelings about that—or anything else. I was usually late to our lunch-time appointments or cancelled them altogether because something needed to be taken care of at work. This allowed me to convince myself I wasn't getting anything out of it and that I wasn't clicking with the therapist. Rather than working to find one I did connect with, I used it as the excuse to shut the door on that kind of introspection. Instead I entered into yet another relationship with a guy whose heart I broke.

Dave had been a coworker for a few years, who decided it was safe to express interest in me now that I was only working at the agency part-time. At a party thrown by a mutual friend, he and I had been chatting more than usual, mixed with some heavy flirtation. As we both swilled several glasses of wine (I had a few more than he did), he acknowledged being a "goner" every time he looked at my legs. I had always thought Dave was sweet and cute in a kind of geeky way, but had never considered him potential boyfriend material until then.

Why that was true, I don't know. He was a sweetheart. Even though we didn't know each other all that well at the time, he had gone out of his way to express his sympathy when Mom died. I also knew him to be a good listener and supportive whenever we would have any conversations of depth. The more I thought about these things, I started to see Dave in a different light.

His amazing encouragement continued as we started to date. The world was swinging into holiday celebration mode, including the extravagant office party thrown every year by the agency. That party was the one time of the year when the advertising business was every bit as glamorous as I hoped. There was champagne, filet mignon, and dancing, at the most beautiful and prestigious country club in the area.

About a week after the party, I started experiencing a dull pain on the left side of my face and neck and in my left ear. Although this was unlike anything I had ever encountered, between my new relationship, finals at school and my twenty hours a week at work besides that, I was far too busy to worry about it. At least not until these bumps started appearing, first on my chest then spreading up to my neck and lower face as well. The pink welts were extremely painful, and perfectly aligned on my left side, almost as if there were an invisible line down the middle of my body. Finally I could no longer ignore this unsightly—and painful—swelling, so I made an appointment with Dr. Silvani, who had been my mom's doctor. He examined the bumps and confirmed it was a nasty case of herpes zoster, better known as shingles, a condition most often reserved for senior citizens, not an otherwise-healthy 26-year-old woman.

Asking a few cursory questions as to what might be the cause of this, he dismissed it with, "It could be anything. Maybe a virus going around. I wouldn't worry about it." For me, it was yet another instance of someone in authority not seeing the damage we do to ourselves when we don't grieve. Had he taken a more holistic perspective, he perhaps would have inquired as to how / if I had worked through Mom's death the previous year. But where I was in life, I was more than happy to hear that everything was fine. The doctor suggested I take aspirin to alleviate the pain and let him know if I needed anything stronger than that if it didn't get better.

Beyond that, I scarcely gave it another thought in terms of how to take care of myself. I was grateful for the additional space the holidays brought into my life with time off from school and work, but even that I filled with constant activity, including many holiday parties. I especially would not miss the big soiree some of my friends had invited me to, a black-tie affair at the Detroit Museum of Art. That evening, I donned my glamorous strapless long black velvet gown, spending as much time applying a heavy concealer to my neck and chest as I did on the rest of my make-up application. After all, I needed that glitz and glamour to help make everything be OK. I could not let the grief literally bubbling up through my skin win.

Nor, it turns out, could I be faithful in a relationship, especially when I was drinking, which was pretty much every social occasion. As sweet and wonderful as Dave was, I found myself still too guarded to truly open up to another person. I kept him at arm's length by cheating on him, lying to him about it, while also talking to him about our future—where to live, how to make the transition. Somewhere in my being I knew I wasn't going to be any more available to him than I had been to Mike.

I may have managed to hide from Dave who I really was, but not from one of the guys I was cheating on him with. Now enrolled in Michigan's Business School on a full-time basis, I had a whole new crew of men to use as a prop for my life and props in my life. Here I was a 5'8" 26-year-old beautiful blonde with a figure even other women envied. The men stepped forward willingly—especially once they realized how I drank and how easy I was then.

Unbeknownst to me initially, two of those men were bitter archrivals as publishers of the two largest publications affiliated with the business school. When I found that out, I confronted one of them with the question as to whether he had pursued me to win the affections of his enemy's latest conquest. He denied this, then followed with the statement, "Wow, even saying that sure gives an indication of how little you think of yourself." I was furious, mortified, and busted. Apparently the façade wasn't holding up as well as it once did.

CHAPTER 12

That gave me yet another reason to run. As soon as school was over, I had unilaterally decided I was moving to Boston, leaving Dave behind, completely bewildered as to what happened. The move gave me a new sense of freedom. I was leaving behind my friends of many years who, two by two, were getting married, settling down, and buying houses. In those years I was becoming a professional bridesmaid, with a closet filled with taffeta and satin dresses to prove it. It was a lifestyle I disdained and wanted no part of. Instead I was now in a city where I could drink without having to worry about driving or answering to anyone who knew my patterns.

This landed me in a life that just escalated all of my vices. My one-night stands continued and increased and now included married men. My drinking caused an argument with my roommate. Now that I was doing a fair amount of business travel, I started drinking on the flights—something I previously avoided because I thought "Only alcoholics do that." I had drunken flings with coworkers and clients—often very publicly. No, life wasn't working in Boston either…

Rather than face it wasn't working because of my behavior, I focused on my career having stalled. At that time, there were very few automotive advertising opportunities in Boston. I was in one of those jobs, so when my boss left and they hired someone from the outside to fill her position, it became clear I was at a dead end there.

I rationalized it was time to move to New York with the stated excuse of getting my career back on track. To some degree it worked. Within a year there, I was a VP on the BMW account heading up all their regional advertising, with three men reporting to me. My job entailed traveling the country as the liaison between the BMW dealers, regional management, and the headquarters team. It was a glamorous, prestigious job that I did very well.

With my engagement to Ed, I had also stepped more deeply into a relationship than I ever had, even though I broke it off several months before the wedding. Instead I lied to myself that having had someone ask me to marry him proved that I was OK. My life was working just fine, thank you, and I had the badges to prove it.

But that wasn't true. The dichotomy of my life was never more apparent than it was at a very elegant soiree hosted by my client, BMW, in May 1991. The party was held the final evening of a weeklong dealer event in Scottsdale, Arizona. Hundreds of people were there including dealers, their general managers, BMW personnel ranging from the CEO to area managers and marketing managers, and the agency contingency. The week had been a success, so everyone was ready to let their hair down on the last night. After drinking from 6:00 p.m. to 1:00 a.m. and dancing in the eighty-five degree heat, two male coworkers and I decided a dip in the pool was in order—but we didn't want to walk the half-mile or so to change into our suits, so skinny-dipping it was. For the first five or ten minutes, it wasn't all that big of a deal. Matt and Woody got into a swim race, we splashed around a bit, and it was harmless fun. When those two decided to get out of the pool and wrap themselves in towels, I decided to head for the hot tub. Unfortunately, as I was sitting there completely bare naked, a line of fifteen or twenty clients, who had taken the time to go to their rooms and put on their suits, strolled out the lobby doors, around the pool, and headed straight for the hot tub. As one by one they got in, I initially convinced myself that the bubbles were strong enough that no one could see anything. One glimpse down proved that not to be the case—I was indeed exposing myself completely. Immediately, I asked Woody to hand me a towel, which I wrapped around me while still in the tub, then sheepishly snuck out of there.

That was the beginning of the end of my glamorous career. I was in that job for another year when my drinking and my shooting my mouth off about other job possibilities made it clear I needed to find another job before I got fired. I did just that—but found the next work situation to be worse. I believe dysfunctional is the best word to describe it.

In the year I was in the new job, my boss had two heart attacks, so he was out of work for several months. My counterpart on the other side of the account was a woman my age who had never worked at an agency before, but was apparently well-qualified due to the skimpy skirts and tight shirts she wore. She spent most of her time leading on our boss (when he was there), a situation that resulted in a sexual harassment lawsuit; he claimed they had had a consensual relationship, she denied any such involvement and accused him basically of stalking her.

I didn't exactly welcome this chaos and tumult in my life, but it served its purpose. I tried valiantly to get upper management to understand what was happening on the account….at least the part of it that I wanted them to see. I certainly didn't want anyone to know that my drinking had seeped its way into many a workday or to know of my own sexual escapades with coworkers. It didn't need to be spoken of that I had gotten very drunk at the client's annual conference in Vegas and slept with one of their married senior executives. I considered it no one's business that I spent the day after my going-away party, an absolutely gorgeous June

Saturday, so hung over that I cursed that the sun was so bright it was painful for me.

One of the agency executive vice presidents did understand how screwed up the situation was on our account and took me under his wing. He recommended me to a peer who owned and ran the marketing services agency his client used. This new job was not prestigious at all—but was a good title and more money.

That was the job where my drinking was really out of control. I thought of myself as a "lady who lunches" with two of my coworkers—which meant the three of us would be out for a two-hour two-bottle of wine lunch at least twice a week. Being such a small agency, at least my extracurricular activities with coworkers were curtailed, but my badmouthing the owners to my clients certainly was not. It was completely understandable they "asked" me to leave the agency by the time my annual review rolled around.

Now the losses in my life took a different form than death. My career, once bright and the defining force of my life, had fallen apart. I had gone from getting hired by the hot creative ad agencies to barely hanging on at small mom-and-pop marketing service firms. I had also moved many times within the city, desperately trying to keep up the front of success while financially keeping one foot out of bankruptcy. It was a life that was not working. It was a life that needed to change.

It was a life I tried to change. After my split from Ed, I committed to therapy. Iris, my therapist, was a pretty classic Freudian as I learned over the years. Once or twice a week for the proscribed fifty minutes, I sat in her office talking about my upbringing and what was going on in my life. Some days I got really honest and told her about my drunken one-night stands. Most days I kvetched about my life. Iris mostly sat silent and expressionless, occasionally offering comments such as "That must have hurt" and "You seem angry." These became such pat answers that I, along with two other friends that were also in therapy at the time, decided we were going to start an alternative band named "You seem angry" with "That must have hurt" as the back-up singers.

I also took to occasionally journaling, mostly recording my days with as positive and sunny a slant as I could muster. My favorite life improvement technique at the time was classic denial. When my life felt really out of control—when the wolves were at the door, whether the wolf was taking the form of an annoyed employer or persistent creditors or unavailable suitors—I would stay in for the evening, buy a better bottle of wine than I normally did for nights in, and set my goals for the upcoming weeks and months. Needless to say, those goals were never achieved—but there was nary a drop of wine left in the bottle by the end of the evening.

Not surprisingly, none of these strategies fixed the problem— and so I ran again, this time to Chicago.

I justified this move to myself in many ways. "It's a cheaper city. My sister's there who doesn't party. My other friends there live a pretty tame life too. I won't have the stress of a big advertising job. It will be closer to Dad, who is finally settling down in Detroit after his many years of running after Mom's death, including 2+ years in the Peace Corps in Paraguay." I definitely thought I'd be able to get my life under control in Chicago.

It turned out I was wrong. Having moved there in early October, college football season was in full gear. Thinking it would be nice to watch the MSU game that first weekend with other Spartans, I tracked down the alumni club and showed up at the bar where they were watching the game. Not knowing anyone there, I of course ordered a beer or two to help me feel more comfortable chatting and meeting new people. By halftime, I was doing lemon drop shots with my new best friends—and took one of them home (another married man) by the drunken end of the game.

I drank my way through that year I lived in Chicago too, with a few spectacularly out-of-control nights. At my next-door neighbor's Christmas party, I hooked up with one of her tennis buddies and left the party for the blues clubs. Closing time came and went, with me holding just vague shadowed memories of the evening. St. Paddy's Day, the night of Dad's cancer diagnosis, I went straight from meeting my sister to the Lincoln Park bars. That night I allowed myself to drink with a fervor that I had been trying to suppress since my move. I needed to kill the pain. I desperately needed to kill the pain—but it did not work.

My next thought was to run again—this time back to New York, which I did just a few months after Dad's death. I was armed with enough of an inheritance to survive for awhile and a little inspiration. The song "Gotta be Bad" by Des'ree had become my rallying cry. That song and a copy of "Our Deepest Fear" by Marianne Williamson began to give me a glimpse of another way of being in the world. My sister had gifted me that poem in a manila folder as she drove me to Midway Airport for my move, my hands shaking and throat closing as I choked back tears reading those beautiful words.

I moved back to New York with such hope. I had missed the city. Where I lived on the North side of Chicago was a lot like living in the suburbs, something I never wanted to do.

Within a week of moving into my sweet little Brooklyn Heights apartment, I was walking down Henry Street on a crisp fall day and had an overwhelming sense that I was right where I was supposed to be. It was a feeling completely unfamiliar to me. I dismissed it as my just appreciating the beauty of autumn in my gorgeous new neighborhood where the tree-lined streets held multi-million dollar brownstones.

On a late afternoon a few weeks later, I decided to head down Court Street in Brooklyn to the local bookstore. I didn't necessarily intend to buy anything, but I have always loved losing myself in bookstores. Lo and behold, that afternoon I did end up buying four books, *The Color Purple, A Drinking Life, An Unknown Woman,* and *A Woman's Life: The Story of an Ordinary American and Her Extraordinary Generation.* I was definitely on a search for something. For a way to be ordinary, a way to be extraordinary, a way to be known, a way to be unknown. I had no idea what it was—but I was determined to, at the very least, make some sense of my life, maybe even (please!) find a way to fix it, to make it work.

With my demented logic, I decided the books were going to provide the key to my life, so I might as well reward myself with "just one drink" at the dive bar on Atlantic Avenue that I hadn't yet checked out. As I sidled up to the bar, placing my bag of books next to me, I ordered my usual Chardonnay and began to look around the place. It was a typical bar, a typical Brooklyn bar. There were a lot of regulars, judging from how the bartender was bantering with them. It was not too long before I was bantering with him the same way, then with the cute guy about three stools down from me. I soon found out his name was Frank, and he was an Assistant District Attorney in Brooklyn. Wow...a lawyer. That was all I needed to decide I should stay for another one...although I was already on my third or fourth by that time. The next thing I knew late afternoon had turned into late evening, dusk had long passed, and Frank was suggesting we go to this trendy, dark bar on Boerum Place. It sounded like a good idea to me. So did the shots we did while at the Boerum Bar.

So did going home with him. That was until we were naked in bed, when all of a sudden he said, "You're nothing but a slut. I should kill you right now." I never sobered up so quickly in my life. Still, I didn't know what to do. This man was a lot bigger than I was, plus it was sometime in the middle of the night and I really didn't know where I was. I knew I wasn't terribly far from my apartment on Henry Street, but I had no idea what direction it was. I realized I needed to change his mind so I went into "girlfriend" mode and became extra sweet and loving, then ventured to say something like "You wouldn't really do that, would you?", to which he replied, "I could never hurt you. I love you." Truthfully, I found that statement almost as creepy as the death threat, but at least I felt a little safer. There was no way I was going to anger this guy, however, so I had sex with him, then stayed awake—fearfully cuddling—until daybreak. I started to try to get out of bed, only to be physically pulled back in, complete with a sweet "Don't go." I dutifully stayed until 7:00 am when the alarm went off, and Frank, complete with hangover groans and moans, dragged himself to the shower to get ready for work that day. I very quickly and quietly dressed and headed out the door, down the one flight of stairs, and onto the brownstone-lined street. Still not knowing where I was, I headed in one direction, then another, until I finally saw the Enterprise Car Rental on Atlantic Avenue off in the distance. Using that as my marker, I knew I could navigate my way home. I arrived at the front door of my apartment at twenty minutes to eight, climbed into bed, and cried myself to sleep.

After that, I vowed I would not drink in public again, certainly not out by myself. I thought that was the solution. It was barely a start.

CHAPTER 13

T here was no denying something needed to change in my life. Big time. Actually, a lot of things needed to change, but it was increasingly clear what had to be first. Fortunately, grace was opening the door to make this earth-shattering shift possible.

In my move back to New York, my real estate agent had been this dynamic, vivacious woman. Jane, then in her early fifties, was a few years into her second life as a real estate agent / actress in Manhattan. Her first life had been as a Long Island housewife. Baffled as to how such a radical transformation could happen and finally desperate enough to ask, I inquired what gave her the courage, the focus, and the commitment to venture down a completely different road than the one she had lived so far. "I don't get it," I said. "You really just left a life you'd lived for over twenty years as a suburban housewife to move into the city and pursue acting." Jane's response was that she was involved in a community of people who lived large, challenged themselves, and cheered each other on to have the life each one wanted. I most definitely wanted what they had so when she invited me to an introductory evening for the personal growth program, Lifespring, I readily accepted.

Totally clueless as to any other option, I registered that night for their basic program, after which I entered the advanced, after which I signed up for the Leadership Program (aka "LP"). We discussed things like accountability, risk, keeping our word—all things I had never given much conscious thought to before. Even more important, we were given the opportunity to clear out a lot of pain, a lot of secrets, a lot of armor we lived behind. I was ready. I was so ready that in the exercise where we revealed our secrets by raising our hand about certain topics (with everyone's eyes closed for confidentiality), I raised my hand when the statement was made, "Raise your hand if you're an alcoholic." I felt deceived when the next question was "Raise your hand if you think you're an alcoholic" as that felt more true to where I was—but in any case, it was out. I had finally admitted the thing I was most terrified of letting anyone know. What to do with this revelation was still unclear to me.

Until a month later when, as part of LP, we had the assignment to write a "Letter of Accomplishment", outlining how our life was going to be different ninety days out—which coincided with the end of the training. The first thing I wrote was that I was going to limit my drinking to weekends, to beer and wine, and to no more than two drinks. Unbeknownst to me, the small group leader to whom I turned in this letter, was sober ten years at the time and recognized that entry as a classic attempt by an alcoholic to control her drinking. His first question to me was, "Do you think you might have a drinking problem?" My answer was a definite "Yes." Next he asked me, "Do you want to go to an AA meeting?" I acquiesced with a very timid, "If you'll go with me"—probably more timid than I had done or said anything in my entire life. That exchange happened on a Monday morning. We agreed to go that Wednesday evening, December 13, 1995. He left it up to me to find the meeting.

By this time in my life, I had had many evenings that I just didn't remember. My memories of the next night were vague for a very different reason. I was completely shell-shocked. I was sitting in an Alcoholics Anonymous meeting. What???!!!!

I remember a very few things about that evening. I remember that my small group leader, a short African-American man, had on an ethnic African hat that I'd never seen him wear. I remember that people were very nice and accepting. I remember that some people were surprised this was my first AA meeting ever. (That thrilled me. I was so proud people couldn't tell what a newbie I was. Apparently, I was managing to keep up the front at least a little bit.) I remember feeling some teensy semblance of hope, yet also not wanting to become a part of this group. I would just show up as much as I needed to, not even sure what it was that I was showing up for. Yes, I knew it was to stop drinking, but for how long? And did I really want to do that? Was I really ready to? I was greatly relieved when someone said all I had to do was not drink today. That I could do.

Fortunately, through Lifespring I now had enough people around me that had gotten sober—really sober—by going to AA meetings that I decided it was worth a try. I found a meeting in my neighborhood in the Heights that met at 7:30 a.m. Since I wasn't sleeping anyhow, I started to attend regularly. I still can see the faces of the regulars there. Cantankerous Hank. Compassionate Joe. Goofy tall Joey. Stylish, accomplished Randi. Acerbic Marsha. Grandmotherly Francine. Lawyer Larry. It was a group of people who, to quote the Big Book of Alcoholics Anonymous, "normally would not mix". But it was a group of people from whom I felt more love and acceptance than I did from my own family. Especially from April 13 on. When I realized and shared that it had been four months since I had a drink, the group broke out in applause—not uncommon in AA meetings—but it was the first time I genuinely felt it and could open to it. I belonged there.

Besides just not turning to a drink whenever life got uncomfortable, the fellowship and twelve steps of recovery introduced me to living my life in a completely different way.

Growing up, my family's modus operandi was twofold: 1) You are solely, completely responsible for your own life and really can not count on anybody else (in any form) for help. 2) Just make it look good.

I was just out of college when I realized how deeply—and harshly—my parents had instilled the message of not counting on anyone else for help. I was in the midst of a diligent, unrelenting, yet still unsuccessful job search. Every major agency in the Detroit area had been sent my resume at least four times; I was now papering even the smallest and most ancillary companies with copies of it as well. Finally, I found out that a friend of mine from my summer job was good friends with the son of Jim Doyle, then president of D'Arcy MacManus Masius, arguably the most prestigious agency in the area. Not only did she know him, the two of them were going to a luncheon the next week where Mr. Doyle would be speaking. I was invited to go along. I did just that, dressed the part, asked a couple of smart questions during the Q&A, and had the chance to hand my resume directly to him at the end of the event. I was hired about two weeks later. I was absolutely elated about this job. How it came about with the help I had received from my friend was a very nice bonus.

About a month after starting my job, I was talking to my Dad, who had been in middle-management at Pontiac Motor Division—the agency's largest client—for almost 30 years. "I just found out that one of my coworkers, a guy I knew from Michigan State, got into D'Arcy through Mike Losh, the head of Pontiac," I told him.

Dad responded, "I'm not surprised. That happens around there a lot. I have been in some trainings with Losh, and probably could have gotten you in that way too." Very startled, and angry that my own father could watch the emotional turmoil my job search had put me through and not make a simple call on my behalf, I asked him why he hadn't done that. His answer was, "I wanted you to learn that we have to do things on our own." I pointed out to him that I did not get my job entirely on my own but instead got help from someone who had been a stranger just months earlier. It reinforced to me how I couldn't depend on anyone else, at least not my family; there might be the occasional gifts of support but it was certainly nothing to expect.

The notion of making things look good was an unspoken but underlying premise learned at an early age. It was reinforced every time my family of seven traipsed down the center aisle at church to deliver the offerings, dressed in our Sunday best, despite the lack of love and connection that existed in the four walls at home. It won out with every straight-A report card or honor roll mention, the badge that was supposed to prove to the world—and myself—that all was OK. The most obvious tangible example of the need to present a pretty picture was in the photos that were taken around our home. For years before the camera was snapped, anything out of place was moved to the side so the photo would show a neat, clean, orderly house—while the reality of the mess lay just outside the camera's angle. It was the perfect analogy to our family. But my greatest hurt from the "Just make it look good" rule had been the mandate to not ever grieve, to not ever let anyone know that I hurt in any way.

It was obvious both of these engrained ways of being were going to have to fall by the wayside in order for me—and my life—to change. I had to ask for help from other people—and accept it when it came. I had to not worry about what others' thought of me or how I looked. It would be necessary for me to heal the grief within me. In order to do all this, I even embraced the path of faith—of not just believing that God existed, but that He/She loved me and wanted the best for me.

A lot of people talk about a "pink cloud" when they get sober. It's a time when everything is fresh and new and exciting.

For some people, this can go on for months, even well into their second year of sobriety. Not me. Once I had thawed out enough and started to chip away at the layers of alcohol that had been my buffer, all the buried grief of my life burst forth as if a fire hydrant, not just a fountain, of tears.

I cried. I cried over Robbie for the first time ever. I cried over the way my beautiful pedigree collie, Barney, had been neglected. I cried even more when I realized that the kids had been just as neglected. I cried over my Catholic upbringing. I cried over abuse in my family. I cried over the way I had treated men and the way I had been treated by men. I cried over the realization that I had been date raped. I cried over the lack of connection to my family. I cried over my parents' being dead. I cried over the relationship I had with them when they were alive, and the relationship I didn't have with them. I cried for every reason and for no particular reason. I just cried.

These tears, unlike the self-pitying wailing that had earned me the identification as "a maudlin drunk" from one of my bosses, were healing tears. They rose from my soul and from my broken heart. After each snot-nosed cry, I would feel lighter, sometimes right away, sometimes a few days later—but it always happened. Still it was not an easy process to go through. Some friends suggested anti-depressants, but even then I didn't believe it was a clinical depression I was going through, and even more important I didn't want to stunt the healing, or even the possibility of it.

Yes, I knew in my gut I needed to allow my healing to be the center of my life. Over the last few years I had taken baby steps in that direction—but my drinking had always been the stockade wall around my psyche that kept any real opening from happening. Now, just as grace had entered to introduce me to AA, spiritual doors opened to bring a profound healing practice into my life. Jane, the woman who had introduced me to Lifespring, also introduced me to her friend, Mark, a sweet ex-rocket scientist (literally) who had just moved into Manhattan weeks earlier. Mark and I instantly connected and started dating just as I was getting sober and he was embarking on a new spiritual path called Johrei.

Johrei, a Japanese practice founded in the 1930s, is the process of sending Divine Light for healing purposes. My first experience of it was at the service where Mark was to receive his Ohikari, the sacred pendant that allows members to offer the Light. I entered a loft office on Spring Street in Soho and was immediately taken by the beauty and serenity of the place, as well as the warmth of the people. Mark introduced me to Larry, the minister, Naomi, an elegant older African-American woman with a vibrant smile and effervescent laughter, Juli, a former model-turned-writer, and a few others. I had no idea how important these people were to become to me in the years following. We then settled in for the service.

I was pretty skeptical about this. The notion of channeling Divine Light for healing purposes was something I had never heard of before—and something that sounded downright weird. Nonetheless I trusted Mark, so I reminded myself to relax and breathe. So far there was nothing I should be suspicious of. These were loving people in a beautiful environment. While all of that was still foreign to me, there was no reason I should be afraid of it.

The ceremony started with offerings being placed on the altar in front of a scroll with Japanese letters. The whole group then said a Japanese prayer / chant, followed by English prayer that, at that time, sounded as foreign to me as did the opening chant. Not realizing the mission of Johrei is to bring about Paradise on Earth, the prayer described a world beyond what I could grasp. It spoke of "boundaries between countries vanish and ancient conflicts disappear as if dreams"; "peaceful clouds move across brilliant skies"; and "through service to humanity, all are blessed with health, peace, and prosperity." I listened dubiously. After a sermon by Larry, he raised his hand, entered into prayer, and channeled Johrei to the entire gathering. I decided to close my eyes and relax into it. After just a few moments of this, the light in the room began to intensify greatly; I felt as though I was being bathed in it. I opened my eyes at that moment to see him channeling directly towards me. My cynicism began to slip away in that moment. It didn't matter my mind could not wrap itself around the notion of channeling Divine Light for healing purposes; it was getting through to my heart.

Between AA and Johrei, which I was now receiving occasionally from Mark, the melting of my heart continued to take the form of tears. Sometimes Johrei would calm me and alleviate the tears; other times it seemed to bring forth a new torrent of tears, but tears that felt even more healing than most. As the summer ticked on, I finally agreed to go back to that gorgeous loft office to receive Johrei again, explaining to Mark between sobs that "I'll go if you think it will help."

CHAPTER 14

With eleven months of not drinking under my belt, things felt like they were falling apart more than ever. I had gone through my inheritance from Dad, in effect breaking a promise I wouldn't be broke in a year, but also knowing that taking the time and space to get sober was the greatest investment and gift I could possibly have made with that money. And I knew Dad knew it too from his new vantage. Mark, with whom I had probably had my healthiest relationship to date, moved back to Seattle for work and to be near his teen-aged kids The tears, which had subsided to an every second or third week bout, were back on a daily basis.

The week I was to celebrate one year of sobriety just intensified my being a "woman on the edge of a nervous breakdown," to quote a movie title from that time. It is not uncommon for people to be overwhelmed with feelings around anniversaries of when they got sober—and that is never more true than the first year. With my actual date on Friday the 13th (December), I had managed to get through the previous Monday without crying—a very rare occasion around that time. As I was getting ready Tuesday morning for the seasonal sales job I had taken at Kate's Paperie, I could already feel myself on the edge of a big crying jag as I headed out my apartment door to be at the store by 10:00 a.m. Dealing with the hustle, bustle, and jostling one gets on the train from Brooklyn to Manhattan certainly didn't help anything. The final straw was walking up the subway steps at the Spring Street Station, one of hundreds of people streaming off the Number 6 train onto the sidewalks above. As I had ascended half the short staircase, a full beer, cracked open enough for foam to be seeping out, fell onto the steps and, seemingly in slow motion, plunked down step by step in my direction. Just as the beer flowed from the can, tears immediately flowed from my eyes. I rushed to the pay phone across the street and called my sponsor, Heidi, telling the story with the exaggerated statement that the gods were throwing beers at me. I finally pulled myself together enough to walk the remaining block and a half to the store, even though I was fifteen minutes late already. After being there less than an hour, that day's floor manager came up to me and kindly and gently asked me if I wanted to leave for the day. I guess she figured I wasn't going to sell a lot of two-hundred-dollar photo albums to holiday shoppers that day. I took her up on that, but instead of heading home, went directly to my sponsor's apartment where she literally babysat me until it was time for my regular Tuesday night AA women's meeting down the street from my house.

There was another anniversary in my life that was adding to the emotion I was feeling. The day right after my first year sober was the ten-year anniversary of Mom's death. I was starting to realize I seem to have a cellular memory of major events in my life, so that too was bringing up all sorts of things. The biggest emotion was sorrow that had probably not been expressed since that occasion when I found the Christmas card I had bought for her. Right behind that, however, was anger that she had denied me (and all her loved ones) the opportunity to grieve and therefore to heal. Not drinking was giving me access to these feelings that had been buried very deeply for most of my life.

I wasn't sure how to get to the other side of all this intense emotion, but I suspected that Robert Frost was right when he said, "The only way out is through." Fortunately by then my feet were firmly planted in two spiritual paths—AA and Johrei—that could offer me guidance during this process.

AA offered me the twelve steps of recovery, as it has for a few million others in its seventy-five years of existence. My shift had started a few months into recovery when I acquiesced to those who told me I couldn't continue to live as the bulldozer through life I had been and expect to stay sober. "If nothing changes, nothing changes," they told me. So I began to develop a relationship with a Higher Power that I could trust with my life—and did. I started to actually have a spiritual connection. Over that first year, I recognized that my life really did work better when I trusted that there was something guiding the flow of my life, whether in business dealings, relationships, or even my own healing process. I learned that when I went through things, not around them in a state of drunken oblivion, they changed. They often changed for the better, but no matter how they changed I could then deal with that set of life circumstances…again, with the help of other people and of God.

With this foundation I could better learn how to deal with the emotions that insisted on expressing themselves in my life, especially the anger. One of the major sources of this anger was indeed the suppressed grief, but it went way beyond that. As I entered my second year of sobriety, it seemed I was angry about every single thing I had cried torrents of tears over less than one year earlier. I seethed over the date rape and over my relationships with men in general. My pulse raced with rage when I thought of everything in my family that had set the stage for the dysfunction I was now grappling with in my life: pervasive alcoholism, the lack of emotional connection (especially between my parents), gender roles that held men as the center of the earth and women as their mere servants and playthings. Yes, this anger needed to be dealt with in the form of AA's fourth step, "Made a searching and fearless moral inventory of ourselves," which then needed to be shared with my sponsor. Sharing every buried emotion, every secret, every shameful act of my life with another person did exactly what it is designed to do. I walked away from our "chat" with a sense of "That's it? All my life I have had to separate myself from the human race over the things I just told another person in one afternoon?" It gave me a level of freedom I had never known.

By the time my 1-year sober anniversary and the ten year marking of Mom's death actually approached, Johrei had also become a regular part of my life, so much so that I was in the six-week membership class and about to step into the service of maintaining the finances for the center. Knowing my growing commitment to this practice and seeing my emotional torture, my minister suggested I might want to enshrine my mother. Normally something reserved for members (of which I would not be for another month), Larry made an exception. In Johrei, enshrinement is the process of having your ancestor's name sent to the Sacred Grounds in Japan to have them prayed for during Ancestor Services and on special anniversaries of their passing, like ten years. I went ahead and did that, hoping that it would bring light to both Mom's soul, as well as my own.

I believe my taking that step at that point opened me to astonishing encounters. My experience with Johrei grew and unfolded. During one session, I witnessed a review of my father's life from his perspective. I felt his pride about how much he had accomplished—raising a family, being financially responsible and able to provide a very comfortable life, something he had not enjoyed as a child. The pride went on to include the degrees he had received, the volunteer work he had done with underprivileged youth, his time in the Peace Corps, and the relationships he had forged with people at Pontiac Motors over the years, including his being honored by the Professional Secretaries Club for his advancement of women. I connected with the love he had for the people who had been most important to him in his life—his kids, Mom, Pat, his sisters and brother and all their families, as well as friends he had had for decades. I also felt the pain of his regret. I saw him—through his own eyes—as a man who had drunk excessively for decades, doing permanent damage to his marriage. I witnessed the pain of his unfulfilled dreams as an entrepreneur at heart, which had stayed buried deep under the responsibilities of a family man. All this ran through my heart and my mind in twenty minutes as I sat receiving Light.

I also had times when I went into the center feeling fine, not expecting any tears to come forth, and was met with twenty minutes of sobbing that started as soon as the person opposite me raised their hand to channel. Oftentimes, those tears felt as though they had been so deeply buried in my psyche that they weren't even my tears; they were the tears of generations past. They were the tears of my mother when she went to live with another family in high school. They were her unshed tears after her miscarriage. They were Grandma and Grandpa's tears over the hardship of raising six children during the Depression. They were the tears of many generations past. They were coming through me to be healed, for them individually to be healed but also for my entire lineage to be healed.

It made sense that I would feel ancestral healing through the practice of Johrei. Being a Japanese practice, one of the central focuses was praying for our ancestors who had left this world. Every month, the Ancestor Service was one of two services held; there was also a larger Annual Ancestor service where the ancestors were actually invoked and people brought their ancestors favorite foods to place on the altar. Since I had been attending both the monthly services religiously, I was surprised when, on the morning of my first Annual Ancestral Service that May, I woke up with a rebellious almost little-kid-like "I don't want to go." After sitting with that and trying to figure out what it was, I decided it was not something I wanted to give in to, so I got ready and headed to the service. I was overwhelmed by the beauty and abundance of the service. A little ways into it, I recognized that my initial hesitation had been that of my mother's. Going somewhat against her initial wish, she knew I considered this service to be for her. Even though she had been in the spirit world for ten years at that point, that perspective remained—until we got underway with the service. The lightening I felt in my being, knowing that was a reflection of the release her soul was experiencing, once again—and not surprisingly—brought me to beautiful, healing tears...sobs, actually. It was the beginning of a long process of honoring my mother's soul and life that I was not allowed to do when she had left this world a decade earlier. This process continues to this day as I more deeply heal my relationship with her.

My experiences with Johrei and the many AA meetings I was attending reinforced an important notion. *My journey was my journey.* Having lived life so far building a veneer of bravado as opposed to building a strong sense of self, I had dismissed the notion that my life had merit—that it was worth being shared with others. In twelve-step meetings, I heard some stories that were infinitely more heartbreaking than my own—and these people still were filled with gratitude for what they had and who they had become as a result of their experience. I also heard stories of people who had had it pretty easy—and yet were bemoaning their life circumstances. All this helped me develop the belief and trust that the journey I am on is exactly what my soul needs. It might not be what any other person / soul needs (almost certainly it isn't) but my acceptance is greater when I have trust that I am getting what I need for my highest good. I have used this recognition as a guiding light since then—both to bolster me through the hard times and as a source of gratitude at all times.

As my spiritual life was growing exponentially, my material life had momentarily hit the skids. I ran out of money and could no longer afford my apartment. My holiday job at Kate's went well and had gotten me through a little time, but it most definitely was not going to support my current lifestyle. I was going to have to move, but how was I ever going to find a cheap enough place that I could get by on a retail salary, assuming I would even be able to stay on at that job after the post-Christmas sales ended?

Blessedly, my faith that things work out was proven true. A friend of mine needed a roommate in a homey two bedroom floor-through apartment in a Brooklyn brownstone, about a half-mile from my current place. That was important to me as my AA meetings, especially my 7:30 am home group, had become my family and my base. Now I just needed to figure out how I was going to pay even the meager rent of $450.

Two options came forth. I had been invited to stay at Kate's with a promotion to supervisor of the photo album department, including a raise to a whopping $12/hour. It certainly was not anywhere close to my previous New York salary but would allow me to keep food in my stomach and a roof over my head.

The other option was more intriguing to me—but also scared me and had its potential pitfalls. BMW, my previous client, was hiring regional agencies as part of a reorganization of their marketing. Before the holidays, they were in the midst of selecting the New York-based agency that would be responsible for the $30 million dollars plus that would be spent throughout the Northeast, with the announcement expected right at the beginning of the year. I decided it was worth calling my old Eastern region client, Roy Steinwolf, to start the process of throwing my hat in the ring wherever the account landed. I had worked with Roy for a little over a year the first time I worked on the business, initially as the representative directly managing the regional business, then as the person overseeing all the regions.

We had worked very well together. I suspect my drunkenness at functions did not escape his notice, but he also knew I was conscientious in my work and excellent at my job. He readily accepted my call and said he'd be happy to put in a good word for me with whatever agency was selected.

In our conversation he also confirmed the press was accurate. The leading contender was a hot new agency that, a few years earlier, had been founded by a creative team I worked with at another agency. My heart sank when I heard this as I knew I could not go to work there. Even though I had worked really well with these two guys, I had also partied way too much with them. Doubtful they would be ready to put such a person in a key role on a major account. Even if they did, I wasn't comfortable that my fledgling sobriety could survive working with people who knew me as the person that, every week, rounded the whole agency up for TGIF at Murphy's Pub. Still I said nothing, thanked Roy for his support, and told him I would be back in touch after I heard which agency had been picked. If my friends' agency did win the business, I had no idea how I was going to explain to Roy my sudden disinterest in the job—especially when it meant picking a $12/hour retail job instead. What I did know, however, was this was one of those things that I was supposed to "turn over" and trust that God would help to unfold in a way that was for the highest good of all. I hoped that would translate into my getting back into a prestigious agency job with a cushy salary, but I didn't see how that was going to happen.

Yet it did. All of the new BMW regional agencies were announced in *Adweek* the first week of the new year. It turned out the agency hired to cover the Eastern region was not the hot new creative shop after all. It was the New York office of the Bloom Agency, a long-established Dallas-based agency that was part of the international Publicis network. The dark horse agency had put together a solidly strategic and abundantly creative pitch that wowed the car company's decision makers. They were to immediately start producing creative work and holding dealer meetings, which meant they needed to get staffed up quickly.

As promised, I called Roy the moment I saw the announcement. He had already forwarded the resume I sent him over to Jim Overend, the group management supervisor who would be overseeing the account. Jim was looking to quickly hire an account supervisor who would be running the day-to-day operations of the business, so he wanted me to call him ASAP and hopefully get in to see him that same week. Roy told me Jim seemed like a really nice guy but forewarned me that he was so incredibly handsome that most people were a little jarred when they first met him. Damn, now that was going to be hard to handle!

Early the next week I went into the agency for my meeting with Jim, only to find out Roy was not exaggerating at all. Standing about 6'2" with wavy salt and pepper hair, steel blue eyes, and a slightly dimpled chin to match his dimpled smile, his handsomeness unnerved me as he walked into the lobby where I sat, even though I had been adequately prepared. Our talk went well, and he scheduled me to meet with three others from top management. Those interviews also went well, not surprisingly since I had had similar responsibilities on the same account before and was being recommended by the man who would be my main client. A week later I got a job offer for $10,000 more than I expected I would be given, an offer I accepted immediately.

Given my growing spiritual perspective, I could not help but notice all the little "coincidences" that had my life turn around so dramatically in such a short time. In one month's time, I had gone from the edge of homelessness and severe underemployment to a new roommate situation and enough money that I could start to dig myself out of the debt I had accumulated over the last few months trying to keep my head above water. I recognized the spiritual intervention, especially since I had recently celebrated a year sober and had just become a Johrei member and was now doing service and offering financial expressions of my gratitude to the center, however meager they had to be at the time. All this made me feel that I was definitely on the right path. It convinced me that the sober, spiritual life based in service, gratitude, and humility (my needed mantra as I ventured back into the ad biz) was serving me infinitely more than my days as a promiscuous, maudlin drunk. It was a path I intended to stay on, and to deepen.

CHAPTER 15

One of the many blessings Johrei brought into my life was international travel. With the mission of the religion being to bring about Paradise on Earth, there have been five prototypes (mini-paradises if you will) created throughout the world—three in Japan, one in Thailand, and one in Brazil. Every year US members voyage to at least one of these Sacred Centers, as they are known.

In the late summer of my first year as a Johrei member, it was announced that year's trip would be to Brazil in late October / early November for their Annual Ancestral service. That made the trip a little more affordable and shorter than the trips to Japan, which was what was scheduled most years. I started to toy with the idea of going. I was now secure in my job, my financial situation had improved dramatically, and I was still very much focused on ancestral healing for my family—still most notably Mom, but I had also become open to the need for healing throughout the full lineage on both sides. Yes, signing on for the trip was in order.

Upon arriving in Brazil, the trip started with a day at Guaraja, a beautiful small beach resort area near Sao Paolo. Our group enjoyed a lovely day on the beach, followed by a wonderful dinner at a churascaria, where we stuffed ourselves with meats so tender they melted in one's mouth. The evening ended with my first attempt at salsa dancing, complete with some damage to my dancing partner's feet. Even before getting to the Sacred Grounds,

I was already loving Brazil and feeling more open to the breadth of blessings life can bring.

As our coach rolled up to the entrance of Guarapiranga, the Brazil Sacred Grounds, I was still skeptical that any place in this world could legitimately be billed as an example of Paradise on Earth. I could see the grounds had been immaculately designed and were meticulously maintained but people being people, there had to be conflict, self-centeredness and all the other foibles of humanity. Paradise on Earth had to be an overstatement.

But it wasn't. The warmth of the Brazilian people overwhelmed me. Their joy, their passion helped me to see the freedom I was missing in my life. Their focus on others in a healthy way gave me insight into how self-centered I still was, regardless of the amount of service I was now doing in both Johrei and AA. The way the people at the Center embraced life and everyone they came in contact with made me believe that, yes, this is what Paradise on Earth must look like.

The main event of our trip, the Annual Ancestral service, was held two days before the end of our stay. People began arriving on the grounds at six in the morning for the 11:00 service. Besides the international visitors, hundreds traveled from hours away throughout Brazil. By ten it did not feel as though more people could fit, yet the flow of people continued and intensified. Our US contingency, honored as special visitors, were seated near the front of the open air temple, so it became difficult to see how many people had gathered by the start of the service.

It was the thunderous chanting that opened the service that let me know the magnitude and the power of the crowd that had gathered. Just as every Johrei service worldwide starts, this one opened with the Amatsu Norito, a Japanese prayer that has the vibration of a chant. I got choked up as I heard the love and dedication in the thousands of voices joined together in honor of their ancestors. I had the sense that my mother was finally fully accepting the prayers being offered for her spiritual evolution.

After the service, a massive community lunch was lovingly served. Around every bend I turned, Johrei was being exchanged, people were sitting in appreciation of the beauty of the grounds, or laughter was being shared between friends who saw each other much too infrequently. By the time I retired at the end of the day, my heart was full.

The next day was our last day, so a big party had been planned for the evening. It was going to be our last chance to say goodbye to the friends we had made. I was especially going to miss Marisa, who stood at about half my height but glowed with a vibrancy I'd rarely seen. Then there was Victor, the gorgeous flirt whose smile looked like the most extensive collection of ivory I've ever seen. And of course Jao, the head of the Sacred Grounds, had won a very special place in my heart as well.

That evening we ate, we danced, we hugged, and we laughed. Near the end of the party our hosts had a special presentation for us. It included a roast of our minister and, to my delight, my being named as the friendliest visiting American. I was presented with a beautiful picture book of the Grounds but it was also decided I needed to have my photo taken with the twenty Brazilian men attending the party that evening. They held me off the ground horizontally, and I had a huge smile on my face. There was nothing seedy or overtly sexual about it. Pure and simple, I was being honored as a woman—a joyous, fun woman these men (and women) had come to care for deeply. My heart grew on that trip about as much as the Grinch's did on Christmas Day.

The sense I had of being appreciated and honored by men for who I am as a person with a value beyond just my sexuality would always have been welcomed. At that time, it was more important than ever. It was the beginning of my prayers being answered.

Overall my life was going extremely well and, for that, I was grateful. The one thing that was missing and that I longed for was a partner, someone who, to quote my friend Karen, "loved me best." Any semblance of romantic life had been virtually nonexistent since Mark had moved back to Seattle, let alone one as precious as what my heart dreamed of.

CHAPTER 16

About seven months after my Brazil trip, I was at a meeting in Brooklyn Heights when I heard a voice I'd never heard before coming from behind me. This man was introducing himself as new to the neighborhood. His voice was deep yet gently melodic as well. I turned hesitantly to see who could possibly possess such a calming, resonant voice—expecting his looks could not possibly be on par with his tone. Fortunately that was not the case. The words had come from the mouth of the most handsome man in the room—tall and thin with beautiful tanned, olive skin, thick dark wavy hair, and the most gorgeous big brown eyes I have ever seen, accented by long, long eyelashes.

This is another instance where I believe something bigger than I was in charge. By this time, I had moved into a beautiful floor-through apartment in nearby Park Slope but was still spending a lot of time in the Heights because I was comfortable there. My friends were there. Had that not been the case, I would not have met Brendan, that handsome man with the mesmerizing voice. On his part, he had been trying desperately to find a room or a share in Manhattan that he could afford on his meager savings and his struggling actor / caddy / odd jobs income. Finding it impossible, someone finally suggested that he look in Brooklyn. On his first foray into the Heights (an expensive area itself), he asked some deli guys if they knew anyone, and they referred him to a woman looking for a roommate. He moved in about ten days after that first conversation. Brendan and I often joked that, while he was looking for a place in Manhattan, God was sitting up at the master computer hitting the "delete" button and saying "There's a blonde waiting for you in Brooklyn." It gave us a chuckle, but also felt very true.

Brendan and I spoke intermittently—whenever we ran into each other—over the next few months. I learned the deep yet gentle melodic voice was matched by his deep, gentle soul. He noticed when it sounded like I had a little cold, or looked tired. He offered suggestions—sweet, unobtrusive, suggestions—on remedies. Over several weeks, I noticed the joy and excitement I felt whenever I saw him. Over Labor Day weekend, I noticed with sadness that Brendan wasn't around. I promised myself I would connect with him the next time I saw him. That changed my life—completely and forever.

September 13, 1998 was a magical night. It was that Saturday when I ran into Brendan early in the evening. My plans for that evening were to go into Manhattan to watch the Michigan State football game with the alumni club, something that was near and dear to my heart and had been a big part of my life for years. I did indeed do that; he just went along.

In reality, he never asked me out that evening, nor did I ask him. Shortly after greeting each other, Brendan said to me, "I'm hungry. Have you eaten?" Apparently we were entirely in sync with each other and he had been wanting to ask me out as well. I had a very brief moment of hesitation before looking at him, and asking, "Do you like football?" When his response was an enthusiastic "Yes," I told him what my plans had been for the evening and he decided to join me.

As we drove into the city, I asked him, "Do you know anything about Michigan State?" I asked the question fully expecting that he would confuse my beloved alma mater with The University of Michigan, our archrival, as most people in the East seemed to do.

Instead he answered that his best friend, Jeff, had gone to MSU and that he had visited him there in East Lansing a couple times. He then paused before finishing the story. "It's actually the only place I've ever spent a night in jail," he revealed hesitantly. Brendan then went on to explain, "We were leaving Mac's Bar when a couple cops tried to arrest Jeff for drunk and disorderly conduct. I started shooting off my mouth, trying to stand up for Jeff. Instead of getting him released, I ended up spending the night in jail too." He regaled me with the whole story, including the bars where they had been that night, bars where I too had spent many an evening. I chuckled appreciatively as I knew it could have easily been my story. Plus my heart was warmed by his willingness to reveal himself a little more deeply, warts and all.

The evening continued with a Michigan State victory over Notre Dame, something I always take as a good sign. Brendan's charming of me continued with a phone call he made to a friend who was a Notre Dame fan, gloating over the win—as he was now officially a Spartan fan. As we drove home over the Brooklyn Bridge, ever elegant in its lines, an equally elegant, beautiful, romantic full moon rose high in the clear night sky. Enjoying the evening so, I suggested that perhaps we should go to the Promenade in Brooklyn Heights to enjoy the view of the Manhattan skyline. We did. We chatted for a while, both of us fidgety and nervous like teenagers, when finally he kissed me. It was a sweet and comfortable connection, just like our date had been and our relationship would prove to be for the years following. After a little more making out, we decided it was time to call it a night. Brendan walked me to my car, giving me one more kiss good night. I told him how much I had enjoyed the evening and giggled how important it was that he was taller than I as he hugged me. He teased me about that for weeks to come.

I have never before or since had a relationship unfold as beautifully and naturally as it did with Brendan—and no wonder. In our journey together, I came to a deep, deep knowledge we have known each other many times before and will again. I have come to an equally deep belief our souls had contracted to share the experience of the years to come—complete with more joy and more sorrow than I had ever known possible. I believe it was all programmed into our souls, so of course it would be easy and natural.

Our early months together were absolutely idyllic. On our second date, he strolled up with his long, languid stride, keeping his normally swinging and twisting hands behind his back, trying to hide the beautiful two roses he had brought me. We grabbed a bite to eat at the local diner, then headed for our Promenade. As we chatted, occasionally kissing, I shared with him that I thought it would be a good idea to wait before we made love. Perhaps it would be sweet to mark his 40th birthday, just under a month away, with that occasion. I could see a little disappointment in his eyes, but he agreed. By the time the evening was over, I was so charmed, giddy, and enchanted, that I changed my mind on the spot and invited him home with me that evening. He stood up, grabbed my hand, and said "Let's go." It was an awkward evening in that it had been a long time since either of us had made love. For me it had been almost a year and for him several years. Although he had been sober a little over five years at that time, he had not had a relationship in sobriety, so this was his first time having sober sex. When one is used to being out-of-your-mind blotto during the carnal act, it definitely takes some getting used to. Despite it all, I knew this was more than sex. I knew this was indeed making love.

The next few months didn't give us a lot of time together as he was in a play and I was traveling a lot for work but we so cherished those moments we did have. I still hold the picture in my mind of seeing him on the street corner, waiting for me for our third official date. We were going to the San Gennaro Festival in Manhattan's Little Italy, replete with games, booths, and lots of great food. Since I was going to be at the Johrei Center right near there, we agreed to meet on a nearby street corner. I was running a little late, and rushing up to see him, when I stopped dead in my tracks. He was looking absolutely gorgeous in his sports jacket, yellow-and-white striped button down shirt, black jeans, and dress shoes. I went up to him and got a sweet hug and kiss, as he grabbed my hand for the rest of the short walk to the festival. We had a lovely evening, including him winning me a stuffed animal at one of the booth games. I was absolutely enchanted and felt cherished.

Another evening that marks as among the most romantic, yet simple, ones of my life was the occasion of Brendan's 40th birthday, just over a month after our first date. He was one of the leads in the Heights Players production of *Desperate Hours*, and had a performance that night, so we knew it had to be a late celebration. I was at work late that evening, and barely had time to get home to buy a chicken Caesar salad and readymade cake before Brendan was to show up. I decorated the cake with the numbers "4" - "0". It was Brendan's turn to be enchanted by my efforts, especially the bubble bath I drew for him. He told me it was his best birthday ever.

He had one other 40th birthday celebration that I joined him for. His parents wanted to come down from Westchester to see his new place and take him out for a nice lunch. Because of his play schedule, they put it on the calendar for the weekend after his birthday. As he and his mom, Gail, spoke of the lunch, Brendan asked her if he could bring his new girlfriend. She was thrilled, and told me later that he very proudly and sweetly informed her that I was a blonde whose name was Ann O'Neil. Brendan shared that with his mom because of her own Irish heritage, in a family dominated by the Italian lineage.

I was slightly terrified about that lunch. I met Brendan and his parents in the Heights, where we strolled down Montague Street, the upscale tree-lined main thoroughfare of the neighborhood, until we settled on Armando's, a nice, very traditional Italian restaurant. His parents sat on one side of the booth while Brendan and I sat on the other, holding hands every moment we could. I quickly realized his parents' relationship was completely unlike what I had grown up with. Between my parents, my mother was usually the more dominant one, the more social one. Not that my father was a wallflower, but Mom was pretty loud. With Brendan's parents, his dad, Joe, was by far the central focus. He was always dapperly dressed, as he was that day in a navy blue suit jacket, tie, white shirt, and khakis. His mother, Gail, who played the supporting role, was neither as well-put-together or vocal. It was also very easy to see that she was the one that Brendan got his sweetness from. She was gentle, supportive, and worked hard to keep things comfortable. By the end of the lunch, I held a sweet affection for these people who I barely knew.

With both my parents having died already and my siblings living all across the country, my connection with family was limited to phone conversations on a monthly basis or so, along with an occasional holiday visit to one of my siblings—usually my sister, Meg. Conversely, family was a very central part of Brendan's—if not, *the* central part of Brendan's life. This was driven home for me a few other times that fall. Brendan and I had taken a day trip north to see the beautiful fall foliage. On our way back from northern Westchester County in the New York suburbs, he wanted to stop in Pelham, to see if his brother Joe was home so I could meet him and his family. I was a little hesitant about popping in unannounced, but was uncomfortable beyond belief when it turned out they weren't home. Brendan went in, called out but realized no one was home, and headed straight to the refrigerator to check out what kind of leftovers they had. I used the bathroom, hesitant to do even that, but otherwise just stood in the living room, asking Brendan if he was sure we should be there. Brendan very quickly dismissed it with a "He's my brother," which clearly meant much more to him than it did to me.

His sisters, Eden and Sheila, were the first family members I met. They had come down to Brooklyn supposedly to see him in his play but I suspect also to meet me. At an early dinner beforehand, he and his sister, Sheila, were debating who was now farther from the rest of the family—Brendan in Brooklyn or Sheila in Darien, Connecticut. Since my whole family had not lived near one another for over twenty years at that point, I couldn't fathom what it would be like to live that close to my family, let alone actually take advantage of that physical closeness. I figured that might take some getting used to.

Not being particularly close to my blood relations, my friends were my family. As such, it was their self-appointed role to screen Brendan. My Brooklyn friends were getting to know Brendan as I was, but my older friends—especially those from when I was living in Boston—were most curious about this new man in my life. Since this particular group of friends and I had lived with our nicknames for years, our rule was that if you were involved with someone very special to you, they had to get a nickname too. Since Brendan had already long had the nickname "Bean," his new one had to go with that. Based on his career as a struggling actor and a charity performance his troupe gave at a homeless shelter, his nickname as christened by my friends was "Soupy"—short for "Soup Kitchen." Although he never liked its origin, he did relish that I had a special name for him—Soupy Bean—that no one else used but I almost exclusively used. That was so true that he once confessed he could tell when I was somewhat displeased with him as I called him "Brendan" then and only then. In his tribute back to me, I became Goldilocks.

Soupy Bean became a key part of our early days together. Since Brendan was always creating—stories, scripts, dialogue, characters—one day I came home to find a drawing of a Superman-like character with an "S" on his shirt. Brendan then explained to me that it was not Superman; it was the superhero Soupy Bean. Soupy Bean's gift was that he could be simultaneously out saving the world and also at his woman's side. All that was needed to activate this power was that she scratch his back with a very gentle, almost imperceptible touch.

As often happens, just as we were really settling in with each other, we had the chance to learn that absence does indeed make the heart grow even fonder. The week before Thanksgiving I had to travel out to Utah for a five-day commercial shoot for my client, BMW. When the shoot had been scheduled, I had seen it as the perfect opportunity to visit my sister in Chicago for Thanksgiving on the way back. I went ahead with those plans despite really wanting to be back home with my Soupy Bean. When we spoke on Thanksgiving Day, I noted how sad he sounded. He admitted that, even at his brother's with the whole family there, he was very much missing me. I said back to him, "Yeah. I can't wait to get home to see you, too. I kind of wish I hadn't planned to spend Thanksgiving here with Meg."

Two days later I flew back into LaGuardia Airport, went home long enough to drop off my luggage and pick up my car, then drove the hour to Larchmont, New York, where Brendan was still hanging out with his family. We agreed I would pick him up from a diner parking lot where he had caught up with some friends. By the time I got there, my heart was beating wildly. Saying absolutely nothing, he took me in his arms and gave me the most loving, tender kiss. Bean later told me that was the moment he knew with absolute certainty he was in love with me.

CHAPTER 17

Months later we were at LaGuardia for our first trip together. I had always wanted to visit Montreal, so we decided to go there take to mark my 38th birthday. It was exquisite. First of all it was the sexual highlight of all our time together. Whether it was getting away from it all, the romance of the city, or the celebratory aspect of it, we made love more times that weekend than during any other time we were together.

The trip was filled with sweetness and goofiness too. We started our mini-vacation with lunch in the garden of this terrific restaurant. The weather was temperate, the décor classic, and the musicians angelic—a perfect beginning to a perfect trip. The photos from that meal remind me of the combination of beauty, love, and goofy fun that set the tone for the whole trip.

Two things Brendan did on that trip made me realize how deeply special he was and how much he loved me. The first was his buying of my birthday present. We had been in a shop where I saw a pair of earrings I really liked. My first reaction was I didn't need them; the trip itself was enough of a present. As we walked a short way down the beautiful blossom-lined avenue, however, they were still on my mind, so I mentioned to Brendan I was going to go back later to buy them. After a sweet smooch on the street corner, we went our separate ways for a couple hours. He was off to a science museum where he could feed his inveterate curiosity; I was off to a paint-your-own pottery shop to feed my burgeoning creativity. We agreed to meet back at our room at Les Jardines in the late afternoon before going out to dinner. Just as planned, on my way back from my pottery painting, I stopped by the shop only to be told by the store owner the earrings had been sold. At first I was disappointed, then I realized what was going on. With a sly grin on my face, I asked if the customer happened to be a thin handsome man—about 6' tall. After a quizzical look, he confirmed that was the case. By the time I got back to the room, there was a wrapped little package waiting on the dresser with a beautiful birthday card signed by Bean de Soupee, aka the French Soupy Bean. With tears welling up in my eyes, I hugged my sweetie close, wanting in that moment to hold him that closely for the rest of our lives.

The next evening just reinforced that sentiment. It was our last night there, the eve of my actual birthday. We had dinner, then strolled around Old Montreal down by the river, with the sun setting and people milling all over, enjoying a perfect summer evening. After appreciating a street vendor's gorgeous painted photographs, watching some street performers, and snuggling on a bench next to the river, we decided to take a stroll to find a scrumptious dessert place. It wasn't long before we stumbled on a small hole-in-the-wall crepe place, with a view of the river from the outdoor tables. No one else was in there, but the crepe sundaes were still calling to us. After we ordered, I excused myself to the rest room, which seemed more like a converted broom closet. To my surprise, Brendan was not there when I came out just a few minutes later. The counter girl explained he had gone to get some ice for her because she was the only one in the store and couldn't leave. She then suggested I grab a table outside. Soupy returned, dropped something off inside the store, which I of course assumed was ice, then joined me at the table. The next thing I knew our ice cream crepes were being delivered, emblazoned by three glorious colorful sparklers. "Happy Birthday" was sung by Brendan and the counter girl. Very few times in my life have I been more surprised and more enchanted than in that moment. I knew that my prayer for a very special partner had been granted.

The only flaw in our Montreal escape had been Brendan's pain. The previous March, Brendan began experiencing a pain deep in his ear. Initially we dismissed it as the result of his being out caddying when the weather was still cold, but it continued on even as the temperature rose. By the time of our trip, his attempts to get a diagnosis so far had included a trip to a walk-in clinic and an appointment with his dentist. At the clinic, they cleared some wax and prescribed an antibiotic, also mentioning it could be a dental problem if it persisted. After that he did venture to his dentist who recommended having three teeth pulled. The first extraction, less than two weeks prior to our trip, had not provided any relief, so Brendan decided it was time to make an appointment at a well-known hospital specializing in issues like his.

His appointment there was scheduled for just over two weeks after our Montreal trip. At the appointment, they found nothing, even with a scope. Brendan's increasing pain was now compounded by the frustration over not having a diagnosis, over not having a clue as to what the source of his growing pain was.

His pain and undiagnosed illness started to take a toll on our relationship. Not knowing his tolerance level for pain and with no doctors coming up with a diagnosis, I began to wonder how sick he really was—or if he was just a wimp or a hypochondriac. His condition started interfering with his already-spotty work schedule, which meant I had an even larger share of our financial obligations. I was feeling put upon.

And Brendan hurt. He began losing weight because he couldn't eat. His voice was starting to be affected, which meant he couldn't audition either. He worked hard to stay positive, but many of the things that brought him joy were increasingly not in his life. He was not in a good place.

We were not in a good place. And we were not dealing with it.

One thing we had established by then was our weekly date, where we put time aside to focus on each other and our relationship. It was our chance to make sure we spent some quality time together. At least that was still in place so on a beautiful late fall evening we decided to go see the Kevin Spacey movie, *American Beauty*. While it was a great film and entertaining in many ways, what really struck me was how far apart the family in the movie had gotten and how destructive their relationship was to everyone it touched. When Brendan came to bed that evening, I was in tears.

When he asked what was wrong, I said, "I'm not sure we're going to make it. This is the first time I'm not sure we're going to make it." He then also broke down and said, "I'm so glad you said that. We need to keep talking. We need to remember we're on the same side." From that point on until the moment of his death, our relationship never again was a question in my mind.

With New Year's 2000 approaching, we had decided in August to go to London for the celebration, assuming that whatever was going on with Brendan would have been addressed by then so it would be a nonissue. Even though this was not the case and the holidays had been challenging, Brendan was still hopeful and so wanting to go on with life that he insisted we take the trip. As planned, we flew out of JFK on December 28 and returned January 2. Brendan would later call this trip "our last really good time."

Although I had a great time too, this trip was made for him. He loved to play the English chap. The Churchill Museum. The changing of the guards. The Underground. The theatre...oh, the theatre. He was absolutely enthralled we got to see the great Vanessa Redgrave in a Noel Coward play. He came away from that more in love with his great love of acting than ever. The millennium celebration on the banks of the Thames was the icing on the cake. Brendan loved meeting new people and was in his glory amidst new friends from around the world.

Unfortunately, the trip had its challenges as well. Our journey back to the hotel on New Year's took several hours since the Underground was shut down for security purposes. It was after three in the morning by the time we finally found an empty taxi and made our way back to our room. While I was tired, Brendan was almost distraught from pain and exhaustion. I instantly collapsed but after a few minutes of not being able to get comfortable enough to rest, Brendan decided to stay up to watch the rest of the celebrations around the world on the "telly", particularly in his beloved New York. Little did we know at that time all that the new millennium would bring.

The return to our hotel that evening appeared a cakewalk compared to our journey back to New York because of his pain. It was excruciating and he could not get comfortable. Fortunately the plane wasn't crowded so he stretched out with his head on my lap. Then he tried to watch the movie. Then he walked the length of the plane. I felt for him so deeply. I think I was starting to *finally* understand how sick he was.

Brendan was also increasingly fearful as to how sick he was. In November, he had started seeing a neurologist who gave him a diagnosis—facial neuralgia—but since the treatment did nothing to relieve his pain, Brendan was increasingly doubtful that was it. Suspecting cancer, he asked the neurologist if he should have an

MRI, only to be told "That won't show you anything." He kept telling this guy the medication wasn't working, that his pain was more intense than ever, only to be dismissed with a higher dose of medication that didn't work.

One night in a moment of vulnerability, he turned to me in bed and said he was getting more sure all the time that it was probably cancer. Knowing how extensive and expensive treatment would be and having no insurance, he said to me with great trepidation, "You might have to let me marry you." My response was less than generous. I said to him, "It's probably not cancer. Even if it were, I suspect my insurance wouldn't cover it since it's a pre-existing condition. Besides that, I don't know how I feel about getting married under those circumstances." My heart still hurts when I think of how I trivialized his feelings in such a tender moment. That is one of the rare, rare times my soul knows I hurt Bean.

Around the same time as that conversation, he started looking for a new doctor. His sister had sent him a list of well-respected physicians throughout the city. He ended up at New York University Hospital with a neurologist who knew to refer him to Dr. Dellacure, an Ear, Nose, Throat specialist. His new doctor did some in-office tests, including a scope of his throat, then sent him for an MRI. He had an appointment on Friday, March 17, to get the results. That was an eerie and unpleasant coincidence for me, as that had been the date that my father was diagnosed as being riddled with cancer. Five years later to the day, my mostly-Italian but a smidgen-Irish partner would also be handed hard luck on St. Paddy's Day.

When I asked Brendan if he wanted me to join him for his appointment, he said no. All along he had felt his health was something that was his responsibility to take care of, so I went to the office as usual for a client meeting that morning and spent an anxious afternoon waiting for his call. Just after two o'clock, my cell phone rang. His quivering voice on the other end of the line stated, "The doctor saw something on the MRI and thinks it's probably cancer. He's scheduled a biopsy for next Tuesday." I took a deep breath and told him I'd be home within an hour. There was no other place for me to be in that moment.

CHAPTER 18

C ome that Tuesday, March 21, 2000, I found myself sitting in the waiting room of NYU Ambulatory surgery with Brendan's parents. They had picked us up that morning in time for Bean to be ready for his noon biopsy. When we got there, Brendan went in to pre-op and I took a seat with his parents to await the news that would define the next several years of my life—and the final years of his. Although I had spent quite a bit of time with his parents in the eighteen months since I first met them, sitting with them under these circumstances was at least as uncomfortable as our first meeting at Armando's Restaurant. Of course that probably would have been the case no matter who I was with.

After a short time in the waiting room, a nurse called my name and invited me to join Brendan in the examination room until he was taken away to surgery. Walking into that tiny room, I saw how frightened and open he was. We prayed for a few moments. Then his doctor came in for a last chat before he was taken into surgery. That short visit in the examination room deeply rooted itself in my heart. It was then I knew at my core that whatever it was, I was with him 100% on it....really, truly 100%. Fortunately, he knew it also.

As much as we shared our fears, frustrations, and feelings about his illness with each other, we also understood it was not possible to fully know what it was like to be in each other's place.

I could not possibly know the level of pain and fear he endured. He could never know the burdens of being a caregiver or my own fear. Nonetheless, we shared these with each other to the best of our ability and supported each other completely. After Brendan's death, I was in a bereavement group where one of the members talked about not ever really discussing her partner's imminent death with him. I was horrified for her as I could not have made it through that time without Brendan's availability, love, and support. His love and caring for me surpassed his own pain.

As minutes then hours passed that afternoon in the waiting room, Brendan's parents and I grew more and more concerned. Surgeons were coming out and giving families good news all around us. The sighs of relief and joy ruled. Then, almost three hours after Bean had gone in for his biopsy, his doctor came out and pulled us off to the side. We knew it was not good news. He gave us that dreaded "C" word diagnosis but also gave us hope it was probably Stage 2 and that 70% of people with this type and level of cancer survived. He began to preview with us treatment options Brendan had, then went in to give the news to Brendan, who was just coming to in the recovery room. At least now we knew. Dr. Dellacure had diagnosed his cancer within two weeks of seeing him for the first time, something many, many doctors were unable to do over months.

A few minutes later I was allowed back in the recovery room to be with Brendan. He asked me if I heard the diagnosis, and I said "yes". Then I held his hand and said, "I'm here, Soupy. We're in this together." He squeezed my hand and gave me this tender, weak smile—all he could handle at that time. His parents joined us a few moments later.

When we got home late that afternoon, Brendan went immediately to bed. He was exhausted, still under the effect of anesthesia, and I suspect needed the escape from what he had just been told. I took my phone and headed to the park to walk, sob uncontrollably, and call my minister for prayers and counsel. I went to bed early myself that evening, joining Brendan who was still sleeping.

The next day I went to work at a job I had started about nine months earlier. Jim, my former boss from Publicis (the gorgeous one who was also an amazing boss), had hired me as the Director of Client Services for the small agency he now led as its General Manager. It turned out that job was a blessing in a much more significant way than professionally. The day after Brendan's diagnosis, I asked the Office Manager to check with the insurance company if a pre-existing condition clause was in our policy, something I thought with absolute certainty would be the case. When Jennifer came back to my cubicle with an amazed look on her face and the statement that there was no such clause, I sat numb for a moment. At that very moment, my dear sweet Brendan was at Bellevue, one of the most difficult hospitals in the city, going through the process of investigating his treatment options and setting himself up as a Medicaid patient.

I immediately called home with the news, but Bean had not yet returned from his day's adventure. After clock-watching the rest of the day, I left work around six (early for that job) and headed straight home. Brendan had gotten there himself just a little earlier, enough time to hear the message but probably not fully digest it. He regaled me with both the harrowing details of being shuffled around from department to department. He also awed me with his story of having felt the nearness of Jesus and how that kept him going. As usual, his heart was on his sleeve. Amidst his fear and his pain, grace was most definitely present.

The discussion flowed to its logical conclusion—we would indeed marry. Making sure it was something I wanted to do rather than feel I had to do, Brendan reminded me, "When we talked about getting married for insurance purposes before, it was something you said you weren't sure about."

I replied, "That is true. I did say that. But that was when it was a theoretical question rather than the reality of what we were facing. I know this is not *just* about insurance. I meant it when I said to you the other day that I am with you 100%."

After I finished that statement, clad in a grungy T-shirt and his Yankee shorts, Brendan got down on one knee. "Will you marry me?" were the next words to come out of his mouth. Leave it to my superhero Soupy Bean to try to bring some romance to a conversation mostly dominated by practicality. One completely and totally founded in love, absolutely, but still dominated by practicality.

When I went to work the next day and told them I needed the following Monday off because I was getting married, one of my coworkers asked, "Who has the shotgun?" My reply was "the insurance company" but both Brendan and I knew it was so much more than that. Being married would also make me next of kin with all the responsibility and privilege that brings. Even more than that, it was supposed to be. We were to be joined together in marriage under unusual circumstances—but still nothing could have been more right.

The next months—and years—really taught me the value of a close family; in particular, of Brendan's close family. Two days after the diagnosis, two carloads of his siblings showed up at our apartment to support Brendan and me, individually and together. They brought bags of take-out dinner and settled in, all six of them.

After dinner, Brendan's sisters turned the conversation to our nuptials. I stated we were planning to go to Brooklyn City Hall and do the Justice of the Peace route. Neither of us had the head space to plan anything more than that. Good thing Eden and Sheila did. As a television producer whose credits included a cooking show, Sheila had worked with a very good restaurateur in Brooklyn Heights. The restaurant was normally closed on Monday. She called them earlier that afternoon and inquired about the possibility of holding our wedding there. Her friend was very open to the idea so the three of us headed out for me to see the venue while the rest of Bean's siblings stayed with him.

The restaurant was appropriately named Rustic. It was simple yet elegant and had a fabulous menu. It was a place I very likely would have chosen for our wedding even if we had had more time. I liked the notion of having a real ceremony and a real celebration to mark the event. My only concern was how much it would cost since it was a nice restaurant and we would end up with at least twenty-five or thirty-five people, mostly Brendan's family. When I mentioned that to his sisters, they informed me their parents would be covering the check. I stood there in silence, absolutely overwhelmed by the generosity we were being shown.

In some ways, the next five days were typical pre-wedding days, in most they were not. Yes, I did the shopping trip with his sisters—but I knew I had two hours in which I had to find my wedding dress. I did manage to find a dress I was content with—but was thrilled to spot the absolutely perfect 1940's style ivory slightly-veiled hat while riding the escalator down. Yes, we wrote the vows, but with the groom in bed resting, trying to get some relief from the agonizing pain. The invitations were of course confined to phone calls. Mixed in amidst it all was the scheduling of an appointment at Memorial Sloan Kettering to get real treatment, a blessed counter to the experience he had had at Bellevue.

The only remaining question was who would perform the ceremony. I wanted it to be led by my minister, Larry, but he was leaving earlier that day for Japan. A friend of mine then reminded me that another friend of ours was an ordained Interfaith minister. I called Laurie who said that she was available and would be honored to officiate at our wedding. I had already designed most of the ceremony but agreed to meet her that Sunday afternoon, the day before the service, to finalize everything.

Brendan spent that afternoon with his brother Joe, Joe's wife, Vero, and their youngest, Manu. Joe brought shirt, belt, and socks to complete Brendan's wedding ensemble, which also consisted of pants I had bought him the Christmas before, now barely hanging on him, and his favorite charcoal gray suit jacket. They went for a walk in Prospect Park while I was in nearby Brooklyn Heights meeting with the minister. Brendan later acknowledged Joe's visit was at least partially brought on by a call Brendan had made to him the previous Friday. In that talk, my precious love had broken down in sobs to his older brother, acknowledging his fear and even some anger. After Brendan shared this with me, I was even more touched to see how well he was being cared for, how well we were both being cared for. I had known his family to be close but until that weekend had not realized how truly deep the heart connection was between them.

When I arrived home after my meeting with Laurie, Brendan had left one of many sweet, sweet notes he gifted me with during our time together. This one acknowledged he knew how much I and others were doing to make this occasion special. His gratitude was obvious, but even more touching was his statement of determination to make the marriage as special as we were working to make the ceremony. His note referred to starting our official life together on an unorthodox note but that helping us to see how truly blessed our union was and always would be. Once again, he was right.

CHAPTER 19

F inally our day arrived, a mere five days after our decision to marry. A lot had been packed into those days, so it felt as though much more time had gone by. Brendan spent the night before our wedding at his parents since they were taking him to his intake sessions at Sloan-Kettering, the world-renowned cancer hospital, that very same day. It was my job to finish our wedding program and transform myself from harried, concerned partner to beautiful bride. As soon as Brendan and I saw each other for the first time that evening, I remember looking at him as he walked in the door, thinking "In about an hour, this man is going to be my husband." Even after having been through a brutal, brutal day, upon seeing me he still greeted me with a smile, hug, kiss, and the statement I was the most beautiful bride he'd ever seen.

On the joyous occasion of our wedding, his day had been made horrific, not only by a long day at the hospital, but also by getting two pieces of very bad news. First he had found out he was going to have to have a feeding tube put in that upcoming Thursday. Even more troublesome, he had been told his cancer was more advanced than had been thought just five days ago. When he had called with this news earlier that day, I heard in his voice how disheartened he was. I also have to admit to taking a big gulp myself. Our initial thought had been we would have this unorthodox start to our life together but the odds were in our favor we would have a life together. This news foreshadowed what came to be—we'd have a life together but it would be far too brief.

Before the ceremony, we snuck away to the Promenade, the site of our first kiss, to have wedding photos taken by Sheila's husband, Dave, an amazing cameraman and photographer. Despite the calendar saying March 27, fortunately spring was in the air and we were able to be out coatless long enough to have the requisite shots taken. With the Manhattan skyline in the background, we got beautiful shots, traditional shots, goofy shots. In one of the photos, the Twin Towers of the World Trade Center are in the background immediately behind Brendan. I've often noted "gone, gone, and gone", referring to that shot as "proof positive of the Buddhist principle of impermanence."

Around 6:30 p.m. the thirty-three guests started arriving right on schedule. At seven, we took our places in front of the minister for one of the most touching weddings ever, if I do say so myself. Since my parents were both dead, I wanted to start the service paying tribute to them and inviting their souls to join us. To do so we played "I Will Remember You" by Sarah McLaughlin. There was not a dry eye in the house as all were well aware of the circumstances of our nuptials and what Bean and I were facing.

Although he was hanging tough, it was obvious Brendan was in incredible pain throughout the service. He got fidgety during that first song as it went on and on. When it came time to say his vows, he could not read them all the way through as the mobility in his jaw was severely limited by the tumor. I was OK with that as the previous weekend we had gone through them and I knew they came from his heart every bit as much as mine.

The ceremony ended after the minister's blessing with the most incredible kiss I've ever had in my life. Despite his pain, Brendan laid one on me, requiring me to catch my breath and get rebalanced afterward.

The reception pretty much looked like that of a typical wedding. The meal was spectacular. Time was spent roaming from table to table, visiting with the guests. Toasts were offered, some touching, others funny. We danced to a funky version of "Have I Told You Lately That I Love You?" One of my friends noted if she ever had a man look at her like Brendan did me during that dance, she would be a very happy woman. And I was, albeit not one without worries.

Yet it was also obvious these were indeed atypical nuptials. The groom, rather than enjoying the feast, was served his own special order dinner of mashed potatoes and soup, which he didn't even manage to finish. The bridal dance was also abbreviated as Brendan did not have the stamina to make it through the whole song. Fortunately, Joe and Vero had gotten up to dance, followed shortly by many of the other couples, so our exit to the table was not entirely conspicuous. Some silliness went on; the fabulous hat that was my find of the shopping excursion, got passed from me to my sister to her stepson to Brendan to Brendan's father to other friends—with all of them posing for a photo in it. Much laughter was being shared, although Brendan was also grimacing from the pain each time he let out—or tried to suppress—a huge guffaw. Finally, the evening ended for Brendan just after nine, as he was completely exhausted from all the events of the day. He insisted I stay and visit a while longer, both to give the guests permission to enjoy themselves and to catch up with our out-of-town guests. I stayed for another hour-and-a-half. By that time, "my chauffeur," Brendan's father, had returned from getting Brendan settled in at our apartment, had loaded up the gifts, and was ready to call it an evening himself—as were most of the people since it was a work night. On my wedding night, I was home by eleven to snuggle with my husband. The snuggling was old, since it had always been a part of our nightly routine, but the husband was new.

As I lay in my husband's emaciated arms that night, I thought of how blessed I was to be with this man, wherever our journey might take us. I thought about never before having felt as safe, physically and emotionally, as I did with Brendan. Nor had I felt as honored, respected, or heard. With him, I was blessed to know true unconditional love. It was both a great gift and subsequently a great loss.

CHAPTER 20

For us, there was no honeymoon. I showed up at work the very next day, because I knew I was soon going to need time off that was more critical than lolling around as a new bride. The first of those days was only two days later, when Brendan had his feeding tube put in. His parents picked us up and drove us to the outpatient surgery area at Sloan-Kettering, where, for the second time in ten days, I sat and waited with them for the surgery to be over. Afterwards, I was called in to recovery to see Brendan and also to learn how to keep the area clean. As the nurse was showing us and moving around the plastic contraption coming from the stomach of my beloved, Bean looked at me and rightly said, "I think you should sit down." He was right; it was the closest I'd ever come to fainting in my life, and I wasn't even the one who was going through all this.

Brendan, on the other hand, stood strong. He was most definitely proving to be my superhero, Soupy Bean. The treatment he was on was extraordinarily harsh. Near the end of it, he confided the doctors had told him, "We're not going to let you die. With this protocol, you will probably feel like you are and you may even want to, but we're not going to let you."

His initial treatment, the ones the doctors acknowledged may have had him preferring death, consisted of three modalities. The experimental aspect was an antiogenesis, C225, which was combined with standard chemotherapy and radiation at least once a day for ten weeks. On the last day of his treatment, Brendan was begging the doctor not to have to go through his last radiation appointment. His skin was burned and leathery from the radiation. A severe rash, best described as the worst case of teen-age acne ever, covered most of his face and chest as a side effect of the C225. He was down to about 130 pounds on his 6' frame as a result of having subsisted on a diet of liquid food going through his feeding tube. It was a good thing they had insisted on the tube at the start of the treatment given how burned his mouth was.

Still, at the end of the three months, we had gotten great news. The CT scan showed the cancer was gone. "There might be a little smidge left" as one doctor put it, without any seeming concern, so we were elated by the news.

What was not causing elation in my life at that time was my job, the same one that had allowed Brendan to get excellent treatment with very little out-of-pocket costs to us. As a small agency, cash flow was always an issue. Add to that, Joe, the temperamental, controlling co-owner and it was definitely a challenging, often frustrating, place to work. My boss Jim was very much my buffer in having to deal with Joe so I was protected. This particular day, however, Jim was on the West Coast for a business trip when one of our account people had a meeting with the Benjamin Moore client. Knowing she had a reputation for being difficult, I had been over the presentation with Gavin, the account executive, and felt our creative work was addressing everything she had wanted. Gavin called me after leaving the meeting and shared he thought it had gone well. There were a few things to follow up on and issues to address but nothing major. I had just hung up the phone from him when my name was being bellowed by Joe from his office. The client had just called him and had not shared the same perspective.

I grabbed a notepad and headed into Joe's office to get one of the worst beratings I ever had in my career. He accused me of having not known what was going to be presented, which I calmly told him was not the case. He recapped the client's input for me, after which I shared with him Gavin's perspective. This only angered him more; his yelling growing louder and more animated. As he launched into "You've got to...", I took a deep breath and simply said, "You are going to have to get your next Director of Client Services to do that, because I quit" and walked out of his office shaking. I went to my cubicle to call Jim and leave him a message as to what had transpired. When he called me back from the airport, he asked me if I was sure this was what I wanted. I told him I would think about it and we could talk about it the next day. I went home and discussed it with Brendan, who was really uncomfortable with me leaving my job at this time, but also understood all I had been through at work and with him. We agreed it would be nice for us to have some time to recuperate together and maybe even take a mini-honeymoon. The next day at work I told Jim I was certain leaving this job was the right move for me.

Good thing too, because it was not long before we realized how much recuperation Brendan needed and what a long, hard climb that was to be. He still could not eat because of the burns in his mouth. He had little energy to be out and about. His speech was still extraordinarily strained and garbled.

At my birthday dinner the week after getting the good news of his being "cured," it was hard to tell his treatment was over. While I enjoyed my Italian feast, he kept me company but did not partake. Given Brendan's energy level, we ended up calling a car service to get home rather than walking the mile or so back as originally planned. Things were a far cry from the glorious birthday celebration in Montreal just one year earlier.

That's how it went most of the summer. We, along with the rest of his family, went to his sister's for the Fourth of July. He napped. We went to Chicago for my sister's wedding festivities.

Given a lengthy flight delay home, we had to find somewhere in the airport he could hang his feeding apparatus for the hour or so it took him to "eat"—preferably as unobtrusively as possible. Come August, we tried to go out on a Saturday evening but about fifty yards down the street, Bean realized his wedding ring had slipped off his skinny finger. He was so upset and agitated by this and his subsequent frantic search for it that he exhausted himself so much he was in bed a half-hour later. I still remember his sweet smile when he woke up as I slipped his ring back on his finger after finding it on the bathroom floor. It was moments like that that sustained me; that sustained us.

CHAPTER 21

The only thing that seemed to flow easily that summer was how quickly I got a new job. It fell into place almost as miraculously as it did when I got my first job back in advertising after getting sober.

Looking forward to some time off, it took me about a week before I put the word out that I was in the job market. A call to one of my favorite headhunters, Eileen Haubenstock, revealed there was an Account Director position open on the Volvo account at Messner Vetere. It was on the National / Brand side of the business, which I had not worked on in an automotive capacity, but I did have equivalent experience on other accounts. That was enough for me to land the position, complete with a better salary and a car allowance for a Volvo. I was thrilled with it all, especially the car allowance. It had been several months since I had wheels and we had been very restricted by that in dealing with Brendan's treatments. Fortunately, his parents were very generous and wanted to be a part of his treatments, so they schlepped him (often us) to every appointment he had. It was going to be nice to not have to rely on them so much.

Just a little over one month into my new position, the job took me to the south of France for a commercial shoot in late August. That would have been a boondoggle I would have loved to go on any other time—but then, I so did not want to be away from my honey for one day, let alone nine. Brendan's ability to speak was still extraordinarily strained, with his communication usually coming out as a raspy mumble. Given this and the fact he was still weak and eating through his feeding tube, we all agreed it would be best if Brendan stayed with his parents for the time I needed to be overseas. In my brief talks with Brendan while on that trip, he started noticing a difference in the pain. He noted the feeling was more like it was prior to treatment rather than merely the discomfort of the burns. I reminded him that his follow-up appointment was coming up soon and we would find out what was going on then.

What was going on was indeed that his cancer had returned. While we were obviously disheartened by the news, neither of us realized at the time how bad that was. Near the end of his life, his oncologist, Dr. Pfister, explained it was that turn that most likely sealed Brendan's fate, but we certainly didn't know—or accept—that at that time.

We investigated surgery as a treatment option but were told it was not viable because Brendan could not open his mouth more than about a half-inch. To even attempt surgery, his jaw would have to be broken, an ordeal he was in no shape, physically or emotionally, to endure. Instead Brendan stepped immediately into the next treatment program, chemotherapy.

As harsh as the previous treatment was, in many ways, this was at least as equally harsh. At least on the first protocol, Brendan had not gotten physically sick. With the chemo, he was nauseous and throwing up on a regular basis. His skin was sallow. He lost all his hair—on his head, his eyelashes, his pubic hair, everything. When I look back at photos at this time, he looked at his absolute worst. In some ways, I think he was. After all, not only did his body have to endure yet more when it was already beaten down, so did his spirit.

Another thing that challenged him was he started spending a lot more time in the hospital. During his first round of treatment, he had only two overnight stays, both known about and planned for. This time it was different.

The first of many Urgent Care visits that resulted in his being admitted was in late October. I had been at a Johrei service for a few hours. On my way home I called to see how he was and he replied "not great." When I got home about an hour later, he was burning up with a temperature of 102. As we had been told to call Urgent Care if it went above 100.5 degrees, we did so. He argued with the doctor on the phone about going in but finally we convinced him. After an hour or so in Urgent Care, the diagnosis was pneumonia, the first of many bouts to come. That visit lasted only three days; they got longer from there.

Almost as soon as he was back on his chemo treatments, he was also back in the hospital. Less than six weeks had passed when Brendan found himself in Urgent Care waiting to be admitted once again. His second day in that stay had been by far his most difficult to date. With his red blood count extremely low, they had set him up for a transfusion. I had not been there for that as I had a big client meeting at work that would not have been good to miss, so his parents came in to sit with him that day (as they usually did, even when I was there). Apparently, the technician who was hanging the transfusion had a hard time finding a good vein—to the tune of three tries, only to have the hospital call in their chief psychiatrist because Brendan got angry. Imagine that, a patient angry because they were needlessly poked and prodded at a time when they were already depleted in every sense of the word.

When I arrived at the hospital that evening, he was upset from the day's activities. His distress came less from the difficulty in hanging the transfusion as it did from the resulting consultation. Being the sweetie he was, he never wanted to cause problems in any way and that was how he interpreted what had happened. After his parents left, we snuggled for a few hours and got caught up on the day, then discussed the plans for the next day.

Prior to his being admitted to the hospital, we had invited a few friends over for a tree-trimming celebration the following day to celebrate my fifth sober anniversary. As usual, Brendan did not want me to miss out so he insisted I not cancel the party. Instead, after he fell asleep around ten that night, I headed out the front door of Memorial Sloan-Kettering, and rounded the corner that clear, cold breezy night as snow started to fall. I had seen a late-night Christmas tree vendor on the street and knew it was my best opportunity to select a five-and-a-half-foot tall full lush tree and have it tied to the top of my Volvo S40. The next stop was the all-night Pathmark right off the entrance to the Brooklyn Bridge, since I knew they had groceries as well. After loading the necessary veggies and dip, cheese and crackers, sodas and seltzers, and plates and cups first into the cart, then ultimately into the car, I finally was pulling up in front of our apartment shortly after midnight at the end of a very long day. I unloaded the groceries, thought about the tree but decided to get it in the morning, and left the car parked on the street. I was done for the day, with another busy one in front of me for the following one as well—but I still knew how relatively easy my day had been compared to that of my beloved.

Even with increasing hardship, Brendan (my Soupy Bean) apparently was still not ready to leave this world. Nor was I ready to let him. At that time, we hadn't even discussed the prognosis with the doctors. I suppose we didn't want to know. Less than two weeks out of the hospital, Brendan was determined to make Christmas as special as ever. I was determined to make it more special than ever.

That October, I had bought Brendan a guitar for his birthday so he could return to his teenage hobby. As we shopped for the guitar, he also lurked around an amplifier the price of a month's rent. I convinced him how unpractical that was—both expensive and far too powerful for our apartment. It took his hospital stays for me to realize how ludicrous that was. He was getting great joy from the guitar, but if he'd have even more fun with an amp to go along with it, an amp it would be.

I wanted to keep this a surprise from him so I ordered the amp and had his sister and brother-in-law stash it at their house until Christmas. On Christmas Eve, when Brendan and I shared our usual romantic holiday between just the two of us, I let him open a package with the cords to the amp as a precursor to what was to come. He first looked very confused, then hopeful. I confirmed with him that there was indeed something to go with those wires and he would be getting it the next day at his brother's. He just smiled tenderly and looked at me with awe. The next day he was just like that teenager who had plucked a few strings and loved that he could create this powerful, reverberating sound. His present was the hit of the party.

With New Year's upon us, Brendan decided he wanted to go to the sober dance held every year in Brooklyn Heights. It was a party where we had danced until our muscles ached just three years earlier. Now pain was his constant companion, not something a result of excessive celebration and joy.

Being at the party was awkward. Few people recognized him even though most knew him fairly well. Even among those who did, many just didn't know what to say. They had heard what he had been going through, some in detail, but it was another thing when they came face-to-face with the damage of the disease and, even more, the treatment. It was hard to reconcile this gaunt, hairless, sallow man with the gorgeous hottie he had been.

While Brendan did not say anything about how he had been received that night, I could see his hurt. The trip home was gloomy for we were still fighting snow that had been falling most of the day, but now it was accented by the heavy silence of Bean's despair. Once we got home, the mood lightened somewhat. We snuggled for a while, then he decided he was going to try to get some sleep. I headed into the living room to let him rest despite my own agitation. Thinking about the fireworks about to go off up the block in Prospect Park, I had a momentary thought to stroll to the park to see them but did not want to be separated from Bean at midnight. Even if he were asleep, I still wanted to sneak in a smooch. Just then the fireworks started and he called to me an inaudible cry—it turned out the fireworks could be viewed, barely, from our bedroom window at the back of the apartment. We both huddled around the window and cuddled up to each other, craning our necks to see the glorious grandeur of the show—denying the likelihood that we were celebrating our last New Year's Eve together.

CHAPTER 22

Brendan was back in the hospital within the first week of the New Year. Everything just kept getting more difficult from there.

With all his bouts of pneumonia, he had missed several rounds of chemotherapy, so it was no surprise when the next round of CT scans showed the tumor had continued to grow. Something else needed to be tried. What that was, no one was sure. We needed to determine what Brendan's best treatment option now was. He was not about to give up. Then I was more than happy not to let him. In retrospect I wonder if I / we did him a disservice by encouraging him to go through grueling continued treatment for what inevitably were just a few months more. Knowing what I know now, it is certainly not a path I would choose for myself.

His doctor at Sloan-Kettering talked about another clinical trial for which he might be eligible. This one called Sugen. Even though Bean knew he was getting excellent care at Sloan, he decided to seek out another opinion just to confirm this as his best option. The process of actually getting that confirming opinion turned out to be a significantly more difficult process than he thought.

The first stop was Mount Sinai Hospital in the city as it certainly seemed it would be easy to get a second opinion there. I called for an appointment for Brendan; we went up there only to sit in the small dingy waiting area for over seven hours, and never see a doctor. Even the receptionist / scheduling staff brushed us off whenever we would ask about the delay. Brendan was so discouraged we just left. When someone called a day later to apologize and offer him another appointment, he was most definitely not interested.

Instead the search for a second opinion took us down to Johns Hopkins in Baltimore to consult with a female physician there who was as much an expert in the arena of head and neck oncology as Brendan's doctor. But what a schlep it was. The afternoon we left, winter weather was already setting in. Since Johns Hopkins was in downtown Baltimore, we decided it would be easier to take the train than to drive. Arriving on schedule in the early evening, we settled into our hotel room for the evening. We had a cozy night, lying around, watching the snow begin to fall, wondering what the next day was to bring.

That evening I shared many parts of the book I was reading with Brendan, a book entitled *Only Love is Real*. Written by Brian Weiss, the preeminent expert in the field of past life regression, this book followed the lives—as in, past lives—of two of his patients who are now a couple. Through a series of regressions with each of them individually, details came forth that revealed throughout the centuries they had played significant roles in each other's lives. Five years earlier, I never would have believed it; given my growing understanding of spiritual connection, I yearned for the book's message. The instant connection Brendan and I felt made sense. More important was that we also saw hope for our future together— whether in this lifetime or another.

With snow falling heavily the following morning, we checked out of the hotel and grabbed a taxi to Johns Hopkins. The intake process went smoothly and quickly, as did his appointment with the doctor. She confirmed Sugen to be Brendan's best possible option. As we talked further with her, we were also somehow able to ask the looming question, that of the time he probably had left. She answered that it was probably six months after treatment stopped working, whenever that fateful day happened. So Sugen it was.

As we walked back to the glass-fronted lobby, we were disheartened, surprisingly less by the news we had just received than by looking out at the blizzard now in process. Well over a foot of snow was on the ground already, and it was still coming down heavily. Our original plans had been to have lunch with my friend and ex-client Patty before going to the train station. Instead it was clear we needed to head straight to the Amtrak station. Patty agreed to drive us there but arrived at the hospital over an hour after expected, since the trip took four times as long as it normally would.

Fortunately, we had enough room in our schedule that we got to the station about fifteen minutes before our departure time. The train left just a few minutes late, but it was standing-room only, overcrowded with all the people bumped off cancelled flights. We managed to get a seat for Brendan, while I sat in the aisle nearby on our luggage propped up on its side. I kept looking over at my sweetie, alternately dozing, trying to read, and glancing around the train and out the window. I wondered what was going through his mind.

By the time we got back to New York several hours later, the taxi line at Penn Station was over one hundred people long and twisted around three times. With over eighteen inches of snow on the ground and it continuing to fall, albeit slightly lighter, I stood in the line, while Brendan went inside for a little while to warm up and try to get some rest and relax but to no avail. I wish he would have honored his diminished state and let me explain to people his condition—obvious to anyone who looked—so we could cut the line, but his pride would have none of that. Almost four hours after we pulled in to Penn Station, we finally walked into the front door of our apartment. Somehow no matter how exhausted and disheartened he was, my Bean was still as sweet as ever.

CHAPTER 23

About a week later, the process began to get Brendan on the Sugen trial. The night before his baseline exam he got little sleep as he had trouble breathing when he slipped into a certain position. I mentioned this to the doctor at the exam, who told us he needed to do an endoscopy through Brendan's nose into his throat to see if there was any blockage causing the breathing difficulty. I could see Brendan cringe when he said that, so I asked if it was absolutely necessary. We were told it was, so Brendan readied himself with grace—as he always did. That is a nasty, invasive procedure to go through, particularly when it's the fifth or sixth time you've had it done.

The finding was the tumor had continued to grow and was now starting to cover his larynx, causing the difficulty breathing when he lay down. The doctor told us he would need a tracheotomy immediately if he was to go on the Sugen trial. Otherwise the tumor could suffocate him before the treatment had a chance to work. After getting a second opinion from his surgeon, hopeful there was some other option, his tracheotomy was nonetheless scheduled for March 28, one day after our first—and only—wedding anniversary.

Amidst all the turmoil of hospital stays, Christmas, and second opinions, the one bright spot was it was very clear we still remembered we were on the same side. At one point in January, Brendan had written a note that said, "I've been thinking. Maybe

I should go stay with my parents for a few weeks." I looked at him with a face that was a combination of surprise, confusion, sadness, and maybe a little hurt.

I asked him, "Do you not feel as though I am taking good enough care of you?"

"That's not it at all," he quickly replied in his strained, barely-audible voice. "This is all just so much for you. You seem so stressed out and unhappy. I love you so much I just want you to be happy."

I hugged him, with tears in my eyes, and said, "Oh my God. Thank you so much—but I'm not going to be happy if you're not here. Yes, it's hard what we go through day in and day out, but the only thing that makes it bearable is you. If you're not here, I'll still be sad for what you are going through, but then I would also be missing you and feeling badly that I am not there for you. That's the most important thing in the world to me." He smiled his sweet smile, held my hand, and looked me in the eyes. That was the last time we ever spoke of not being together until the very end.

So here we were, celebrating our anniversary with his family and preparing for another surgery. Since I was still working at the time, the plan was for Brendan and me to move into his parents' one bedroom apartment so they could be there with him during the day. They would then go stay at their son Joe's at night so Brendan and I could have as normal of time together as possible. It was on our anniversary eve that we headed to his parents in the suburbs. Brendan's brother, Joe, had driven out to Brooklyn in his SUV because all the medical equipment needed by that time— feeding pump, ventilator, humidifier, suction machine—would not fit into my small sedan. The two of them led the drive, me following behind in the car.

Our actual anniversary day saw all the siblings coming by to congratulate us and wish Brendan well the following day. It was a somber celebration. Brendan was quite frightened by the prospect of the surgery, understandably so. He was cheered by my gift to him, an engraving and resizing of the wedding band he had been unable to wear since the previous summer. His gift to me was a beautiful sapphire and diamond pendant, a surprise since Brendan was usually very thrifty (read: cheap) but I'm sure he knew it was the most extravagant piece of jewelry he would ever buy me. We had photos taken that day, but I couldn't bear to add them to our wedding album as I had originally intended. Brendan still was completely bald, sallow, and visibly disheartened. I knew he would not want those photos preserved in a celebratory way.

The next day, Brendan and I arrived at the hospital with his parents and got Brendan checked in and sent off to surgery, then settled in for the long wait to hear if the surgery was successful. Just after noon, they called my name and informed me Brendan was out of surgery, that it was successful and event-free, and Brendan was in recovery. When I finally got to see Brendan, it was clear he didn't agree with that assessment. He was visibly agitated and surly, only one other time had I seen him more so. Now totally unable to speak even though there was a contraption on the end of the trach that theoretically should have allowed him to do so, he motioned for his notebook to write something. What he wrote directly contradicted the report, "Most traumatic experience of my life. I could feel everything." While he was supposedly out during the surgery, he claims to have felt the knife actually cutting his throat, an experience I cannot imagine. No wonder he was angry.

Brendan ended up spending a few more days in the hospital than originally anticipated. The day he was scheduled to go home, it turned out he had a bit of a fever, compliments of the onset of yet another round of pneumonia. What was supposed to be a two-day hospital stay had turned into almost a week. At last came the time for him to check out and his Sugen trial to finally start.

While we were still staying at his parents following his tracheotomy, I had gotten a phone call at work from my sister that Uncle Burt, Dolores's husband, had just died of cancer. I hadn't even known he had been diagnosed with it, but when I heard of his death I was completely overtaken by the news. I went in the bathroom at work and just sobbed. I got through the rest of the day and resumed my sobbing when I was safe in Brendan's arms—as scrawny as they were by that time. I acknowledged being angry at the power of the disease of cancer, but we both knew the heaving sobs were more for the very real possibility its power would soon overtake Brendan once and for all.

That following weekend we were still staying at his parents. I went back to Brooklyn for the day to pick up mail and catch up with my friends while his lifelong Spartan best friend, Jeff, came up from Maryland to visit him. When I arrived back to his parents' apartment that evening, both his friend and his parents had already retired to their own places. Brendan was waiting for me with one of the sweetest messages I ever read:

"Sat.—My Goldilocks—

It's about 8:30 and I'm waiting for you. I hope the day doesn't have you too tuckered out. I'm glad that you got to see your old pals. I had a good time with Jeff today. Did you know he drove all the way up today just to see me! What a pal, why we even had lunch together, he lasagna, me Osmolite mix. Really we had a nice talk. As good a heart to heart as one could have to another over a word processor.

You know time may go by but the spirit of friendship doesn't. I wish everyone could be as lucky and have the embarrassment of friends that I do. Then my thoughts turn to you my delicate peach. I just love ripe peaches and when I can eat again, they will be the first fruit with you, because everything we do is shared...laughter, tears, I felt for you so much through your crying on Tues. night. It again reminds me that this is our illness, and not just mine; our life, not mine; ours to give and share. God has given us the bitter with the sweet, Why? He may or may not reveal. But in the meantime let's share all that comes our way and get rich on it. Love—Soupy"

It amazes me that such generosity of spirit could come from a man who had been through literal hell for over a year. A man who more often than not these days threw up through a trach, an experience that was frightening to see but I'm sure all the more frightening to experience. A man who was in his third round of treatment, all brutal on his body but not marring his soul.

CHAPTER 24

H is generosity was proven in his writing to me again months later, after it was undeniably clear to him he would die. So committed to me and my happiness, he wrote a list of things I was to do after he died:

"Travel"
"Stay pretty"
"Watch your money"
"Fall in love—Choose wisely"
"Keep up with your photography"
"Keep a picture of me around for a year"
"Stay in touch with my family for a year"

A dying man's wishes for me. My dying man's wishes for me.

Yes, our love was extraordinarily strong and we were as committed to each other as we were to ourselves. Our *American Beauty* lesson had been reinforced big time. This is not to say we didn't have some disagreements; we just had the fortitude to work through them.

Most of these challenges came up in the area of work. Brendan obviously and understandably could not work—but he was feeling guilty about that…and I suspect somewhat bored as well. My already demanding job was just getting more so as there were a lot of major changes going on at my client, including them moving their headquarters from the East Coast to the West Coast. This understandably had our agency management a little nervous, and therefore the pressure was on to be on our game all the time.

With the move into my in-law's apartment, my life became that of a commuting professional with a terminally ill spouse. By eight every morning I was on the train, spent a busy, stress-filled day in the office, then was hopefully on a train around six, getting home just before seven. Even though this schedule only lasted about three weeks, it was enough to make me realize I needed to take time off from work. I even thought of quitting I was so fried, but then realized that with the Family Medical Leave Act, I could take a leave for up to three months without danger of losing my job or our insurance.

This idea concerned Brendan. A lot. While he knew I wasn't doing all that well and the stress was starting to get to me, he had always been financially conservative and somewhat fearful. He was concerned how we would get by without my salary for that time. It was also hard to assure him that our insurance was not in any jeopardy whatsoever.

We had started this conversation a couple times earlier since he had been diagnosed with his second bout of the cancer, but I had always backed off fairly quickly because my situation was tolerable—not easy, but tolerable. But now, with the commute added to it and more aware of his limited time, I became insistent that I take this time off.

Thinking of this process makes me aware and grateful how each of us took care of ourselves. We did of course care for each other and consult with the other a great deal around our needs and our fears, but the final decision for what each of us needed was ours and ours alone.

So with that, Brendan gave me his blessing as I went into work to request a leave as soon as that could be feasible. A few days later, the car was packed up for the reverse trip to Brooklyn where he and I would resettle as his Sugen treatments continued.

All this time we still continued to hold out at least some hope. Foolish? Perhaps—but we knew no other way. There were times when Brendan did acknowledge the very real possibility of his death, enough that his will was done and a health care proxy put in place. The denial was strong enough, however, that we continued forward with the purchase of a house in upstate New York.

From as soon as Brendan and I got together, it was clear we both wanted to settle into a home. As Brendan's condition declined, that desire increased. Brendan would have preferred to buy an apartment in the city. I preferred to buy a house upstate. Although we did look at places in the city, we ended up purchasing a small 1860s farmhouse in Hillsdale, New York, a small town in southern Columbia County, a little over two hours north of the city.

I had seen this place listed in *The New York Times* three weeks in a row starting in January. Finally, I went up there in February to look at it. I immediately fell in love with it and convinced Bean to go up there with me to see it the following week. His response? "I think it's perfect for us. The right size. The right price. Good location."

Bean's sweetness came through loud and clear during this process. He was incredibly apologetic I had to shoulder the burden for buying the place—getting the mortgage, arranging the inspection, everything. I understood completely. After all, it's hard to accomplish much in this world without being able to speak. He also took to the notion of being a "country land baron" as he referred to himself with great charm. As an inveterate knowledge seeker, his latest quest was to learn all he could about small farm animals we could potentially keep as pets. His search quickly centered on rare goats, evolving into many print-outs of specific available goats. He especially related to one runt not likely to be adopted, and therefore not likely to live, giving him the name "Fido." I suspect Bean knew he might outlive Fido some but not by long.

Brendan ended up being at the house on no more than three or four occasions. The closing was on June 1. I was in attendance with a Power of Attorney for Brendan, who was at one of his Sugen treatments in the city with his parents. They all came up the following day. There was joy that weekend.

Soupy took pleasure in his time at the house, as infrequent as it was. He relished sitting outside, even when the hammock fell when he was resting in it. He enjoyed sitting in the living room watching the Yankee game. He was particularly keen on checking out the local golf courses, getting on his knees to evaluate the greens and, I suspect, pray he would one day play that course. Somehow we were even more close than usual when we were up there. I remember one night crawling into bed about an hour after Brendan had. It was the first time he cuddled so close it felt like he was trying to crawl into my skin. The other time this would be the case was the last full night of his life.

I also made one other major decision while in this fragile state, one that proved critical both to my getting through the loss of Brendan and to the big turn my life has taken since then. Since my spiritual life had continued to grow through the Twelve Steps and Johrei, the previous year I had started to consider entering an Interfaith seminary. Milagros, my Lifespring good buddy who subsequently became like a surrogate mother, had attended the New Seminary years earlier and shared with me some of the blessings she received from it. In the spring of 2000, as a new bride now dealing with my husband's illness, treatment, and a demanding full-time job, I promised myself that if I was still contemplating enrolling a year later, I would do so. Well, I was, so I did. I sent my application, including an essay on my spiritual life to date, in to the New Seminary in March. I received a phone call from the admissions director a week later and, after a brief conversation, was told that I was accepted. I, Ann Elizabeth O'Neil, was officially on the path to becoming a minister.... "How did this happen?" was all I could ask myself.

CHAPTER 25

C ome the end of June, Brendan finished the ten weeks that constituted the first round of the Sugen trial. The follow-up CT scan showed the treatment had miraculously shrunken the tumor ever so slightly, but enough that he was eligible to stay on the protocol for another round of treatment. This news strengthened that tiny, almost imperceptible thread of hope to which we clung ever so fervently. This hope, however, wouldn't last much longer.

The week of my fortieth birthday was to be his first treatment in Sugen—Round 2. Even though Brendan was quite weak at this stage, he wanted us to have a party up at the house for my big 4-0. We invited his family, my sister and her family from Chicago, and several of my closest friends. I headed up there after his Tuesday treatment to get the house ready, with the plan he would stay with his parents who would bring him up after his treatment on Friday, the actual date of my birthday. The bash was scheduled for Saturday.

Just like most everything in our life for that year plus, it's not the way it happened. I got a call from Brendan's parents on Thursday that he had a slight temperature. Just over an hour later I got another call it was up more. By the third call they were on their way to the hospital as it had surpassed the 100.5 cut-off and the doctors told them to bring him in. I spoke to Bean and got his orders (via his parents) I was not to come down; I was to continue preparing for the party and waiting for news from them as to what was going on. I tried to do that for about an hour but knew my place was at Brendan's side. Dressed in the T-shirt and casual shorts I had worn all day, I walked into Urgent Care at Sloan in the early evening, only to find out Brendan was still waiting to be seen by a doctor. About two hours later came back the verdict—the usual culprit, pneumonia, was back again. Brendan needed to be admitted.

As soon as those words were out of the doctor's mouth, Brendan started crying and used all his effort to eke out, "But it's my wife's birthday." He finally gave up and wrote it as his speech was still inaudible. The doctor and I convinced him he needed to be admitted, that he would only get sicker without immediate antibiotics and not be able to attend the party anyhow. His parents went home, and he and I waited for a room to be assigned. We were still there at midnight, when he realized it was my actual birthday. Lying on the gurney in the middle of Sloan-Kettering's Urgent Care Ward, clad in the cut-offs and navy blue polo shirt he had on when they realized he needed to be taken in to the hospital, he squeezed my hand and hummed the most unintelligible but touching round of "Happy Birthday" ever. I leaned over and kissed and hugged him, knowing every moment with him was the best gift and celebration I could ever have. Shortly after, he drifted off to a light sleep, still on the gurney, while I sat nearby waiting for information about an open room. About a half-hour later, one was available, the admission process was completed, and he was wheeled up to his room, a double but with no one else in it. Once he was settled in and sound asleep, I drove to our apartment in Brooklyn for some rest myself. Even though I got there at almost two in the morning, I went through the routine of picking up the mail and going through it as I tried to wind down.

I spent most of the next day—my fortieth birthday—in his room at the hospital. Throughout the day we found out the treatment plan for this round of pneumonia, as well as the possibility it would result in him being off the Sugen trial, his last hope. With all this, he still insisted I go up to the house for the party, especially with my sister coming in from Chicago and friends coming from a distance as well. I thought of the statement "The show must go on" and knew where his insistence was coming from. Finally, it was agreed his parents would stay behind with him and I would return first thing Sunday morning.

Unfortunately, everything happened so quickly his siblings were not clued in as to what was going on, so they showed up expecting to see Brendan and be celebrating both my birthday and the news there was still hope for their beloved brother. Oh how things had changed! Still, we all tried to put on our party faces despite the update and absolutely sweltering weather. Thank God for his numerous little nieces who sweetly focused on the badminton game and the birthday cake and ice cream. Brendan's brother-in-law captured all of it on a video for Bean, which was also replete with much, much well-wishing for the patient. While inclusivity was the goal, its effect was actually just the opposite because it continued to remind Brendan how much he was missing out on.

The day finally came when Brendan was released from that particular stay. There was still a sliver—a tiny sliver—of hope. The plan was to monitor him, then resume the Sugen treatment if all seemed well. It did not.

CHAPTER 26

M y work leave was over. Three months had gone by and the path of Brendan's disease still was not fully evident to us, so I headed back to work for what proved to be a very short stint.

Because of my leave and the move of the client's headquarters, I was assigned a new responsibility, that of covering the Southern region. My third day on the job, I was invited down to Atlanta for a big regional meeting, where I would meet all of the clients I would work with regularly, as well as my new direct reports. Brendan's parents had picked him up from our place the evening before so he would not be alone for the two days I was to be gone. When the alarm went off at the ridiculously early hour of 5:00 a.m. for me to catch an eight o'clock flight, I was the only one putzing around our apartment. Still too early to call his parents' home by the time I boarded the flight in New York, I took the flight, got off the plane, shlepped through Atlanta's huge airport, and met up with the car service before I had the chance to check my voice mail.

By that time, there was already a message from my father-in-law telling me Brendan was back in Urgent Care. As I was on my way to the meeting, I decided the only appropriate thing to do was to show up, introduce myself, and explain the situation and excuse myself.

I arrived shortly after 10:30 at the hotel where the meeting was being held. With it already underway, I snuck in the back of the conference room, deduced who Courtney and Alex were (my two employees), and sat myself down next to them. The Regional Manager, John, was up at the front, giving the purpose and agenda for the day, as well as recognizing the "special guests" with them that day. The day's guests of course included the agency, so John made a point of noting that most of the people surely recognized their agency regulars but also introducing me to the group, even though I had not yet been introduced to him.

At the first break, I explained to Courtney and Alex about the call I had just gotten, and asked for their perspective on how John was going to take that information. I was relieved to hear he was a reasonable, understanding man. I then approached him and explained the circumstances, to which I got a prompt, "Get out of here." I called a car service and did exactly that, perfunctorily meeting a few of the area managers in midst of it all.

Even though I was back to the airport by two, planes were cancelled and delayed so I could not get on another flight until five that afternoon—which ended up not leaving until almost six. Finally, after an interminable anxiety-filled day, my cab pulled up in front of the familiar Memorial Sloan-Kettering around 8:30. It turned out Brendan's day had been as long and stressful as mine; he was still sitting in Urgent Care with his parents when I arrived. He was simultaneously relieved to see me and angry as hell at me. I completely understood even though he was the one who had wanted me to return to work, whatever the assignment.

He had had his scariest episode to date and had lost the ability to breathe as his trach had gotten completely filled with phlegm and been difficult to remove. It was then I promised Bean I would do my very best to be at his side when his time came but if I wasn't, he was to know my heart and soul were absolutely there. He acknowledged that to be his fear and where his anger

157

of the evening came from. We kissed and made up. I spent the night with him in the hospital after he was once again officially admitted.

That was his last stay at Memorial Sloan-Kettering. His first day in, he shit in his pants and cried. "How did it get to the point that I'm crapping in my underwear?" was what he wrote in his ever-present notebook. I told him he was really sick and it was understandable. A few days later I was returning to his room from a ten-minute walk around the hospital, only to be asked by a physician I didn't recognize to please not go in. They were about to do something to try to raise Brendan's dangerously low blood pressure by breaking up the phlegm in his chest, a procedure that might be hard to watch. I explained to him I was Brendan's wife and intended to be by his side in anything like that. A few days after that, Brendan was in isolation because of the latest strain of pneumonia. We all masked up and gowned up to sit at Bean's side.

Then came the critical conversation. There was absolutely nothing more that could be done for him at Sloan-Kettering. Sixteen months and three treatments into it, Brendan got his death sentence. Initially Brendan's wish had been to die at home "if it does not jeopardize the chance of my recovery and does not impose an undue burden on my family." I wanted to honor those wishes and began looking for a ground-floor or elevator home for us since soon Brendan would be challenged by our stairs and yet would not stand for confinement, even in his own home. The Sloan-Kettering staff consistently explained Brendan would be much, much better off at Calvary Hospital, where they focus on palliative care for terminal cancer patients. He would be kept more comfortable than he could at home, and his death was significantly more likely to be peaceful and nonviolent given all the medications and machines and tubes he was on. Finally, Brendan and I agreed to look into it further. We both watched a video on the hospital, and I went for a visit there with my sister, Meg, who had come in from Chicago to help me with all this.

I was so grateful for her support. Brendan's family, all of whom lived locally, had been a tremendous help and had welcomed me into their clan so readily and completely. Whatever I needed—for me or for Brendan—was handled by his family. This took the form of siblings spending time with Brendan when I had to be elsewhere, his parents covering large chunks of out-of-pocket expenses, and even his sisters dragging me away every once in awhile to ensure I got a break.

But I was still very aware it was Brendan's family, not mine. I had only known them three years, so I didn't necessarily let them in to the core of who I was or what I was experiencing. My twisted sense of humor rarely, if ever, got shared with them—yet it had always been what I relied on to get me through the tough times. To keep the peace I diminished many of my religious and political beliefs. Plus, to some degree, I was always in danger of slipping back into the "Don't cry. Behave" rules of my youth, particularly when Gail would use the phrase, "We have to be strong for Brendan." Spending almost two weeks with my sister allowed me to relax a little; especially since she was still as efficient at getting things done as she ever was.

CHAPTER 27

T he decision was made to admit Brendan to Calvary Hospital, especially since they allowed family members to stay overnight with their patients. He had initially wanted to go home for a day just to see our Brooklyn apartment one last time, but we were talked out of that. The reasons given were room availability, insurance, and changes to his care I didn't yet know how to implement, but I suspect the reality is we would not have made it to Calvary in the Bronx if we went by way of Brooklyn, at least not anytime soon.

Since I was on leave from work again, Brendan and I quickly settled into his 120-square-foot room at Calvary. Initially I thought it would be Bean settling in and I would be occasionally taking advantage of the overnight visitation rights. That was not the case. Between Brendan's somehow covert reminder I was to be with him when the time came and the distance between Brooklyn and the Bronx, it turned out I was there almost every night; there were maybe three nights when I stayed in Brooklyn. That was completely OK with me.

It was also clear if this was to be our home, a home it would be. Brendan had me bring some of his favorite books. One of his friends gave him a cool rock-band poster to decorate the room, another a brightly colored cotton throw to make it even homier. The wide window sill soon was decorated with cards, knick-knacks, and flowers. Brendan also insisted he would not be living in a hospital gown so I packed up a supply of sweats, shorts and T-shirts for him to don daily. It was indeed our new home, especially since we were together.

Our life was pretty simple the first month at Calvary. Brendan was still able to get around easily, even tethered to an IV pole for his medications. Most days we woke up around eight. The doctor came by on her rounds shortly thereafter. After that, I would help the aide clean Brendan and get him dressed for the day. By that time, his parents would have arrived with Brendan's *Post* and *New York Times* and we would all sit around, read, visit (Brendan via notebook), and even go outside in the courtyard if the weather allowed it. On special days, I would wash Brendan's hair or massage his feet and just watch the relaxation take over. He so loved the special pampering.

It was one of these run-of-the-mill days that holds one of my simplest yet most beautiful memories. Brendan and I were sitting reading, he in bed absorbed in the day's papers and I in the chair next to him lost in a re-read of *Only Love is Real*. Without even looking up, he just held his hand out to the side and grabbed mine and held it tenderly. In a lot of ways, it seemed surreal that we were at a hospital for patients 95% of whom would not be in this world within three months.

It was moments like this that made me aware of how unnecessary our voices can be, of how much babble we have in our world. Gentle touches such as the one Brendan and I shared that morning—especially when combined with the looks we often exchanged—spoke more than most conversations I have had in my lifetime.

As September rolled around, everything changed. The first event was his cousin's death. A healthy, vibrant, elegant woman in her 40's, she had taken the dog out for a late night walk, never to return. She had been struck by a hit-and-run driver and left in the ditch to die. Needless to say, a family that was already shaken was shaken even more.

Only to be shaken along with the rest of the world on the fateful 9/11. Three days earlier, I had attended my first class at the New Seminary. I felt very blessed to be in that environment but was all the more honored to be so involved when the nation got caught up in the furor of blaming the entire Muslim religion for the events of that day. While I understandably did not participate in the healing of the aftermath (with the exception of prayer), I felt comforted to know that many of my classmates and New Seminary alumni were giving service at Ground Zero and throughout the city, doing whatever could be done to support and help New Yorkers with the grief, terror, and anger they were experiencing.

I knew my job was primarily to be present with my very ill husband. Grace ensured I was with him during this tragedy for on Monday, September 10, I had headed home in the early afternoon for my weekly journey back to Brooklyn to get mail, do the laundry, catch up on life chores as his parents stayed with him during the day. Around seven that night, exhausted and hungry, I called Brendan to see how he would feel about my having one of my rare nights in Brooklyn and getting an early start the next morning back to Calvary. I expected he might take issue with the idea but thought I'd give it a try anyway as I knew he'd be sound asleep by the time I got back there that night. Even though he could not speak his answer, his "Awww" had a tone to it that made it clear he really wanted me back with him that night. I am so eternally grateful I made the return trip that evening instead of waiting for the morning. I cannot bear to think of how upset Brendan would have been without knowing where I was at the time the planes hit and the Towers subsequently fell, particularly since the drive back would have had me in the vicinity of the chaos.

Instead, I was sitting on the edge of his bed at his side. We had just awoken a few minutes earlier and were starting into the day's routine when one of the aides came in and told us that a plane had just hit the World Trade Center. Being the insatiably curious man he was, he automatically wanted the TV turned on so we could see what was going on. Our assumption was that it had been an accident. We turned the TV on just in time to watch the second tower being hit. It was then we knew it was not an accident.

Things were in turmoil that day at Calvary Hospital as they were throughout New York City. One of the neighboring patients' sons was downtown for a seminar that day. We prayed for his safety. Brendan and I started thinking about people we knew who worked in the World Trade Center and fortunately could not come up with many. The one close friend of his was home when we called, fortunately having been running a little late that morning.

The next day we found out one of his sister's lifelong best friends was missing. She and her new husband had been by to see Brendan two days earlier and bring him a prayer card. It was then we had found out she was four months pregnant. Initially, Brendan's family did not want to tell him that Helen was missing, but I knew he would want to know. He prayed as fervently as the rest of us for her to be alive—which of course she wasn't.

Over the next couple weeks it became clear Brendan's condition was worsening. His energy was waning. His face was more and more swollen and deformed by the tumor. He started taking in less food. He was also more determined than ever that I keep my promise to be at his side. So much so that on the rare occasions I left the hospital, I would find he had conned his visitor to take him down to the main floor to await my return, much to the chagrin of the staff.

He also started to really come to grips with the notion of his own death...finally. He asked to speak with one of the priests at his parent's parish, a contemporary meditater with a less-than-traditional Catholic viewpoint. After their conversation, Brendan wrote to me, "I'm going to miss you a lot." When I asked what he meant, he wrote that Fr. Gatt had explained the afterlife is more similar to this world than we normally think. Brendan took that to heart and anticipated normal human emotions over our inevitable separation. I do not necessarily share that viewpoint but was touched immensely.

Brendan also began to get clearer and more specific on his dying wishes. I had befriended another of the overnight visitors, a woman whose partner was there with lung cancer. She and I often inquired as to the state of our respective partners. I saw her one Friday only to be told that Tom, her partner, was increasingly agitated and had started a fight with her the night before. Knowing she was in need of some peace and suspecting he was as well, I offered to channel Johrei to him, explaining to her this was my primary spiritual practice and a healing practice that often provided great comfort and calm to people. Over the next two days, I channeled to him twice, with the second time being at the moment of his death—unbeknownst to me it was that imminent. After that, Beth explained to me Tom had indeed calmed not only at the time of receiving the first round of Johrei, but was calm and coherent enough later that evening that they could reconcile and say a proper good-bye to each other. When Brendan heard that story, he told me that's how he wanted to leave this world—with my channeling Johrei to him. Weeks later, he did.

Yet apparently he had one more birthday he had to celebrate.

CHAPTER 28

I am a definite believer that people leave this world when they are good and ready…and only then. Before that was to happen, Brendan intended to celebrate his birthday, complete with a party.

The celebration started first thing in the morning when Dr. Kogan, his staff physician, came in with a card and a Beatles book for him. He was touched but I was even more so. For this woman to gift him with something so perfectly chosen for him when she had already given him so much made me choke back tears.

At Calvary they provide patients celebrating their birthdays with cake and ice cream. All too often it is shared only with the staff and perhaps one or two family members who visit. For this momentous occasion, the patient lounge was decorated with balloons, streamers, and refreshments as we needed to take over that room to accommodate the twenty people who came to pay homage.

Homage is the only word to describe it. Fortunately, Brendan was still completely coherent and therefore his usual self—as gracious a host as can be. He sat in his wheelchair as one by one siblings, in-laws, aunts, friends all came up to him to shake his hand or hug him. He, the Jets fan, even nonverbally chided Jeff for his choice of a Giants cap that night. (How dare he!) With deep gratitude, Bean opened his cards and gifts. I couldn't help but wonder if any of the gifts would be put to use in what were most certainly his final days.

Brendan was completely present as stories of shared memories were awkwardly bantered about. They started as an attempt to convey how important he was to those present, to be able to capture the depth of love we all held for him. Once again, I suspect the words were inadequate but that he still got the message.

To make the celebration complete, Brendan was determined to eat. Having not had a morsel of food in over a year and a half, the cake and ice cream were too much for him to pass on. With a determined, voracious look in his eye, he set about to cut the cake. Knowing it would make no difference at this point yet not wanting him to choke, as would have been likely had he taken a normal bite, I helped him get an infant-sized taste of the cake then the ice cream. Surprisingly he declined the second teeny helping; the first round had been enough for him. Being the Italian he was, he just needed the taste buds to be exercised one more time. Food and much love were at the core of his 43rd birthday party.

There are many photos from that celebration that remind me of the love that existed for Bean. Some are of the whole gang, others are of him with family members. My favorite one is of him and me off to the side; I am holding his hand and playing with his hair while he softly gazes down.

Now that his birthday had been adequately celebrated, there were two other goals Brendan set his mind to. Having been tethered 100% of the time to an IV pole since he entered Calvary, he wanted his freedom. He wanted to be able to walk around completely unencumbered and intended to make certain that would happen. The process of changing his meds and nutrition schedule started the day after his birthday, so by the end of the following day he could walk on his own—albeit with support from another. The nurses were extremely concerned to see this as he had become incredibly frail, but there was no stopping him nonetheless. One of them said to me, "He shouldn't be walking around," but clearly she had not felt the resolve in his body I did when helping him to steady himself.

After having accomplished that one, Brendan decided he wanted to go home. I was informed of this decision on my return to Calvary after an afternoon away. As I was approaching his room, I heard his father say, "She should be here any time. We'll talk to her as soon as she gets here." When Brendan wrote out he wanted to go home, I had two thoughts. The first was consideration about what "home" he was referring to as I have long believed that, when a dying person says they want to go home, they are not referring to any home on this earth. My belief is our end-of-life wish to go home is to our spiritual home, the one we share with the Creator. The second thought was remembering his desire that his last days be at his home in the physical world. As it was becoming increasingly clear those days were upon us, we discussed where that home would be.

Most of Brendan's family wanted him taken to his parents' apartment since it was convenient to all of them. I was pretty clear that would not work for me but also heard everyone's concern about Brooklyn not being practical. We all compromised on the house upstate, with the understanding his parents would be staying there with us. We conveyed this to the Calvary staff, who promptly and efficiently worked with the hospice facility up near our house, one I volunteer with today. By Wednesday, it was decided he would be moved the following Monday.

Pretty much everyone in Brendan's family—including in-laws and nieces—had come to visit him at least once in his almost three months at Calvary, as well as many, many friends. The one exception was his oldest niece, Julia, for whom I knew he had a special place in his heart. As quite a few of us were sitting around Brendan's room talking about the move to our house, I asked Joe,

Brendan's brother and Julia's father, "Where's Julia been?" He answered uncomfortably that she'd been a little busy, adding that dealing with death has always been difficult for her. I told him I understood that but "tell her to get her ass here anyways." I knew she would regret it if he died without her seeing him again.

Joe immediately called Julia, sharing my exact statement with her. Hearing the words repeated I cringed, hoping they were not too harsh. Julia agreed to make the short trip from Pelham that evening. In about an hour, she arrived at the door of Brendan's room with a couple of her sisters in tow. Her sisters decided to join me down in the cafeteria for dinner to give Julia some time with Brendan. As we sat, Gabrielle once again defended Julia for not having yet visited, explaining that her heart was tender—something I know and have always loved about her. I merely answered that I knew she would regret it if he died without her having a chance to say good-bye, thus the command performance. After dinner, we went back upstairs to relieve Julia, who was ready to go. With eyes filled with tears, she gave me a big hug as she left, whispering a barely audible "thank you".

The transition plan we had all agreed to—Brendan's parents, the Calvary staff, and me—was for me to go up to the house Sunday to make sure all the equipment was in place and the local hospice ready to take over. He would be transported by ambulance Monday with his parents driving alongside. Almost immediately the shadow of death appeared at the door. Agitation set in, liquid feedings were refused, and the shutdown of his body began.

CHAPTER 29

B y Thursday, I asked his doctor if she thought he'd last until Monday. Her solemn and earnest reply was, "I don't know." He did not. That night his agitation was full force. They had begun administering medication to calm him somewhat—which worked for a brief while with every dosage. That evening he was restless, tossing and turning, pulling at all the various devices attached to his body: trach, feeding tube, and mediport. Around midnight I asked Brendan, "Do you think you would get some rest if I got into bed with you?" He looked me straight in the eye more intently than I'd ever seen and nodded his "Of course." I did and miraculously we both slept through the night until the doctor came in to do her rounds the next morning.

I had been surprised to see Dr. Kogan come in because a quick glance at my watch showed 6:40 when her rounds usually started after eight. It turned out it was after eight and my watch had mysteriously stopped at 6:40…actually it turned out to be not so mysterious after all.

That day Brendan was completely out of it. His parents and I were at his side all day, increasingly aware of time clicking away, yet I just recently realized I never spoke to them about what it was like to be losing a son. I had been so wrapped up in my own grief I diminished theirs. It was several years afterward before I came to believe the death of a child—whatever the child's age—is almost certainly the hardest loss to face.

Nonetheless, without speaking anything more definitive than "Call us if anything changes," his parents left the hospital around seven that evening. I immediately called my minister to say prayers as I knew Brendan's death was imminent. (I suspect his parents knew as well.) I then settled in to unfocused reading for a few hours, only to have Brendan awaken with one of his bouts of agitation around ten. After I had talked to and calmed him somewhat and the nurse had administered medication, Brendan fell back asleep. I then went down to the chapel, and sobbing and weeping uncontrollably, asked God to please take him, to please release him from the suffering that had become his life. I then went upstairs to write in my journal and settle in for a few hours sleep before awakening just prior to Brendan's next state of agitation.

In this bout shortly after 5:00 a.m. he was fighting to get out of bed, to walk toward the door. As feeble as he was, it was still difficult for me to hold him in place while the nurse came and gave him another shot of medication. Immediately after that he looked me deeply in the eye then lay back on his pillow. It took me a few moments to realize that look was the last one he would ever give me. His eyes shut and his breathing slowed dramatically. I held his hand, and said, "Soupy, my Soupy. I love you so much, and I am going to miss you so much—probably more than I can even imagine. But you have suffered enough. It's OK to go." A few tears came out of the corner of his eyes and I wiped them away. I then called his parents to say "Brendan's getting ready to go" then went back to holding his hand and channeling Johrei to him as I promised him I would do. The only distraction to this peaceful scene was the aide in the room, who mumbled "That's the most beautiful thing I ever heard" to the words I shared with Brendan. It was a sweet sentiment, definitely, but a little annoying nonetheless. I didn't exactly want a commentary on my last few moments with my beloved.

I do not know the exact time of Brendan's death, but I do know it was very close to when my watch had stopped twenty-four hours earlier. I'm not even certain if it was before or after his parents' arrival. His mom thinks he had already gone, but I don't know for his spirit was still definitely there awaiting their arrival, as was Spirit with a capital S. I have never in my life been more clear there is something on the other side than I was in the moment of Brendan's passing. Just recently, I finally attempted to describe this experience to one of my spiritual teachers. I likened it to being taken into the foyer of the spirit world by Brendan. It was total bliss, total love, total "AAAAAHHHHH"—yet I knew I was, for then, just a guest who was not to stay. I was privileged to have glimpsed the other side while remaining firmly and fully in this world, thanks to the great love I shared with Brendan.

In truth the shadow of death had first appeared the previous Sunday. It was that night I saw Brendan get out of bed, pause at the door, and turn around to wave good-bye to me. This scene startled me awake, only to have me look over and see him sleeping peacefully in his bed. I am certain that was the beginning of his transition out of this world.

The morning of Brendan's death, a few of his brothers and sisters came by the hospital before we left to view him for the last time and help pack up our things. I was already appreciative of the care and respect he had gotten at Calvary, now I was even more so of the space we were given in spending time after his expiration. I sat on the edge of the bed, looking at the bony body that had been my husband. His left jaw was hugely distorted by the tumor that had now grown out of control. His beautiful thick dark brown hair had grown back in and fell over his forehead. Those beautiful brown eyes were closed, but it was as if a slide show of all the moments I had looked into them flashed through my head.

I was grateful to have the time but also found it awkward to be sitting around the room with much of his family with his body in the midst of it all. As I glanced at the pile of his possessions his family had surreptitiously packed up, the three golf irons he kept in his hospital closet just to have them nearby caught my attention. I placed one of them in his hands, stating I knew he would want to hold them for one last time. This elicited an awkward chuckle from many of the visitors telling me that yes, it was definitely getting to be time to clear out. My father-in-law had already had the necessary conversations with the staff about transporting his body to Fox Funeral Home for them to handle the cremation. All his possessions were in boxes and bags with his siblings ready to carry them out. I took a deep breath and bent over to kiss my Soupy Bean on the lips for the last time. His family, already standing outside his door in the hallway, shuffled around slightly with awkward tenderness.

It was October 27, an incredibly beautiful crisp fall day with the foliage bursting colors in a late peak season. The sky was a magnificent blue to offset the reds, golds, and oranges of the leaves. As we left the hospital, I said to Brendan's brother, Joe, I was going to turn on the classic rock station—Brendan's favorite type of music—and know that whatever song came on was Bean's message to me. What came on were the last two lines of the Stones "Start Me Up." Those lines are, "You make a grown man cry. You make a dead man come." I had to verify that those were indeed the lines I heard, then chuckled appreciatively that Brendan was enjoying himself in his new realm.

With none of us really knowing what to do with ourselves, Brendan's sister Eden suggested we go over to her house, which was nearby. We did. The rest of the family, as well as many of their lifelong friends, arrived as we sat in the sun on her front porch.

On one hand I was aware that Brendan was supposed to be there; on the other I was aware he was.

After a while of sitting around visiting, occasionally crying, I realized how many people needed to be called. I had already spoken to my sister that morning from the hospital, but the rest of my family needed to be called. Our Brooklyn friends hadn't yet heard the news, as well as other friends of mine and some of Brendan's newer Brooklyn friends who did not know his family. I retired to the back yard and started letting people know that Soupy was no longer in this world with us. That process made it feel even more real, as did the reaction of Brendan's niece, Vivian. A beautiful girl with long dark, dark brown hair, big eyes to match, and olive skin, her response of sympathy was so dramatic yet genuine as she walked into the back yard that I finally allowed myself to realize the depth of what had happened.

As mid-afternoon rolled around, I realized I needed to go face my new life—alone—in Brooklyn. Brendan's family clearly was not comfortable that I was heading out, but I insisted it was time for me to start the trek back, reminding them I was going to have to do this at some point. I also assured them I had already made plans to get together with a bunch of my friends that evening so I would not be alone. What I didn't mention to them was that I would be attending the anniversary / Halloween party of my AA home group. It was most definitely not that I was in a celebratory mode; it was simply that I needed to be sure not to be alone and to try to remind myself that my life did go on. I had also lined up friends to stay the next couple days before my sister's arrival scheduled for Monday.

I was touched by everyone's love that night. The friends I had invited to join me coddled me. Other attendees did so also. I was even pardoned for a social blunder—stunning a rather shy man who had come to the party dressed as the Grim Reaper. I had taken it upon myself to inform him that I had already seen him once that day and didn't really care to see him again—my lame attempt at levity. My real chuckle, a gift from the Universe, was when the song "Start Me Up" came on and I once again got to hear those words "You make a dead man come." I thought, "Wow, twice in one day. That's been awhile."

CHAPTER 30

I didn't spend a lot of time in my body the following week. Physically I showed up for things, but my heart and mind were so overloaded I checked out. I needed to.

Three of my four siblings were scheduled to come in for the services. My sister, Meg, arrived Monday, my brother Joe on Wednesday, and my brother Dennis late Thursday evening. To keep us together and minimize driving, we all settled into a B&B in Larchmont, New York, Brendan's home town and where the service was to be held. Just blocks from the Long Island Sound, it was a gorgeous huge old mansion with an enormous front porch, complete with white wicker rocking chairs. On the nicer evenings, we all sat out there. On the chillier ones, we were in the eclectically decorated spacious living room. I'm not sure if we were the only ones in the inn, but we certainly were the only ones who took advantage of the public spaces. Besides my family, my good friend Naugie came in for the whole weekend of the service as well, sharing an old-fashioned double room with me. The love and connection from my family, something I was not particularly used to, was proof positive I would get through this ordeal; I would indeed be carried—by Spirit and humans alike.

The real task of the week was to plan the service, a task made infinitely easier by the fact that Brendan had left fairly detailed instructions about the service. His directions were that it was to be held on the Saturday following his death, it was to be a memorial mass only as he was to be cremated, and it was to be followed by a luncheon in the church hall. The only song he required be played that day was "Keep On Rockin' in the Free World." It was months before I realized that was another way he was reminding me—and all who loved him—to continue to fully live life. It was as if he continued his list of things he wanted for me.

Even though his parents and I had very different spiritual perspectives, everything fell into place easily...with a little negotiation. We included enough scripture and Biblical references to keep them happy. I added in a song from *Jesus Christ Superstar* for balance, plus chose a very non-traditional poem for the bookmark to serve as his mass card. It read:

> If my parting has left a void,
> Then fill it with remembering joy,
> A friendship shared, a laugh, a kiss;
> Ah, yes, these things I too will miss.
>
> Be not burdened with times of sorrow;
> I wish you the sunshine of tomorrow.
> My life's been full, I've savored much,
> Good friends, good times, a loved ones touch.

This reading reminded me of his statement "I'll miss you" and his note about the "embarrassment of friends" he had. Just as he orchestrated much of his service, it seemed he also chose his marker.

As it had become increasingly clear Brendan's death was imminent in the last month, one hope I had, but kept to myself, was that he would hold on long enough for the 9/11 memorials and funeral masses to diminish. That may sound callous but so many New Yorkers attended so many funerals in those weeks that

I was afraid Brendan's service would become "just another one". Nothing could be less true.

The service was to start at 11:00 a.m. on November 3, the first Saturday after his death—just as he had instructed. That morning the sky was overcast, with light rain threatening. Brendan's family and my family arrived shortly after ten, hoping Brendan would have a beautiful celebratory send-off, complete with ample friends and family. We had prepared enough programs and bookmarks for about 250 or 300 people. Not enough. As one of Brendan's friends pointed out when the church filled with over 700 people and turned out to be standing room only, "Just like an actor. He had to go out playing to a full house."

The program was entitled "A Celebration of Life" and that it was. There was joy. There was laughter. There were tears. There were beautiful tender memories shared. There was recognition of Brendan's faith. There was acknowledgement of our love.

Fr. Gatt, the priest who had spoken to Brendan in his final days yet still did not know him well, captured him perfectly in the sermon. His first reference was to Brendan's soulful eyes and strength of presence. He recalled walking into his room at Calvary and seeing the shell of his body, but being gripped by him—first by his firm handshake then by his gaze. He went on to describe Brendan as a lotus flower, beautiful even at first glance but all the more so the deeper you look.

By the time we emerged from the church, the sun was out and another crisp, beautiful fall day was upon us. A luncheon was held in the parish hall, with most of the mass attendees sticking around for that. One of my friends called my behavior at the lunch manic and I suppose it was. I was pulled in so many different directions, talked to by so many people, and was fervently trying to be present to it all without having a clue how to be. Having not yet learned specific techniques on how to be in my body, I just wasn't. As the end of the lunch drew near, I thanked everyone for coming and requested they keep Brendan alive in their memory by thinking about what they loved most about him and inviting that trait more fully into their own being. It has become my favorite way to honor those who have passed. For me, it has been Brendan's gentleness that I have tried to emulate.

Brendan's brother, Joe, invited the attendees back to his home after the lunch. The party continued well into the evening with many, many stories about Brendan shared as well as many, many drinks consumed. It was there we decided to play the one song Brendan himself requested for his good-bye, "Keep on Rockin' in the Free World."

A little ways into the party, I retired to the den with my friend Naugie to watch the Michigan—Michigan State football game, a long-time tradition between the two of us. It was also something Soupy would have wanted as he often just watched me watching my Spartans. I realized this at a sports bar during a basketball game versus Duke. Brendan had gone to the bathroom while I was glued to a close game. I was half-aware he had been gone quite awhile when, at a commercial break, I glanced around to see him just standing about a hundred feet away. I motioned him over, when he explained he was so happy watching me that intently captivated that he hadn't wanted to break my focus. That comment was rewarded with a big hug and kiss. I remembered that day as the game kicked off with other mourners reveling in the background.

Not only was the game important to me, I also needed space: from the partying; from the many people I knew perfunctorily; from the manic behavior lots of us seemed to be experiencing, perhaps as our own denial of mortality. In the relative calm on the sidelines of the party, I was able to connect with Brendan, especially feeling his presence with the Michigan State victory, made possible by a stunning last-minute pass with no time left on the clock. Immediately prior to that play, I jokingly had invited his spirit in to play quarterback for my team. Apparently, the superhero Soupy Bean was still taking calls.

CHAPTER 31

L ost and befuddled is the only way I can describe how I felt after Brendan died. Here I was back in my apartment on Tenth Street in Park Slope, a place I had not lived in for almost three months. I had stopped by weekly so it was not unfamiliar, yet sleeping there was unfamiliar. This was the apartment I had moved into on my own four years earlier, yet that truly became a home when Brendan moved in just over fifteen months later. Now I was once again living there alone—only now it had the remnants of Brendan that needed to be dealt with. His clothes hung in the closet. His guitar and amplifier sat by the computer desk he had moved in. His medications—methadone, morphine, and Oxycotin—filled an entire kitchen cabinet. All of this would need to be dealt with, some things sooner than others.

My friend Karen was the person who graciously agreed to stay with me the night Brendan died. When we got up in the morning, finally coherent and cleaned up by noon, she asked me if I was hungry. My response was to look at my watch. It was the only answer I could come up with. My body was numb and therefore wouldn't allow any signals to come forth. I had no way of knowing if I was actually hungry; I needed the structure of the clock and other people to remind me what I was supposed to be doing at that time. I could so identify with the Tom Hanks character in *Sleepless in Seattle*, who, when asked what he was going to do after the death of his beloved wife, said, "Get out of bed every morning and breathe in and out all day. And after a while I won't have to remind myself to do it."

It was a few weeks after Brendan's death before I really had to face the horrible emptiness. The logistics of the service and the presence of my out-of-town family kept me occupied for the first week. Traveling back to Chicago with my sister for Thanksgiving, with a stop in Detroit to visit some family, also helped keep me from facing the loss of Brendan.

What astonished me the most was I began to realize it wasn't that I entirely lost him; it was that our relationship took a different form. True, I ached for his touch and to look into those eyes that held such love. Yet his presence was unmistakable.

At dinner with my friend Irene on my Midwest journey, I casually mentioned "He's here, you know." Irene had only met Brendan on one occasion, but had felt a strong connection to him when they met, appreciating his calm demeanor with the explanation, "He's easy on the nerves." Laughing, she then added, "And for women like us, that's important." How right she was. Perhaps since she had captured his essence so quickly and beautifully, Brendan's spirit joined us at the table. To my statement of his presence, she simply said, "I know." Other friends were put off by such declarations, some skeptical, others frightened. Even the skeptical ones had a hard time dismissing a gift I received from Brendan's spirit just under a month after his death.

I headed out to visit my in-laws the Saturday after Thanksgiving, having just returned to New York the evening before. They had piles of condolence cards they wanted to share with me, plus I think we both needed to establish our relationship on its new terms and see what was to become of it. The drive there didn't start out too smoothly. As I was on a side street about to pull off onto 278 in Brooklyn, my car was bumped by the woman behind me. We both got out and had a pleasant exchange as she was extremely apologetic and there was no damage done. Still, it added to some discomfort I was already feeling. The discomfort continued as I got teary-eyed thinking of all the times Brendan and I had made that trip together. Well, apparently we still were.

As I drove along in heavy traffic on I-95, just after the exit to Calvary Hospital where he died, I started changing radio stations to distract myself. I flicked onto WFUV, the Fordham University radio station he often listened to for its independent leanings, one that I rarely listened to. A song came on that immediately captured my attention from the first note. The words then followed, capturing my heart for eternity:

> I'm over on the other side
> Where life and death softly divide.
> Left my skin and bones behind
> Now I'm over on the other side.
>
> Can you feel me there with you?
> My breath is gone but I'm not through
> Loved you then and I still do
> From over on the other side
>
> I can fly...really fly
> Below the Earth all through the sky.
> Tell them all I did not die.
> I'm just over on the other side.
>
> It's good here on the other side
> The sweetest songs....the bluest skies.
> Thank you for the tears you cried
> But it's good here on the other side.
>
> I can fly. Really fly.
> Below the earth—all through the sky.
> Tell them all I did not die.
> I'm just over on the other side.

The world is smaller than a needle's eye
Where life and death softly divide
When you leave your skin and bones behind
I'll be waiting on the other side

I can fly. Really fly.
Below the earth—all through the sky.
Tell them all I did not die.
I'm just over on the other side.

(Reprinted with the permission of Don Conoscenti)

Hearing these words, my mouth fell open and, while still driving, I began frantically searching for a pen to write down the information the DJ identified; the song was "The Other Side" and it came from the *Paradox of Grace* CD by Don Conoscenti. And grace it was. There is no way that message came from other than the spirit of my Soupy Bean. Confirming what I felt in the moment of his passing…that there is most definitely a place we go to and that it is not far away.

I continued on my trip to his parents, trying to communicate to them this beautiful song, this beautiful experience…with marginal success.

The song was definitely not the only time I felt Soupy's presence. For several months after his death, he was most definitely nearby.

One blessing that seems to have come from Brendan's death is I now experience a much greater access to others who are in the spiritual realm. This has proven to be a blessing for not only me, but others who have been able to "co-connect" with their loved ones with me, particularly as I have delved deeper into healing work.

One friend of mine had not felt any connection to her mother since her death over two years earlier, despite the two of them having been close. When I gave her a healing, her mother's spirit immediately came forth. The day after the healing, my friend called. She wanted to thank me for facilitating this opening, realizing she could now experience an ongoing relationship with her mother.

Another friend's deceased mother also showed up loud and clear at the beginning of a healing session. I almost laughed at how she came forth, announcing her presence with the statement "Esther here." The guy receiving the healing was a little awestruck by his awareness of her during our process.

I find it interesting so many of these connections for others involve their mothers, when my connection to my own mother's spirit is still faint. Despite the opening Johrei offered, it is very, very infrequent that she "shows up"—but she did one time, very powerfully, shortly after Brendan's death. Early that following January, I made an appointment to see Lynn Kreaden, a Core Energetics healer, who I had worked with off and on. I felt called to see her to deal with the issue of grief and loss, so of course I just assumed it had to do with Brendan since he had passed so recently. Yet when Lynn invited me to allow whatever spirit to come forth that wanted to, it was clearly Mom that was present. Lynn then invited me to say whatever it was I needed to say to her. The words that came forth were "I'm sorry I wasn't there for you more." Next was "I'm sorry you weren't there for me more", recalling many times in my childhood when I hadn't gotten what I thought I needed. Still being the one who was carrying the dialogue, the next words were "I'm sorry you weren't there for yourself more," which is when I most deeply touched the sadness of my heart and sat in stillness.

Just a couple of breaths later, I received a message I knew came from Mom herself. The words were "The only thing that matters is that you learn to be there for yourself." I knew no truer words had ever been spoken, that I had never been given a richer teaching from Mom. I have shared the story of this healing and this message with many women since then, especially with my sister, Meg, since I know those words were every bit as intended for her as they were for me. As I left Lynn's office that wintry afternoon, I walked through the freshly fallen snow in Central Park, basking in the stillness and peace. Just over fifteen years since her death, my mother had given me a priceless gift.

CHAPTER 32

I experienced grief after Brendan's death like I never have before. With the earliest big losses in my life, that of Robbie and Mom, I had no space, no permission, no guidance to grieve. I was told to get on with life as completely and quickly as I could, both directly and indirectly in watching the other people around me.

At least with Dad's death, I had enough space around the loss and the circumstances of my life that I could feel the sadness, the pain, and the emptiness that comes with grief. The emotions then were still alternately numbed and stoked by my ever present friend, alcohol. Besides that, my spiritual life was nonexistent, as was my inclination to really letting people know what was going on in the deep recesses of my heart and my mind.

I now lived my life very differently, and it was continuing to shift and expand more all the time. As I grew spiritually and emotionally, how I healed changed as well.

The first year after Brendan died I was in a bereavement group, started individual therapy with a grief counselor, continued in Interfaith seminary, sat in a Buddhist sangha, practiced Johrei, and read many books on grieving. I also created a photo / memory book of Brendan and wrote and held a one-year anniversary service. It took all of this—and good old Father Time—to heal.

Each of these things helped in their own way. The bereavement group offered the gift of camaraderie. It was in seminary I could be held. Through practice, sangha allowed me to rediscover the preciousness of life. It was through Johrei I realized what a blessing the whole journey of Brendan's illness and death were in my life.

I was brought to Gilda's Club, a cancer support organization founded in honor of comedienne Gilda Radner, through my friend, Karen, who was working in development there. When Brendan was alive, he and I both attended an introductory meeting outlining all their services. He opted not to pursue support there because of the frustration he had in not being able to speak. I went to one caregiver support group but did not feel it was particularly helpful. At Karen's encouragement, I attended a bereavement group to see if that would be a better fit. It was... most definitely.

When I started in the group, there were about twelve of us, anywhere between six and ten who attended in any given week. Coincidentally, the majority of us had lost partners who were robbed of their lives in their 40's. Through our sharing in the group, we all came to love not only our own beloved but each other's as well. We shared the ache felt by the one left behind. Some of us had been through long illnesses with our partners; others had had a very short time to get used to the fact that they were soon to be widowed. Most of the newly widowed were also dealing with learning the ropes of being a single parent; a couple of us (me included) were more focused on healing as fast as we could so we could "get on with life," including replacing the blessed partner we had just lost. Despite the differences in profession, life circumstances, and how we lost our beloved, we united in our grief and our desire for healing.

As each of us shared the stories and qualities of our relations, we all felt the love, respect, frustration, hardships, and blessings. We connected around our confusion that the world went on while the bottom of our own world fell out. We expressed our frustration about the ongoing media attention lavished on those who died in the World Trade Center, while our grief was every bit as strong as those whose loved ones had perished in that way. We also dealt with the new realities of life in this world and supported each other in this process.

The group was a godsend, as only in AA had I gotten to sit with others who shared such a similar, difficult challenge as the one I was currently facing. In both cases, that of dealing with addiction and grieving, I was facing down messages I had heard as a child—that we must not be "defeated" by either of these challenges (meaning they should not be recognized in any way), and that, above all, we must not share them with others. These untruths had already captured too much of my life.

The group was led by a very elegant fifty-ish woman, Lew. She was compassionate, nonjudgmental, and could hold the space for anything that came forth. I also appreciated the valuable lessons she shared, such as the predictability that a very light, almost jovial session would follow an intense session, simply because that is the way we as humans work. We can't stay in the darkness forever; we need to be reminded of the possibility of joy, lightness, and connection at that level as well. The other lesson I got from her was delivered rather harshly (which she did apologize for), but it was valuable nonetheless.

Coming from my family of suppressed emotions, I finally had gotten used to my own feelings—thanks largely to the ongoing torrent of tears I shed in the early days of my sobriety. This still didn't necessarily mean I dealt well with the emotions of others. When one of the more repressed women in the group had finally broken down and let out some tears, I handed her some tissues, only to get a sharp reprimand from Lew. Towards the end of the session, after hearing out the feelings Sherry was having, Lew apologized for the harshness of her reaction, but also explained her rationale, which made sense. I had never thought of such well-meaning actions as offering a tissue, giving a hug, even placing my hand on another's back when they are upset as likely to stifle the emotions that are coming out. Rather than seen as offering supportive comfort, it can be physiologically and emotionally interpreted as a blanket designed to smother the flames of emotions that are arising. I learned a valuable lesson in that.

I continued in the group for just over a year. By then, I had talked through Brendan's illness and death enough that it no longer gripped my heart like a vice. Besides that, much of the original group had also matriculated out and into the world. David and I were the last hangers-on, and both came to the conclusion that, when Lew left and another facilitator came in, it was time to take that step ourselves.

The arms of seminary carried me through much of the grieving process, even as I learned firsthand that "spiritual people" can be just as challenged in supporting someone in their grief as anyone else. The most dramatic evidence of this was a woman, Mary, who was in my study group. I still cannot begin to tell why we had such a conflict, because I don't know. I do know that loss was also an issue for her as one of her daughters had died as an infant. Rather than making her more empathetic to what I was going through, however, it made her judgmental towards me—extremely judgmental, as well as ultrasensitive to anything I said or did.

After trying to resolve our difficulties on our own, we ended up calling on one of the deans, Susan, to facilitate. On a Sunday afternoon, they both came to my apartment for what was an amicable but unfruitful discussion. We had not found any common ground for us, so the resolution ended up being that I switched study groups. This was ultimately unnecessary because a few months down the line, just prior to our first year retreat, Mary dropped out of New Seminary to get an online ordination and begin preaching. It taught me that not everyone is committed to genuine healing, even those in the ranks of ministers and ministers-in-training.

The only other instance I recall of feeling as though people were not able to connect with the grieving process—whether it was mine or their own—came during the May class. The agenda for that day included Death & Dying in the morning, and twelve-step recovery in the afternoon. The usual opening of a prayer and a heart-opening song already had me tender and vulnerable, especially knowing what was to come. So when Allan, one of the deans and a former opera singer with an understandable occasional flair for the dramatic, got up and said, "Today we have a bit of a heavy day, but it's important that we learn how to support other people in their journeys in these areas," I reacted. That statement was definitely true, since as ministers in training, we were there to learn to support others in their journeys, but it still stung. It felt to me as though these two topics were the ministerial equivalent of "The Scarlet A" if they were part of our own life. When the sharing opened, I was one of the first up, registering my complaint with the statement, "I am a widow. I am an orphan. I am a recovering alcoholic. This day is my life," a comment that was met with utter and complete silence.

As the teaching went on that day, I opened to the possibility of a new perspective on death. Ariel, the grief counselor I was working with who also taught that day's class, offered her belief that "every death is perfect." It was a concept I had to sit with for quite some time before even considering it to be in the slightest bit feasible. Not because of Brendan's death. I could see in many ways how his passing was perfect, albeit years premature in my view. It was Mom's death I could not accept as anywhere close to perfect. I remembered her anger and frustration at being alive while not able to eat, talk, or do anything.

I still have not fully embraced the notion every death is perfect but it does remind me that, being human, my understanding of what is happening at the spiritual level is limited. This has brought me to a prayer I use often: "May everything that happens today be for the highest good of all. If it be Thy Will, may I see that. In all cases, may I trust that." Today I am willing to consider the possibility that every death is perfect, whether or not I would judge it that way from my limited human perspective.

The other thing I learned during that day is the importance of using words such as "dead" and "deceased". Ariel explained how we often turn to softer words such as "lost" or "passed on" to try to soften the blow of such a huge loss in our life, when of course the very thing we need to be doing is to face the loss head-on and embrace it completely.

Blessedly, it was a very rare experience to feel alone, separated, or isolated during my seminary experience, quite a relief since that had been the all-too-familiar feeling around grieving during my younger life. Instead, seminary provided a perennial hug—either physical or psychic—whenever I was in class or around my fellow students. It was a group that would fully appreciate the song "The Other Side" when I played it for them and would understand when I wept uncontrollably during Josh Groban's "A Breath Away" with the reference to "my forever love." It was a special few who held my heart and my hand when a naïve sister droned on endlessly by how blessed she was by the people who loved her unconditionally, her parents and her partner—all of whom had left my physical world by then. Another sister held me in a giant bear hug as I sobbed during a class on forgiveness as I realized what a burden my sense of not being enough had become. Somewhere buried deep inside I believed that if I had been enough, Brendan would have found a way to heal, a way to survive. Those tears of forgiveness came out for both of us—forgiveness for myself that I couldn't have been more and forgiveness for Brendan that he didn't live, he didn't survive.

It was the first group with whom I felt safe enough to put it all out there. The incident of sharing, "I am a widow. I am an orphan. I am a recovering alcoholic" was one of those times. Yet that was just a precursor to what was to come in the second year of seminary when I gave a sermon entitled "How Do I Heal?" That sermon was:

> It has been said that pain is the touchstone of all spiritual growth, but how do I heal from pain enough to touch the sweetness and grasp the hope of growth? How do I heal from the pain of having found a very special partner with whom I felt safe, honored, and cherished—only to watch him die three short years later? How do I heal from not having felt safe, honored, or cherished as a child? How do I heal from much too much loss in life? I wish I knew. I suppose I start by honoring it all. By letting it fully overtake me once again, complete and all-encompassing in my body and in my soul.

> How does one heal from betrayal? How does one heal from having a man who supposedly loves you raise his hand to you? What do I know of healing? I know pain.

> Yet it is exactly that ability to touch the pain that gives me the ability to heal. To know there is another way.

> I heal by sharing my pain. I heal by knowing it's not real. As intense as it may seem, there is nothing real about it. It is intangible. It is

impermanent. It is tasteless, odorless—yet I honor it anyway. I honor it as my own. And I honor it as the world's.

In honoring it as the world's, I know even more pain. Because even as I share my personal experience of suffering, I take on other forms I have not known personally. I take on hunger. I take on the degradation of women throughout the world. I take on war—and all forms of violence.

In opening to the suffering of others, my compassion builds for myself and others. I understand those days when I can't quite get it together as much as I would like. I understand the hardness in the eyes of my neighbor, my brother, my teacher. I even try to understand and reach out to the person I don't like—the inauthentic one, the helpless one—knowing I have the same pain and suffering and fear as she.

As it's said in the Upanishads, "Who sees all beings in his own Self, and his own Self in all beings, loses all fear." With this loss of fear comes the opportunity for joy. The softening of my heart that allows that connection with another person allows me to share their joys. It allows me to share appreciation for the everyday miracles—a beautiful sunset, a baby's smile, a perfectly timed call from a friend. It allows me to focus on the beauty. It allows me to even find the sweetness of the pain, knowing it comes from awareness.

I guess that's how I heal. I guess that's how we all heal.

For years I thought that sermon was too much for my classmates. There was a heaviness and an intensity in the room afterward that was not common for our gatherings. Based on the class reaction, I felt exposed and vulnerable. It was not until I saw some classmates almost ten years after our graduation and one of them mentioned to me how much that talk had impacted her that I realized I was being carried and accepted even more than I knew.

The sangha I joined taught me how to really sit with my pain. How to sit on a cushion for twenty minutes and bring my attention back to my heaving breath when my mind would wander to how much I missed my beloved, the gentle man who had brought so much to my life. Every Wednesday evening I would schlep to the Upper West Side to Allan and Susanna's beautiful high-rise apartment, which would become our sanctuary for the evening. The support from seminary extended to this group as well, most of whom had recently been ordained. One particular evening sticks in my memory. During the dharma discussion, one of the men was expressing deep appreciation for his partner in his life. I sobbed and sobbed, still remembering to bring my attention back to my breath, whatever jagged, shallow, choked form it happened to be coming out in. Besides offering unconditional love and guidance, sangha taught me how to be present in the physical world at a time when I truly didn't care whether or not I was even still alive.

My long-time practice of Johrei brought the light of illumination. Since Johrei is a healing practice that, from my human perception, did not heal Brendan, I held a grudge. It failed me in what I needed most from it. One year after Soupy's death I finally saw the miracle of it all. I remembered the gift of channeling to a near-stranger as he made his transition. I remembered Brendan telling me that was what he wanted as he passed. Finally, I even realized how little trauma there was in his actual transition because of his awareness to the end. He absolutely went through some fighting and struggle, but the fact he was fully awake and aware when he looked at me for the last time before closing his eyes was a gift to both of us, a gift I believe wholeheartedly came from how much Divine Light he had received during his illness.

Yes, a collage of therapies was most definitely required to help me heal over the loss of the shining star in my life.

Only one task loomed that was directly related to Brendan's death. A few months after it, I was still sitting with his ashes, uncertain as to what to do with them. When I had asked Soupy if he wanted them scattered, his answer was "No" as he clearly stated he wanted me to keep them (him) with me. I was a little uncomfortable with that as I did not see myself as a widow with the urn on the fireplace mantle—especially at my young age. I was left with the dilemma of how to honor his wishes and still be true to myself. Walking in the yard at our house upstate, the answer finally came to me to bury his ashes at the house, giving him a peaceful resting place at the home he didn't get enough chance to know while alive.

A plan was made with his family to bury the ashes on Sunday, April 28, six months and one day after his passing. His parents and all his siblings drove up for the day. As everyone settled in, we opened the ritual with my playing "The Other Side" for them, something many of them had not yet heard. As I shared the circumstances of how that song came into my life, there was an awestruck look on many of their faces. After the song we said some prayers and went out in the steady but light rain to do the actual burial.

I had started digging the hole the day before to keep the task as simple as possible. I had chosen a place at the base of a hill and in the shadow of a beautiful flowering bush as Brendan's final resting place. The only marker that day was the rose bulbs planted around the urn. Several months after the burial, I ordered an angel statue, not realizing it was so tall, standing over three feet. After that got knocked over too many times, I discarded that in favor of a simple garden stone with the word "love" and an engraving of a dogwood fairy on it. I came to find out later that particular type of fairy was representative of eternal love. How true!

Our day of commemoration ended with a lasagna dinner, as Brendan would have chosen himself. It had been a solemn day in many respects, but also very forwarding. I knew I had honored his wishes, had shared his message that "he did not die; he's just over on the other side" and taken a step forward in being true to myself in how he was kept in my life.

CHAPTER 33

What I hadn't counted on was how challenging it was to have focus and structure in the midst of grief. I was in this weird place where my enthusiasm about the possibilities of life could hit an almost manic realm. That was then dashed by the heaviness of overwhelming grief that would come up out of nowhere. A Yankee game could bring on a day of crying, driving past a golf course could have me space out to the point where I lost the next couple hours of my activities. It was an unproductive place, understandably unproductive, but not in my plans at that time.

I was trying to start a business. I left my job on the Volvo account about six months after going back to work. I now described advertising, which had once been my dream and my passion, as soul-sucking. Even though my employer had been generous and understanding with my need for time off during Brendan's illness, it was still a business where three-hour meetings were held to determine whether the driver in the commercial should be wearing a long-sleeved button-down or a polo shirt. Having gone through the last two years of my life, this did not gel with what I now considered important.

Still seeing myself primarily as a businessperson, I became increasingly interested in the spirituality in business movement that was gaining momentum. I attended conferences, created business cards, and enrolled in coach training, all hoping to bring greater consciousness to corporate America. Where I was in life, I needed greater consciousness myself—a common symptom of the bereaved.

One other thing occupied my life—or at least my mind—and that was dating. I was lonely. I missed my partner, and I was craving sex, as the last time Brendan and I made love had been almost ten months before he died. Still, I was definitely conflicted. In some ways, Brendan's death brought back the steel armor that had surrounded my heart until I met him. In other ways, the cellular memory of how beautiful and magnificent a deeply shared love can be and how much it truly enriches life reminded me to stay open to that possibility.

Not that I was in that place when I started dating. A guy friend of mine from the neighborhood with whom I shared an obvious—but unacted upon—attraction had returned from a few months overseas just after the New Year. He had witnessed me grappling with Brendan's illness for over a year, and had been distantly, and yet appropriately, supportive. When we first ran into each other upon his return, he merely inquired, "And how are you?" Whether he meant it this way or not, I read his words as a kind way of saying, "Did your husband die?" I did not have a sense he was coming on to me, but his inquiry opened a nice conversation. It provided a somewhat distant and appropriate way of opening the door to seeing what existed between us. After sharing a few lunches and walks in the park, initially awkward but nice, I invited him to see Robin Williams at BAM for our first real evening date. That was just a few days before what would have been Brendan's and my second wedding anniversary. I noted to my sister how strange it felt to be dating someone else on that date, then dismissed it laughingly with the recognition that other people were dating by their second wedding anniversary, even without having lost their partner to either death or separation.

Surprisingly enough, in some ways Jordan, this first man I dated after Brendan died, was probably less affected by my distance than others in the next few years were. While the armor was definitely thickest at that time, I was at least fully aware of it—and honest about it. When we first started dating, Jordan asked me what I was looking for and I honestly answered: "A sex friend. Someone who I trust and like to have sex with." Even after he replied he thought he wanted something more, we embarked on a six-month relationship on my terms. It was all I could give and I knew it at that time. In retrospect, it was the perfect rebound relationship—solid friendship, some romance, good sex, and open communication as to where each of us were at all times.

How to navigate learning to date again was a fairly common topic at our bereavement group. Many of us were grappling with it and all in our own way. Jay was the group's inveterate flirt. He emitted a low level of desperation; it was clear he did not want to return to the bachelor life. Paul, one of the newer group members as I was leaving the group, married his wife's best friend about six months after his wife's death. Nothing had gone on before she died, but their shared grieving brought them together. Marilyn, another group member, was ready to play the field and enjoy the freedom that she had not had for over twenty years. I myself felt as though I was a cross between all these people and the rest of the group as well.

In the summer after I left my job, a realization of exactly where I was got put into an art project entitled "Stories of My Heart." Page by page it goes...

The
Stories
of
My
Heart

Ann E. O'Neil
8/29/03

I spent
many, many years
trying to
find my heart
&
share it with someone.

Then
Finally one day
I did!
He was sweet
she knew me
she loved me
& we cared for each other.
Our love grew.
Our hearts grew.

But he died.

And my heart
cracked.

I am trying
to heal my heart.
I hope it doesn't
take many, many years.

I want to
share it with
someone else.

CHAPTER 34

S urrounded by friends, family, classmates, and others in recovery, I was finally going through the grieving process, not around it, and was healing as a result. I was soon to learn this healing and our connection was still being honored by Brendan on "the other side."

This came during a spiritual journey to Japan with Johrei. Even though I was disillusioned by Brendan having not been cured, I did have a deep gratitude for the love and spiritual healing the practice and the organization had offered to both of us during his illness and to me after his passing. It remained my spiritual tradition so I eagerly anticipated a visit to the three Sacred Grounds in Japan, remembering my experience with the Brazil trip. I was also very happy that Mark, my old boyfriend who had introduced me to Johrei seven years earlier, would be on the trip. I had seen Mark infrequently since he moved to Seattle and was looking forward to reconnecting with him.

The timing of the trip was determined by the date of the Annual Ancestral service in Japan. We landed on June 29, my 41st birthday, and rested and prepared for the service on July 1. That I was going to have the opportunity to pray for my beloved in a service with thousands of people on Sacred Grounds brought me much joy. The service was beautiful and comforting but did not bring the level of healing I had hoped for, certainly not nearly as much as I had experienced in many other grief-related activities. As the trip wore on I began to realize I was actually feeling Brendan's presence less than I usually did. Maybe it was my connection to Mark. Maybe it was that I held expectations about connecting to Brendan. Whatever it was, I needed to sense him near, and I didn't.

As we went from Sacred Grounds to Sacred Grounds, I expected maybe this was where the spirit of my beloved would connect to me, as he had so clearly and beautifully in the earliest days after his passing. The elegance of the Atami Sacred Grounds overlooking the Pacific Ocean was enriching and inspiring, but did not support a connection. From there, we went to Hakone, a very natural and simple Sacred Grounds where I connected deeply with the spirit of Meishu-sama, the founder of Johrei, but not with Brendan. The last Sacred Grounds we visited were in Kyoto. It was there near the end of the trip in the midst of a bamboo forest I finally said a prayer for Bean's spirit to reveal itself to me. I said that prayer with great fervor and intention, but still had some doubt that this trip would move my healing forward, as I so longed for it to do. I should have had more faith.

The next day, two days before our flight home, we visited a Buddhist temple, the Ryongi-Temple, also known as the Rock Garden. As we rounded the first bend in the lush moss garden, I caught a glimpse of a beautiful placid lake and walked toward it. In a short stroll, it became clear to me that at least 70% of the lake's surface was covered by lotus flowers in full bloom. I instantaneously remembered Fr. Gatt's sermon at Brendan's memorial mass, where he drew an analogy between Brendan and a lotus flower. Brendan was indeed showing me his spirit was still very present in my life and I could access him whenever I needed. To this very day, most remnants of Brendan are relegated to the memory trunk I specially selected then packed away. A beautiful photo of the lake and the lotus, however, hangs in my bedroom.

There were two other blessings from that trip. One was the time I got to spend with Mark. As it became clear we were both going to be on the trip, I had originally asked him if he wanted to be roommates. Just a day later, I called him to tell him I didn't think that would be such a good idea after all, that it might distract from the purpose of our journey. He very graciously accepted my sudden and complete change of mind, laughing it off with the statement, "You are a blonde after all." Chuckling at Mark's sweetness and dry sense of humor, I was appreciative of his understanding. We spent most of the trip with each other—and Mark's roommate, Glenn. It was all as it was supposed to be.

The other gift was the clarity I received on a life question I was facing at that time. At the first year intensive for the New Seminary just three weeks before this trip, the director and most of the staff dropped a bomb on us the last morning with the statement they were resigning. There was great discretion in how they handled explaining their decision to us, but that left a lot of questions. Needless to say there was confusion, turmoil, and even somewhat a sense of betrayal among our class. I think it is safe to say none of us were completely undisturbed by the announcement. After all, since our class had met the first time the Saturday immediately before 9/11, we had bonded. Many of my classmates had volunteered together, and all of us who lived in the city held the seminary as our sanctuary and calming salve from the emotional chaos of New York in the days that followed that tragedy.

As the announcements were made, it was mentioned offhandedly that Diane Berke, the director of the seminary, was hoping to start a new Interfaith seminary with some support, financial and otherwise, that had already been pledged to her. We had no way of knowing whether that could get off the ground in the three short months between the school years, yet we were invited to take that leap of faith that something would be there waiting for us on the other side. On the other side there was pressure and some manipulation coming from the remaining New Seminary staff to complete our second year with them. I think I had a little more distance from the stress of this decision than many of my classmates. Part of that distance was having already gone through a split with Johrei, resulting in the Izunome Association with which I was now associated—and seeing that one come out fine. The other part of it was that I was still very much in the grieving process, and many things in life just didn't matter all that much to me. This was one of those things, but I was still relieved when, while writing in my journal in my Tokyo hotel room on the very last day of the trip, I came to the conclusion the teachers were what had made my experience so far so healing, beautiful, and safe. I wrote that I would indeed be making the leap.

Come the following September, I entered my second year of seminary at One Spirit Interfaith Seminary. Miraculously, all had indeed come together and a new organization had indeed been born. There was permanent classroom space, a curriculum in place, and staff and students ready to kick off the new year.

CHAPTER 35

After a year filled with a lot of changes, a lot of growth, a lot of hope, and a lot of tears, the one-year anniversary of Brendan's death rolled around on a Sunday. It had been a long, long year.

The day started with my friend, Milagros, and I up at the house in Hillsdale. We were to be venturing back into the city for two different celebrations of Brendan. For the first, we were to be meeting his family at the Sunday mass at Calvary Hospital, where he had passed, then having a brunch at his sister Eden's, the very place we had all descended on exactly one year earlier. It was a much chillier and more overcast day than the previous year had been. I was looking forward to connecting with his family, although the notion of a Catholic mass wasn't really speaking to me—until the priest got into the sermon. For whatever reason, Fr. Michael had chosen the sermon of "The Three Kinds of Love."

In the sermon, he described the first level of love as one mostly of convenience. He explained that in this type of relationship your styles fit, life is easy, there is no challenge to being together. Intimacy comes easily, albeit superficially. He cited the second level of love as the one lived by most partners. As time goes by, your connection deepens and solidifies. You know the person is your #1 supporter, and you theirs, and there are some challenges. Still there is not anything extraordinary about this love. It does not have a "to the stars and back" quality to it. The third level of love Fr. Michael called a folly kind of love. He talked about how uncommon and blessed a love like this is. He talked about the joys of a love like this and the pains of a love like this. It reminded me of the reading from *The Prophet* that had been a part of our wedding and so beautifully captured the rewards and challenges of our marriage:

> When love beckons to you, follow him,
> Though his ways are hard and steep.
> And when his wings enfold you yield to him,
> Though the sword hidden among his pinions may wound you.
> And when he speaks to you believe in him,
> Though his voice may shatter your dreams as the north
> wind lays waste the garden.
>
> For even as love crowns you so shall he crucify you.
> Even as he is for your growth so is he for your pruning.
> Even as he ascends to your height and caresses your
> tenderest branches that quiver in the sun,
> So shall he descend to your roots and shake them in their
> clinging to the Earth.
>
> Like sheaves of corn he gathers you unto himself.
> He threshes you to make you naked.
> He sifts you to free you from your husks.
> He grinds you to whiteness.
> He kneads you until you are pliant;
> And then he assigns you to his sacred fire,
> that you may become Sacred bread for God's Sacred feast.

The description of the folly kind of love captured the depth of what existed between Brendan and me more completely and beautifully than anything had. Until then, the only account I had heard about the uniqueness of what we shared was eloquently offered by Brendan's best friend, Jeff, in Bean's eulogy. Jeff had talked about an evening at Calvary Hospital near the end of

Brendan's life. Jeff and Brendan's brother Joey had come by to spend some time with Bean and watch the Yankee playoff game. I took the opportunity to go home and do a few chores. When I came back that evening, I was so happy to see Brendan—as usual. I went to the side of his bed where he had been dozing and took his hand. He awoke, and the look of tenderness and love between us sent the other two macho Yankee fans out of the room in tears. In that moment, they too knew it was a folly kind of love, even if none of us yet had those words. It was nice to be given the "folly" term.

Following the mass, I was still shaky from the miracle of that message, as we all headed out to Eden's home for brunch. It was then I brought out a memory/photo book I had completed. The intro said:

> This photo album/memory book is dedicated to a truly wonderful man, Brendan Miles DiBuono. It is being created with great love and gratitude for all he brought to life.
>
> It is also being created because of a suggestion that doing a creative project that truly captures one's essence is a way to both honor and bring closure. How, exactly, does one truly capture another's essence though? Certainly photos and memories help. Thinking about his passions works, as does remembering his sense of humor. And his gentleness. And his eyes—definitely those beautiful, deep, soulful eyes.
>
> So I embark on this project to capture the essence of Brendan—my Soupy—with great doubt that it's truly possible to do so. After all, an essence is a spark in the universe—rarely consciously detectable but always everpresent. Nevertheless, I will do my best: with love and tenderness.

His family was incredibly touched by the photo album of Brendan and his many loves. They made me promise to make mini-books of the photos for them. The books were their Christmas presents the following year.

After the brunch, I headed out to the city for what I had initially thought would be the real honoring, but it turned out the whole glorious day was. Having been too broken to speak about Brendan the previous year at his memorial service, I chose to have a one-year service at the Johrei center to speak my piece on what this wonderful man had brought to my life. Being that it was the end of a long day and not their faith, I was surprised and inordinately touched when his parents walked in and joined me and some close friends for the service.

After an opening song and prayer, I invited the attendees to participate in a candle lighting ceremony with the following invitation:

> "You may have noticed this candle up here, decorated with many words. This symbolizes the light Brendan brought to this world. The words are the traits that best capture Brendan and his preciousness. They are: gentle, heart of gold, curious, goofy, handsome, passionate, grateful, faithful, and creative. Please feel free to come up, take a candle from the basket, light it, and take it back to your seat."

I then went on with the main message, my one and only public tribute to what this man had brought to my life. The message went:

> I thought it would be appropriate if Brendan's light were shining brightly in all of us as I share my memories of him. At his service last year, I was not in a position to speak of what he had meant in my life, everything was too fresh. So I thank you for

being here with me today to bear witness to the story of our love.

Brendan did indeed bring me the love I had always dreamt of having. It may sound corny but I realized this was true when he played "my song" for me. To me, the most romantic thing possible was to have someone choose a song just for you—and he did. It was an ordinary day with both of us just hanging out at home when he played it for me. I suspect he never knew how much it meant to me. The song was a Johnny Winters heavy rock-a-billy tune named Miss Ann, definitely not the ballad I would have expected but very Brendan. The main words were "Miss Ann, you do what no one else can." It ended with "When I'm with you, Miss Ann, I'm living in Paradise." We really did get to touch Paradise when we were together. If I shared with you all the blessed memories I have of special times with Brendan—the special looks, the way he took care of me and let me in to take care of him, the silly fun—we'd be here all night.

I then went on to talk about each of the traits on the candle, evidencing many of the stories throughout this book. The close of the core part of the ceremony was my prayer:

Infinite, all-loving God and my sweet Brendan—
Thank you for the blessing of having had Brendan in my life.
Thank you for all we shared; thank you for all he taught me;
Thank you for who he was.
I ask for your guidance and strength in helping me to move forward with the life you have left me here on Earth to live.
I ask that Brendan and the life and love we shared be integrated into who I am today, but not be the whole of it.
I ask that Brendan's death be an experience I draw upon, but not the only one.
I ask that I step into the person this has allowed me to grow into—

Fulfilling Brendan's wishes for me (that I travel, enjoy financial comfort, keep up with my photography, fall in love again, and stay pretty),
And my wishes for myself (that I be of service in my new career, and find it, my creativity, and my relationships fulfilling and rewarding).
God, thank you for the whole of this life—for the times of joy and of sorrow; for the times of great love and those of loneliness; for the "on" time and the "off" time. May I be of service to you and my fellow beings throughout it all."

Our society seems to allow one year for grieving…at the outside. It turns out I was all too ready to get onboard with that, shut the door, and leave Brendan behind. It was in this spirit that I planned the marking of his anniversary, motivated by great love but also by wanting to shut down the pain and move forward. It was a beautiful service—an honest and heartfelt one—but also a premature one I came to find out.

I quickly learned one cannot set a clock on grief. I also learned, and continue to do so, that having healed from the loss still does not mean the door is slammed shut, sealed, and padlocked. There are times the memories come flooding back. There are times the pain seeps out. Fortunately these times can also bring back the love full force as well.

It was one of those times in the following summer that I walked by the burial site of Brendan's ashes and stopped to say a prayer. Following the prayer I said, "I know the remains of your body are here…but where is your soul?" As clear as day the answer came back, "It's in your soul." A truer statement never came to me in my life.

It was also one of those times I wrote a letter to my deceased love:

I need to tell you that I can't believe how much
I miss you and how intense the pain can still be.
That night you died—as you lay dying, when I
was holding your hand telling you how much I was
going to miss you, I had no clue of how much I was
going to miss you, of how true that statement was.

I think this way of describing you just came to me.
You were absolutely, positively my favorite person
in this world....But, Soupy, I want to get on with
my life. I know you're in my soul—and I want you
to stay there—but I need for there to be a little
space. I guess that may be impossible: for you to
be in my soul and for there to be space, but I'm
thinking of the feeling I got in last December's
healing session—that you were going to give me
a little more space so I can get on with my life. I
don't know who's having the harder time letting
go—me or you. I suspect it's me. But I do remember
that time after you talked to Fr. Gatt and said, "I'm
going to miss you a lot." That was the sweetest thing
anyone could have said—that even in the bliss of
heaven, I'd be missed.

This letter was followed many months later with the poem:

Am I hanging onto you?
Or are you hanging onto me?
Or, worse yet, am I just hanging on to hanging on?

CHAPTER 36

I t was in this state, this two steps forward—one step back process of healing, that I had the chance to make a big life change. It became clear that one of the previous changes, embarking on a freelance career while in the midst of the grieving process, was not successful. I did not have the structure or the motivation I needed to make it work. I needed to get a job…big time. Just as this became imminently clear, a plum job in my old field of advertising opened up. Plus it offered me the chance to move to North Carolina.

Not that it had been a goal of mine to do so. I had sometimes even joked with friends I needed to live north of the Mason-Dixon line to be happy. But at this point in my life, North Carolina offered a lot. A great job. An opportunity to get to know my brother, Dennis, and his family—including his five children—better since they lived just a few hours away from what was to be my new home. In many ways it gave me the opportunity for a fresh start—so I thought.

Unfortunately, this proved to be another case of me taking myself with me. I thought I was much more healed from the loss of Brendan than I was. It took an evening out with friends at a benefit concert to realize how profoundly true this was. When the woman onstage started in on the song, "How Could I Live Without You?," dedicated to her husband for their anniversary, I became aware of how raw I was. I managed to choke back tears for the first chorus, but by the time that phrase was uttered again, I had to run out the front door. My friend stopped me just as I was getting in my car, ready to drive off, and just held me in a close bear hug as the too-familiar tears poured out of my eyes and my soul. Two years after Brendan's death, clearly I still did not know the answer to how I could live without him. I was still grappling with how to live a life that truly fit me and did not include the love of my life.

My transition to North Carolina was not easy, even aside from the grieving process. Being a woman who happily lives in either a city or in the sticks, I get itchy with too much time in the suburbs. The first weekend in the Triangle area, I called back to my buddies in New York fretting, "I spent my first Saturday night here at a mall." A few weeks down the road, I had met some people (mostly in AA) and was starting to connect, even making a friend or two. One of these women invited me to see the play *Salome* at the University of North Carolina; it was a decent production. That gave me some comfort until I spoke with my friend Mario who had just seen the same play on Broadway, starring Robert DeNiro and Marisa Tomei. Hearing this just took my mind back to all that New York had to offer, all that I was missing. In some ways my transition was helped by me traveling back to New York for the remaining three months of seminary, but those Sunday night flights back to Raleigh-Durham were not happy ones for me.

After ordination, I really tried committing myself to being there. I had gotten in contact with another Johrei member who lived in the area, and we were having regular get-togethers at my loft offering Johrei to people. I preceded those with a shopping spree at Whole Foods so the evening was always a festive, lovely gathering. These soirees started with about four of us but grew to eight to ten before I moved from the area. We eventually also taught a membership class so four of the regulars received their

Ohikari on a visit by Larry, my long-time minister. That weekend also incorporated a flower arranging class with his wife, Azusa, so my loft overflowed with beautiful arrangements put together by each of us. One of my favorite pictures is of my friend Niki just gleeful with the beauty and fun of that day.

The Johrei gatherings gave me some spiritual community but still nothing as consistent or expansive as I would have liked as a newly ordained minister. I was also still active in AA and had people in the meetings I attended who meant a great deal to me, but I didn't feel a strong spiritual focus there either. I was hopeful this was on the verge of changing when I saw an ad in the weekly *Independent*, the alternative free newspaper in the Triangle area. Taking up approximately one column inch on the back cover, it stated "God seekers, God doubters, God followers wanted to establish creative new church." I very excitedly dialed the phone and explained to the woman on the other end of the line I was an Interfaith minister looking for the opportunity to connect with like-minded souls. She then answered she was a United Methodist minister who was lately feeling the church was too restrictive. When I asked her if the church she was establishing was decidedly Christian, she replied, "Oh, absolutely" as though there could be no other way. After another five minutes of conversation where she very subtly declared the superiority of Christianity over other religions because of being "filled up with Christ" versus being empty, I thanked her for her time and wished her luck with her church.

That attitude of Christianity as the only, or at least superior, path was one thing I had been concerned with as I considered moving there. The other thing had been the South's reputation for its racism. I certainly hoped those days were over, but unfortunately I found that to not be the case. Going to the local gas station for my morning Diet Pepsi one Sunday, I was in line behind an African-American gentleman, dressed nicely but comfortably as though he were either on his way to or from church. After he had paid and headed out the door, the older white man behind the counter said to me, "You know, some of those black people have really good hearts. Not all of them—but some of them." Absolutely aghast, I took a deep breath then said, "Well, some of the white people do too." It was the only thing I could think of to say. This certainly didn't seem to be the place for me.

Come the beginning of my second year there, I was increasingly unhappy, which made me feel isolated and lonely and miss Brendan all the more. It was in that mode and that place I wrote:

> Soupy, Soupy, Soupy—I can't believe how much I still miss you. I'm in one of those times when it's especially intense—the spring and the fall seem to do that. I suspect it coincides with your diagnosis/ our anniversary and your birthday and deathday. It all becomes so vivid….I need to trust you're where you're supposed to be. I was thinking of the quote I saw that if tears could build a road, I'd build a path and bring you back home with me. I don't think it would be the right thing to do, but I think I would with how I'm feeling right now. I miss you so!... Soupy, I need to know I have your love and support right now. I am so sad. I am so lonely. I feel like I've really screwed up my life. Please help me…however that looks.

Part of my isolation came from being separated from Brendan's family, as they had become a key part of my life over the last five years. This was even truer now because Joe, my father-in-law, was in his last days. He had been diagnosed with cancer in his back and bones and was dying. The call with the diagnosis had come when I was at the posh Santa Monica Hotel on a commercial shoot for Audi. While spring was still weeks away back East,

I was taking a brief break out by the pool when my cell phone rang. It was my sister-in-law, Sheila, who said, after some cursory greetings, "I've got some bad news. Dad has cancer and it doesn't look good." She then broke into tears for how unfair it was that a man as giving and loving as he would have to suffer like he was. I knew he had been in pain recently, but I had no idea it was that serious. Hanging up the phone, I cried a few tears myself and strolled across the street for a walk along the beach. I sat by the ocean, thinking about the power of its beauty and the pain it can also cause. It was a lot like life.

Joe and I had a bit of a difficult relationship. We had very different perspectives in life, and we both tended to be vocal about those perspectives. Dear sweet Gail, Joe's quiet and submissive wife, spent so much time trying to get him to change the subject whenever we came close to religion or politics, which was fairly often. Our difficulties were compounded by both of us being take-charge kind of people. The day we were settling Brendan into Calvary, we both were trying to get him set up with where his IV drip pole should go. One of us thought one side of the bed, the other thought the end of the bed. After witnessing this for a while, Brendan wrote in his ever present notebook, "Now I know why you guys have such problems. You're too much alike." To that comment, I shot him a look of displeasure and made the statement, "You'd be wise never to say that again." He of course had a valid point.

Despite our difficulties, there was love and respect between Joe and me—albeit sometimes deeply buried. I know he was grateful for me in Brendan's life and I was appreciative of all he and Gail did for both of us. I also respected his talent, his commitment, and his dedication to his family. I got a huge surprise after Brendan's memorial service when my brother Joe told me that Brendan's father had referred to me as one of the most spiritual people he knew. That was heartwarming, as was his leading the pack to make sure Brendan's family showed up en masse for my ordination. The man may have been a control freak beyond all I've ever met in my life, but he had a very sweet tender side to him as well.

Knowing Joe's time was coming to an end, I flew up to New York over Memorial Day weekend to see Joe and say my good-byes. I traveled out to their garden apartment in Larchmont, and entered to find Gail alone in the living room, for by then it was difficult for Joe to get out of bed. After a brief visit with her, I went down the hall to their bedroom to say hello to Joe. He was twisted and in obvious pain, but still charming. He graciously accepted a few minutes of Johrei, but then made it clear he wanted his rest. I thanked him for all he had done for me and for Brendan, to which he offered, "You have a good life." I left the room holding back tears. That was the last I ever saw of him. I got a call a few weeks later that he had died on the same day as Gail's sister a few years earlier. Both had died at Calvary Hospital, the same place as did Brendan. Less than a half hour after getting the call about Joe's death, I was driving and heard the song, "I just want to celebrate another day of living. I just want to celebrate another day of life." I got the message. One thing Joe most definitely did was celebrate living and celebrate life. The next day I was on a plane north to attend the wake and funeral.

About a week after attending Joe's funeral, I was on a plane again, this time to travel to Alaska for a long-dreamed-of vacation that I had booked months earlier. The plan was that I would do the Alaskan Adventure eight-day hiking and camping trip, despite not being in the greatest physical condition, then spend three days in Seattle on my way home visiting Mark, my ex-boyfriend and Johrei friend. The Alaskan part of the trip itself turned out to be less than spectacular. Between wildfires they were having and unseasonable clouds, the joke among the five participants, two couples and me, became "That's where you'd normally see XXX (usually McKinley)." Beyond that, our guide was a physical education teacher who thought the real purpose of the trip should be boot camp rather than vacation. Fortunately, the trip ended on its high note with Mark and me enjoying a nice visit in Seattle. He showed me the sites from *Sleepless in Seattle* and took me to his favorite sushi restaurant.

One thing traveling has often given to me is a shift in perspective. This trip was no different; as a matter of fact, it may have been one of the more extreme examples of it. Prior to my trip, as my note to Brendan's Spirit stated, I had been feeling very stuck, very unhappy. There were a lot of things I didn't like about my life—where I was living and my job being the two biggest ones—yet I wasn't seeing a way out. I had very little financial cushion. I didn't want to take just another job in advertising, even if I could find one back home in New York. I was feeling pretty hopeless.

After a week of camping, hiking on glaciers, and soaking in the beauty of God's creation, I had the strength to make some choices. I knew my Higher Power had always taken care of me when I was living in line with my heart, so I summoned forth the strength and chutzpah to hightail it out of the South and back to the home where I belonged. It took two months for that to happen but it was set in place on my first day back to work when I delivered the news to my boss I would be leaving.

CHAPTER 37

The transition back to New York wasn't as smooth as I had hoped. First of all, "home" was going to have a different address than I had originally intended. My plan in moving back was that I was going to open a book and gift store oriented towards personal and spiritual growth. The specifics of this—where it was going to happen, how it was going to be funded, all that—were still up in the air. Originally I had thought I would move full-time into the weekend house Brendan and I had bought up in Hillsdale. When it turned out that some pretty significant repair work was way behind schedule and over budget, I returned to Brooklyn once again, finding a beautiful floor-through apartment in a limestone one block from my old place.

The work on the house was stressful. The previous Christmas I had visited, only to find water damage and mold, compliments of a leaky roof. Not having a clue how to deal with such matters, especially from 600 miles away, I had hired a friend's boyfriend to handle the job as project manager, knowing he would be hiring a friend of his to do the work with him. Unfortunately, I did not do my own research in this process and found out the hard way this guy was horribly unreliable. They left the house entirely open and uncovered during rainstorms. They started work I had not authorized but said I might want to do down the road after this project was done. Ultimately, he claimed to be out of money with the roof not even half built. At least I knew not to throw good money after bad so I found someone to finish building the job.

The blessing of this debacle was that, somehow, this was not feeding my sense of being alone in the world. It did not reinforce my earlier notion that I had screwed up my life. Perhaps I was beginning to identify normal life challenges from the special challenges of grieving, something I hadn't really been able to do for the previous couple years.

On the outside, it looked as though I was settling in nicely to my life back in the old 'hood. I had started dating Pete, a man I had known from when I lived there previously. I was working part-time at One Spirit, helping them develop their nascent retail efforts and their overall marketing. The plans for my own store also were gaining ground. I was writing a business plan and looking at potential locations for the store.

While I was open to anywhere in the Hudson Valley, Kingston was the name of the town that kept sticking in my mind. After an initial online search showing very affordable commercial properties in the uptown section, I decided to make a trip up there on a Sunday afternoon. After a gorgeous spring drive with the top down on my Audi TT, Pete and I pulled into the area, only to find a ghost town with virtually no one on the street. I had just said to Pete, "I guess I can strike Kingston off the list" when I heard someone call out "Don't I know you from Brooklyn?" It turned out a casual friend had, unbeknownst to me, moved up there about three years earlier. She showed me around town, introduced me to some town visionaries, and talked about planned developments. None of the buildings I had found online fit what I was looking for, but there was one with a sign in the window with work being done in the store area. Peeking through the window, I saw the beginning of exposed brick and almost 1000' square feet, completely unfinished: no floor, no ceiling, no walls. Based on there being a second floor, it sure looked like this building met all my specifications. After jotting down the real estate agent's number, we hopped back in my little convertible to find a place for a celebratory dinner, then headed home to Brooklyn. My dream was starting to become a reality; at least this part of my life was moving along.

Other parts, not so much. Between my new work situation and a financial drama of my sister's I was allowing myself to get dragged into, it became clear that perhaps there was another level of self-work that needed to happen. After talking it over with a few friends and Kim, a new therapist I was starting to work with, I decided to enroll in Chit Chat, a five-day program at Caron Foundation that focuses on codependency. I arrived there in the sticks of Pennsylvania on a Sunday afternoon, was told where my room was, met my roommates, and was informed we would start with a get-acquainted exercise that evening.

I was an observer for the early part of that exercise, very engaged in the interaction between the counselors and one of my peers, but an observer nonetheless. As I sat in the circle, holding my hand in front of my mouth in what had become a common pose of mine, one of the counselors looked at me and asked, "Who told you growing up that you couldn't or shouldn't speak?" Looking at him perplexed, wondering how he knew that, he pointed out my unconscious covering of my mouth. In answer to his question, I thought of how my family had dealt with grief. I also thought of the family disease of alcoholism, and the day in and day out soul-harming teasing. There were a lot of times the message to stay silent came through, usually covertly but clearly enough anyhow. I knew it was time for that to change.

The bulk of the Caron program is psychodrama, where each participant acts out a scene from their childhood that was life-changing but not in a good way. I worked with my relationship with my brothers and how my mother was absolutely, positively unwilling to protect me or stand up for me in any way. This is the hurt that felt most right to work with, yet it took the events of the twenty-four hours prior to my psychodrama to confirm this.

A dream I had the night before showed me that my mother and relationships with men were what primarily needed healing. In this dream, someone was offering me a fabulous business opportunity. I was walking around an office suite trying to finish a big presentation, but my mobility was limited by my mom holding me in a bear hug from behind. When I finally did manage to break free from her, I went out into the reception area, only to see one of my male peers stretched out naked on the couch. I chuckled with my cohorts how accurate that portrayal was of my life—that when I have felt on the other side of Mom's grip (literally or figuratively), I had often instead been distracted by romantic escapades.

The other indicator I was on the right track with my scenario was in the man I had selected to represent my oldest brother, Tim. Jeff was a New York City cop who had been half-hearted in his participation so far that week. Most of us were connecting deeply, but Jeff, being the consummate clown, held everyone else at bay. Yes, he was the ideal stand-in for my aloof brother Tim. The only thing was that Jeff, who was also scheduled to do his own psychodrama that day, snuck out in the middle of the night rather than face whatever it was he was carrying in his psyche. I thought of all the ways I—as well as everyone in my family—checked out rather than faced our problems square on.

During the actual acting out itself, one of the counselors made a point of making sure I saw the role of alcoholism in my family dynamics. He wasn't even particularly focused on my own alcoholism as compared to the underlying way it permeated all my family's interactions and informed who we were to each other.

By the end of the week, I felt great awareness and healing around family interactions, and was just as impacted while witnessing or participating in the psychodramas of my friends, particularly those around grief. One woman took herself back to her grandmother's death in her childhood, and the confusion, helplessness, fear, sadness, and aloneness she felt at that time— questions unanswered, feelings uncared for. The healing I experienced through her psychodrama was deeper than much of the grief work I had done in my life, certainly deeper than I had known prior to Brendan's death.

By the time Friday rolled around, I felt a greater hope and possibility for authenticity in my life than I had ever known. I found the courage to start going by AnnE, a name I had been toying with for several years but also knew it wouldn't be readily accepted by everyone. I realized my time at One Spirit had come to an end; that I would finish up the projects I was working on but that I needed to shift my focus to my store, to my dream. I left that week knowing I was ready to step up in my life.

CHAPTER 38

Whom I was no longer living every day defined primarily as a grieving widow, I was still aware of the need for healing in my life. I knew I was still healing from the loss of my beloved, as well as other losses I still carried, but I also sensed that healing could be more than just that; it could indeed be a journey towards wholeness and self-acceptance. Given all the woundedness that had been alleviated with Johrei and Core Energetics, energy healing was something very appealing to me. So when my One Spirit classmate, Lisa, enthusiastically told me about this powerful healer, Veena, from Singapore, I was intrigued. Hearing she was only going to be in town for ten days, I booked a session with her.

When the day arrived for my session, I drove out from the city to the home in Bridgeport, Connecticut where she was seeing clients. I grew skeptical as I got off the expressway and navigated the back roads there. I found myself in a neighborhood just one step up from slums. The bungalows were small, and kids were running around in the streets, playing in sprinklers and fire hydrants to try to stay cool on the sweltering July day. It was not the setting I anticipated.

Finally finding the right home, I parked in the driveway and headed for the front door. I was greeted by Veena's friend whose home it was. She explained that Veena was running a little late and invited me to sit at the small Formica table in the kitchen while I waited. The home was clean, colorfully decorated and a bit funky—all in all, very comfortable. I began to relax a bit.

Veena surfaced minutes later from the back bedroom where she had set up her healing table to see clients. Not knowing what to expect, I was comforted more by meeting this compassionate, Light-filled but also very "normal" Asian woman. I followed her into the room where we had a very pleasant but brief conversation before we got into the session. I reminded her I had been referred to her by Lisa, who thought it would help me through my prolonged grieving process. Without much more discussion than that, she invited me to lie on the table and relax.

The beginning of the session was pretty mellow. I felt light. I felt relaxed. I felt safe. So far so good. This was all in the realm of what I knew and felt comfortable with. About twenty minutes into it, things shifted. I became aware of a heaviness, a darkness in me. I didn't know what it was or how long it had been there, but I knew it had to go. Instinctively I started rocking my hips and bending my knees. Veena encouraged me to continue my movements as her hands moved more rapidly around me and over me.

A few minutes into this, I realized I was in the exact position of a woman giving birth. My knees were bent into my chest and I was sweating, screaming, and working to push something out of me. Veena, my "labor coach," was alternately propping up my back, holding my hand, and clearing the energy around me. This intensity only went on a short time when I started to feel some relief, as though a physical entity had left my body. I started to relax and let my breath return to its normal pace as Veena finished the healing. Both of us were exhausted but gratified.

I still don't know for sure what was released that day. Veena told me with great certainty I had been carrying an entity in my body. I was very skeptical then and still remain a bit so, despite having had other sessions where the physical release was palpable and even seemed to take a specific form. My logical mind wants to dismiss out of hand the notion of entities, "off planet beings" and other things of the like. I just need to remember I don't need to know. I only need to be open to letting go of anything that is not serving me—thoughts, energy, blockages and whatever else.

Later that year, I was offered another chance for a spiritual pilgrimage to Japan. I jumped at it for two reasons. One is I thought it would be an auspicious launch to my new business to be focused on my spiritual practice for ten days, as I had been told for years that the spiritual precedes the physical. Getting a tune-up at the spiritual level would hopefully prepare me for the blessings and challenges to come as a business owner. The more important reason, though, was that my long-time friend, Mark, following a dream, had moved to Japan several months earlier, and I wanted to see how he was doing, especially since the trip coincided with his birthday. He joined our travel group for much of the trip to each of the Sacred Grounds, then I travelled to Narita with him to stay on another weekend and really explore Tokyo.

While it was wonderful to catch up with Mark and spend his birthday with him, some of his behaviors and comments struck me as odd. One thing was that Mark had wanted to spend the bulk of a Sunday, after exploring beautiful sacred land, watching *Kill Bill* movies. That was not how I knew this peaceful, quiet man, who spent so much time offering Johrei to people, including using it to help me through one of the most emotionally challenging, upsetting, and draining times of my life. Another perplexing incident was a strange statement he made as we were getting ready one morning. Out of nowhere he commented, "You know I don't keep friends in my life for more than ten years, don't you?" My reply was, "So you're telling me I'm not going to see you after next March," to which he replied, suppressing his adorable half-smirk, "Yeah, pretty much."

There was one more thing that struck me as odd on Mark's part. For his birthday dinner, Mark chose one of the few Italian restaurants in Tokyo, hidden on a quiet side street, the whole scenario rather romantic, which was not where we were at the time. During the dinner, our conversation turned to relationships, something Mark had always had a great aversion to and been very open about it, even when we were dating. Out of nowhere, Mark acknowledged he felt like he was getting ready for a relationship, but had no idea how that would come about living in Japan. I simply reminded him that when Spirit wants something to come forth, it will and probably not until then.

By the time I was scheduled to leave, I was ready to do so. The trip had had not left me with the clarity and spiritual connection I experienced during my first trip to Japan.

CHAPTER 39

Two months after my return from Japan I received a call at home late on a Saturday morning. Picking up the phone, I heard a young man's voice ask if I was Ann O'Neil, Mark Nelson's friend. Very curious, I said "yes". This young man went on to say, "My name is Eric. I am Mark Nelson's son. I am calling to tell you that my dad is in a coma."

I gasped, then asked, "What happened?"

Eric explained, "He had just rented a bike from the hotel where he was living. Just as he pulled out of the parking lot, an elderly gentleman, not seeing him, ran into him. He's been in a coma since."

It turned out Eric's sister, Trish, remembered my name from having met me a few years earlier when the two of them visited Brendan and me in New York. Mark's family found my name and phone number in his computer and was primarily calling to get hooked up with Johrei contacts in Japan, knowing Mark would want that. It was ironic they had to call halfway around the world to find people just a few kilometers away. I told Eric I would go to the New York center and let the minister know what had happened. One of us would be back in touch with him with the names of people in Japan who would channel to his dad, or he may hear directly from local contacts. He informed me he had his dad's cell phone; that was the number where he could be contacted.

Still in shock from Eric's phone call, my phone rang again about an hour later with another voice I did not recognize on the other end of the line. This one was a woman with a German accent introducing herself as Mark's girlfriend of over two years. She explained she had met Mark through work since he was working for Boeing and she was with one of the airlines. She had been completely aware of my visit to see Mark and seemed rather nonplussed by it, even though she knew all about our relationship throughout the years, including the fact we had dated. She then went on to tell the story of flying to Japan once she heard of the accident, and meeting Mark's whole family—parents, children, sisters—for the first time, all of whom had also been completely unaware of Mark's involvement with anyone. She spent days regaling them with story upon story of their relationship, complete with a photo album of all their travels and celebrations. I hung up dumbfounded. There was a part of me that was at least glad there was someone US-based from whom I could get updates, but the more I thought about it the more disturbed I became. How did I know this was true, especially since just two months earlier Mark had strongly implied he was not seeing anyone? My mind was reeling.

After those two calls, I headed straight for Izunome Association, the home of Johrei. Two things had to happen. First, I needed to work with the minister to make the necessary communications to get someone to Mark's hospital room as soon as possible. The other thing, growing in its importance, was that I needed to sit in peace and quiet with everything I had learned in the last few hours—from the accident of a very dear friend to the secret life he seemed to be living. The secret life grew more complex after Japanese Johrei members found out about his accident because a Japanese woman he had been dating a few months earlier came forth, and everyone realized that relationship must have been going on at the same time he was involved with the German woman. Yes, there was more to Mark than I had ever guessed… than anyone had ever guessed. His family, especially one of his sisters and his kids, brought great levity to the situation as they started referring to him as the "international man of mystery."

Once at the center and receiving Johrei, the floodgates of tears opened fully. I had cried some after Eric's call, but that had been interrupted by the next call, which frankly brought forth confusion and disillusionment with who Mark was and how well I knew him. By the time I was settled in the chair opposite Minister Marco sending me Divine Light, I was back in touch with the Mark I did know. I remembered how sweet he was when we dated, despite his own discomfort. I remembered the beautiful statue of a man and woman with hearts connected that he gave me for my birthday years earlier, with the card signed "love, love, love" as I had been teasing about his inability to use that word. I thought of our first trip to Japan and the bamboo print I had given him, which I saw beautifully framed in his apartment just months earlier. I thought of when he dropped me off at the airport, dressed in a white shirt and blue jeans, immaculate as usual. I remembered the hug he gave me after he got my luggage out of the trunk. Never in a million years would I have guessed that would be the last time I would see him. I hadn't believed it when he predicted an end to our friendship.

As the days went by, I started to toy with the idea of going to Japan to see him, a move that was discouraged by his family. Trish explained, "You know my dad. You know he would rather have you hold onto the memories you have than for you to see him like this." I knew she was right.

As Christmas and New Year's rolled around and Mark's parents and kids stayed on in Japan, the doctors there were still not willing to give any prognosis on whether there was a chance for recovery, so his family made arrangements to bring him back to Seattle to have him assessed there. Within days of his return, I got a call from Trish he was given no hope for any appreciable recovery. They decided to remove his feeding tube. I received a call the following Saturday he had died the previous day on Friday the 13th, something Mark's humor would have loved. There would be a memorial service in Seattle ten days later. His daughter invited me to speak as a friend and fellow Johrei member, one who had shared that path more closely with him than any other. I told her I would have to let her know as I was about to close on a building that would be the future home of my store and I was not certain I would be able to make the service.

Much of that weekend I spent at Johrei continuing to release tears of another love lost and praying for guidance as to whether I should join his sister and his daughter in eulogizing him. It felt strange to be given this honor when there was another woman who certainly seemed to have a larger role in his life than I did. When I thought about it in the context of honoring Mark's commitment to Johrei, however, it became clear I should be there, so I called Trish and told her I would let her know of my flight details soon. The following Monday I got a call from my lawyer we would be closing on the building for my store that Thursday, January 19, so I could travel out Sunday with no problem.

I almost didn't make it to Mark's memorial service—for it seems I narrowly escaped my own death in the interim. To celebrate the purchase of my building, I had a nice dinner out, then settled into the upstairs apartment that was to become my new home, having already given my Brooklyn landlord thirty days notice. Just as I was drifting off to sleep on my blow-up mattress shortly after 11:00, this loud shrieking alarm startled me awake. I walked around the apartment, unable to figure out what it was, then realized it was coming from the store area. I headed down the apartment stairs and into the cold winter night to the front door of the store, unlocked it and plugged in the work lamp that sat amidst the debris of half-finished construction. I had happily bought the building in that condition so I could build out the store as I liked. Navigating my way to the back where, on the wood frame of a supporting wall, a carbon monoxide alarm had been plugged in, I merely reset the alarm and figured I would address it if it went off again. As a precautionary measure, I did open the window in my bedroom despite the 20-degree temperature and bundled up for the night's sleep.

The next morning I was slated to meet both the building inspector and my contractor at the store to start the process of getting the necessary permits. My contractor called, stating he was on his way but would be late, shortly before the building inspector showed up. Jim, a very nice portly man with a kind smile, was understanding and decided to start looking around himself as we waited for Andy, my contractor. As he started to poke around the street level space, he got a look on his face and said he'd be right back. Although carbon monoxide is odorless, something had made him think there might be an issue with it in the air, even though I hadn't mentioned anything about the alarm going off the night before. He brought the machine that measures the carbon monoxide in the air into the store and it registered thirty as soon as he brought it in. Another reading elsewhere in the store space showed fifty; as we descended the stairs to the basement, the machine read almost one hundred. It was in the basement where the source of the problem was found; the furnace was hooked directly to the chimney. The bricks of that unlined chimney were collapsing inward, blocking a vent and forcing all the air back into the furnace and creating the poisonous gases. My inspector had pointed out that the furnace hooked up directly to the chimney would need to be remedied, but didn't point out how quickly it needed to be addressed or that it could be fatal.

Heading upstairs to the apartment, Jim noticed a hole in the brick bathroom wall opening to the culprit chimney. Taking a reading in the apartment, he looked at me and said, "I don't know why you're alive. With readings at these levels, you shouldn't be. Somebody's looking out for you." I had a sense Mark was already helping from the other side, understanding it might have been his time to go but that didn't mean it was mine. The rest of the day was spent with three Kingston fire trucks at my newly bought building, blowing out the carbon monoxide with industrial size fans. The meeting with my contractor finally happened, with us talking about the new priority of getting a new boiler installed and this one disconnected as soon as humanly possible.

Once everything was as secure as it could be and plans were in place to install a new furnace before anyone else spent time in the building, I returned to Brooklyn to get packed for my trip to Seattle and to write a tribute fitting to Mark and his commitment to Johrei.

The memorial was a beautiful service. I got reacquainted with Trish as well as met Mark's parents, his sisters, his ex-wife, his son, and his German girlfriend, as well as other friends and coworkers. They were all appreciative of what I shared about Mark and his faith. His kids put together a terrific slide show set to the song, "I Can't Drive 55" to honor Mark's race car driving days. Out at the sanctuary where his ashes were placed, I gave a few minutes of Johrei on a bench near his ashes, knowing Mark would want it no other way.

A little over a month after Mark's passing, a poem came to me out of nowhere. As I wrote it down, I realized it was not from Brendan as I initially thought, but Mark, who chose to remind me of the blessing of living in this world. It reads:

> Take a breath.
> You can do that.
> Be grateful;
> Enjoy it.

Really let the air come in and feed every crevice
of your body.
Feel it feeding your very being, your life force.
Then let it go, releasing it fully back to the world
with peace and gratitude—
Knowing another waits in the very next moment.

Someday this won't be so,
Then you'll join me.

Yes, Mark was continuing to be my spiritual teacher, although he had always claimed I was his. It also reminded me of hearing the song "I Just Want to Celebrate Another Day of Living" after my father-in-law Joe died. As beautiful as I know it must be on the other side, the spirits I knew and loved there were reminding me to be fully here.

Grappling with Mark's death a couple months later, I once again decided a Core Energetics session might help to move some of the grief, sadness, and confusion that still existed. As I started the session with Lynn, her reply to hearing about Mark's death was simply, "A lot of people are going to be choosing to leave now." At the time I thought that statement was rather cold (I still do, actually), but now I understand it more fully. Yes, as whatever we are going through in this physical world accelerates, causing even more chaos, many people—consciously or unconsciously, actively or passively—may decide this round of their existence is done. That realization has since actually offered me comfort, both in remembering that death isn't something that is done to us but rather something our souls tune into at some time…whenever it is that they are ready.

CHAPTER 40

One thing I've noticed is the passing of someone to whom I'm connected often increases my connection to others I've loved who are now in the spiritual realm. Whether Mark's death brought on an opportunity for more healing around my grief about Brendan, I don't know. I just knew there was indeed more healing to be done.

Brendan had been dead more than a year longer than we had been together, yet I still thought of him as "my forever love" as the Josh Groban song says. I also increasingly feared this would preclude another deep earthbound soul connection. I remembered my writing, "Is he hanging on to me? Or am I hanging onto him? Or, worse yet, am I just hanging onto hanging on?" Even rereading our wedding vows I found some truth to the hypothesis a friend had offered—that when one loses their life partner, they are left as one person walking the path that had been intended for two. After all, Brendan's and my vows did not say anything like "until death do us part." Instead they talked about our souls being together forever. Even the minister in her final blessing stated, "Their destinies shall now be woven into one design."

How does one move beyond that when the other is gone? Is it even possible—or is the loneliness of the solo path inevitable? I so wanted to heal more deeply and open more fully to the possibilities in my life—but what was that to look like? There must be another leg to this journey; another leg with no map, perhaps no guidance even. That is, until Brendan himself guided me to an answer in a dream I had on Easter Eve 2006.

I woke up Easter morning completely disoriented, having dreamt Brendan was still alive. In the dream, I had not actually been with him when he died; instead he had been sent to yet another hospital while we all accepted the inevitable conclusion he absolutely could not hold on. In the dream, however, I came to find out miraculously he had lived. He had not gotten any better than he was while in Calvary, but somehow had still survived these four plus years. Nor was he expected to get any better. I was expected to choose between continued devotion to the man whom I loved with all my heart and soul, knowing I would give up my own life in the process or forging a new path for myself, one with healing, fulfillment, and the possibility of love again. That was when I awoke—still without the answer. I sobbed and sobbed like I had not in a long time.

When I spoke of this dream with my therapist, she suggested I consider a spiritual practice known as a cord-cutting ceremony—if that felt right to me. It immediately did. Having not participated in such a ritual, I was not entirely sure what to expect, but I did understand it was based on an acknowledgement that sometimes the tight bond we have with another can hold us back in our own life. The dream I just had certainly reinforced that concept. I hoped—and trusted—this ritual would allow me to move beyond any restrictions I still carried from my marriage. After all, Brendan himself had encouraged me to go on with my life with his list of things to do, especially with his statement, "Fall in love—Choose wisely." So in preparation for the cord-cutting, I started writing the story of the love I shared with Brendan. I instinctively knew I had to once again let into the depth of my being all that those years had been and what they had held. Only then could I really release them; now it was time for the cord-cutting itself.

I arrived at my therapist's healing space and walked in to the scent of sage and the sound of beautiful healing tribal music. I was greeted by Kim with a huge hug. We exchanged a deep look, a reminder to me I was being cared for by my sister, a beautiful, loving sister. We then went to the patio out back where she asked me to write any fears I had about doing the cord-cutting. I wrote:

> "I am afraid I am releasing the only true soul love I will know in this lifetime."
> "I am afraid I will completely lose my connection to Brendan and his soul."
> "I am afraid Brendan and others will feel I've abandoned him."

With that, we burned those fears, literally and figuratively. I no longer believe them to be true. After that, I also chose to burn our wedding vows, honoring both Brendan and me for fulfilling them as fully and as beautifully as we did yet acknowledging they were no longer valid. We then went back inside to continue the ceremony.

When working with the heart chakra during the actual ceremony, Kim herself was sobbing quietly. She said, "He's gone. He's not at the end of the cord. I've never had that happen where the other soul was willing to go. He loves you so much. He only wants your happiness. What a love you shared." A folly love indeed.

The ceremony was indeed just what I needed. It allowed me to acknowledge that I had done the work to grieve and to heal. To borrow Elizabeth Neeld's words from the book, *Seven Choices*: "It was at this moment that I recognized that the work of grieving was over. Not, of course, that I believed I would never feel sadness again, or longing or pain. Not that the experience of his death would not be a part of me forever. Not that issues, particularly about myself, that had been revealed, though not caused, by his death were not present for me to continue to grapple with. But what I now realized was that my life was no longer dominated by the presence of loss....I did again take joy in living. I did have enthusiasm and energy. I felt full to the brim with possibility... Yes, I had done the work that was necessary to be able to say, "I have grieved."""

The time had come for me to step fully into *my* life, a life that had not been shared with Brendan in any way. It was to be a life of my own creation, a life I believed that my beloved was supporting from the other side, even if he would have been fearful of it had he lived. Yes, that's what I wanted, a life beyond his comfort zone because I choose to live a life beyond my comfort zone. As Eleanor Roosevelt advised, "Do something every day that scares you."

I may not have lived my early years that way, but working through the grief that had restricted me opened a fuller experience of what is possible in life. It was very much like my recognition that opening more fully to sorrow opened me more fully to joy as well. Learning to fully embrace the death of those I loved also allowed me to embrace my own life, as well as to love more deeply. To love without fear.

CHAPTER 41

Fortunately, the foundation for my new life was already being put in place. My store, Inspired!, opened its doors on July 2, 2006, and opened the door for me to much in life. Because it was a book and gift store specifically oriented towards personal and spiritual growth, and we held related events, it brought me many opportunities for both. It invited me into a more formal expression of my ministry than I had imagined. It prodded me to share my experience with grief more openly with others, including what I had learned about healing from grief and the beliefs that had served me in grappling with life and death. It opened me more fully to relationships, in all forms. It introduced me to deeper healing.

The first opportunity my store brought me to be more ministerial was an invitation to write articles for Benedictine Hospital's cancer newsletter about how I had coped with my husband's illness and his subsequent death. As a new bookstore owner, I shared all of my favorite books, from *Only Love is Real* to *A Year to Live* by Stephen Levine to *Life Lessons* by Kubler-Ross. In those few months around the time of the articles, at least a dozen women came in who had read them and could identify, most who had recently lost their own husbands to cancer. We spoke of tender goodbyes, of the first days of trying to reorient to life—watching the world go on as if nothing has happened when you know it will never again be the same. My heart ached for them yet I could understand that was indeed what was going on…my heart ached *for them.* My own ache, my own pain, had largely dissipated. It would always be enough in my heart that I could deeply connect with someone in their loss, but it no longer ruled my every day. It didn't even hold a strong grip when it did rise from deep within. Yes, my life was once again my own.

One major blessing from writing the articles and connecting with those women was I was able to more clearly see how I had healed, what it was that allowed me to do so. I realized it had been a twofold process. I had done the psychological work of dealing with the reality of Brendan's death and feeling and expressing the grief. I had also been given the gift of continued spiritual connection with Brendan—a gift I recognized and readily accepted. This holistic approach came to me naturally, but it was not one I had seen outlined anywhere. Most of the books and articles I had read on the subject either focused on the psychology and emotion of grieving or they focused solely on keeping your loved one in your life by maintaining a relationship with their spirit. With the perspective of hindsight, I realized either one of these modalities alone could not have gotten me to where I was. I needed to find my own path, one that acknowledged the blessing of an ongoing relationship with Brendan's spirit but that was thoroughly rooted in the need to take responsibility for my own life and my own healing.

Another belief I developed and/or embraced more fully during this time had to do with the cycle of life and death. I have always believed in reincarnation, but that didn't mean I gave much thought as to how or why the cycle went on. I hadn't focused much on the soul's overall purpose, even as my spiritual life grew. How or why people came into my life had been of little importance to me. I most definitely didn't consider how much free will my Spirit had in its evolution.

This issue had come to the forefront when Brendan was dying and I was reading *Only Love is Real*. As mentioned earlier, I could see we had a soul contract to love and to be together for his final days. This helped me to open to the notion that everyone in my life might be there for a specific purpose for the higher good of all.

In reading another book that talked about the major paths in our life, I started considering the role death and loss had played in my life from a different vantage point. Rather than viewing myself as a victim, as the woman who was an orphan and a widow by the age of forty, and who had a whole slew of losses besides those, I started to consider that possibly my Spirit had said "yes" to a life of loss. That perhaps my Higher Self knew this path was what I needed for a bigger heart, greater compassion, and whatever spiritual growth I am to experience in this incarnation.

The belief I now hold is that our Spirit chooses and agrees to our life lessons in each incarnation. God / the universe / Divine Spirit then supports these lessons in the unfolding of our life in the gentlest and most loving manner possible...which doesn't always look gentle and loving when one is resisting what one is supposed to learn. I also believe the people in my life are there because our paths are converging to support both of us equally in the unfolding of these lessons for the ultimate Soul purpose of enlightenment, or what I view as complete loving reconnection with the Divine. This viewpoint has helped me to joyously accept—even celebrate—the hardships along life's path, believing with every fiber of my being there is great value in what they bring to my life.

This belief has not only served my life. It seems to have helped some of whom I have offered it to as a possibility. One of these was a guy, early twenties, who came into the store late on a Saturday afternoon. With Uptown Kingston's Saturday attraction of the Farmer's Market having been closed for hours already, there were as usual very few people on the streets at that time and nobody besides me in the store. I was taking the time to straighten up and move a few things around when this young man I had never seen before walked in. As was my usual way, I gave him a friendly greeting as an acknowledgement but gave him his space to browse. After he had been looking about ten minutes through the various sections—Spiritual Growth and Practice, Healing, Conscious Living—I asked him if there was anything in particular he was looking for. He answered there was nothing specific but said it in such a way that we began a conversation, and I shared some of my favorite passages with him...Pema Chodron's writing from *When Things Fall Apart*, a couple words from Tolstoy's daily thoughts book, a few other things that came forward. After we had been speaking close to an hour, I also offered him Johrei, as I often did in the store. When he asked very skeptically what that was, I explained it as the channeling of Light for healing purposes, noting it could also be considered a blessing or a silent prayer. Somewhat hesitatingly he accepted and sat down across from me. I offered the usual twenty minutes of Light, then gently touched him to let him know when the session was over. He opened his eyes, gave me a gentle smile, thanked me, and got up to leave. At the door he paused a moment and explained he had been brought into the store by its name, Inspired! He then added he had been "so much in need of inspiration I wasn't sure life was worth living" before saying another thank you and leaving in a considerably more peaceful place.

I stood at the counter a moment longer, in shock at what he had just said, recognizing it to be a confession he had been considering killing himself and could now see some hope and possibility in life. So much came flooding forth. The importance of offering possibility and invitation instead of pushing. The way God brought the two of us together for both of us to receive a gift, a blessing that day. The full realization that my store was indeed my ministry. I might have a counter instead of a pulpit but that I was serving God and humanity to the best of my ability. The store was indeed fulfilling its mission "to offer tools and encouragement to individuals."

The store's ministry showed itself in other ways as well. It was evident the afternoon a woman came in explaining she had had an unsettling afternoon and needed to find some peace. She had gone into the beautiful Dutch Reformed Church down the street, but that didn't do it for her. She had sat briefly in the Peace Garden but that wasn't it either. Leaving there she remembered the store and came in. She chatted briefly, browsed some books, had a cup of tea, and left feeling rejuvenated.

Our monthly poetry readings, led by my dear friend Jerrice Baptiste, offered many a chance to deepen their connection with Spirit. Her own poetry reminds me of that of Rumi and Hafiz, with an unabashed love for God and His many gifts. One month she had shared a poem on growing up in Haiti, hiding while hearing gunfire not far from the front door, followed immediately by one of these glorious tributes to the Divine. It made me think of the strength of the human Spirit. It also deepened my gratitude for Jerrice having invited me to facilitate a ritual celebrating her connection with the Divine just months earlier. The blessings were plentiful in my life!

I have often said the store was my greatest example of so many spiritual principles, most notably that of the Law of Attraction. The first time this was unquestionably evident was two days before the opening. Everything was still in disarray with half-unpacked boxes of books sitting amidst the workmen's remaining tools and ladders and painting supplies. The telephone guys had installed the phone the day before, but it didn't seem to be working. I was an absolute basket case as to how everything that needed to get done would. Realizing my state of mind wasn't helping, I gathered together everyone there to take a prayer break. We held hands while I said a prayer of gratitude, acceptance, and opening to God's Will. As soon as I concluded with my familiar "and so it is," the phone rang, proving that my worries were indeed unfounded. I chuckled, said an overarching thank you, then went back to work.

One of the poetry events also reminded me of how the Law of Attraction was working in the store. I had been becoming increasingly aware that when I stayed entirely focused on the store's mission, things were fine. My mental and spiritual state was good; often even sales were even adequate then. It was while I was in one of my fearful modes that my friend Sandy read her poem "Enough". In it she went through her day and outlined how there truly was always enough—from the hot water to the coffee to the food to the conversation to the friendships. It caused me to reflect that I did indeed, for that very moment, have enough. I may or may not in a week or a month or a year, but in that moment I had everything I needed.

CHAPTER 42

Another series of events we had at Inspired! truly changed my life forever. As I was in my office one day with one of my employees covering the front, a woman I had never seen popped her head in and introduced herself as a friend of someone I knew from One Spirit. Nancy and I ended up having a pleasant chat. She mentioned she did healing work and might want to offer an introductory evening at the store sometime if that was okay with me. As my criteria for events was whether they supported the store's mission and this one definitely did, I said "Sure, just let me know when," explaining ideally she would book it the middle of the month prior so I could include it in the store announcements.

Nancy followed up and scheduled her first Introduction to One Light Healing Touch evening a few months later. Whenever possible, I sat in on the store's events and this was one I did not want to miss. After all, so far all my experiences with energy healing had been very positive, whether through Johrei or other healings I had.

The first introductory evening, Nancy co-facilitated the event with Penny, another teacher of the One Light Healing Touch work. With about a dozen people showing up between Nancy's efforts and the store invitees, the event was a popular one. Nancy opened with an explanation of how energy works and offered the definition of healing as being "anything that brings body, mind, and soul more in line with each other." She then led us through a grounding meditation and chanting. It was a beautiful evening but at that time I had not even begun to think of healing work as something that might become my vocation.

Nancy offered the intro evening several more times after that. The second event some of her close friends came; I was glad to meet many of them and be reacquainted with another as I had done some consulting work with her. I still did not think of this work as for me. By the time she held the third intro evening, my life was a mess. I had become completely overtaken by the responsibilities of the store, a breast cancer scare, and what I thought was certain impending financial doom. At the end of the session, as Nancy invited us to check in with any messages our heart may have for us, the words came forth loud and clear, "And how are you taking care of yourself?" I had to acknowledge "It pretty much sucks." I immediately signed on for the next six-month class, totally not knowing how I was going to pay for it—but also trusting that other major life changes had worked out in similar circumstances when I was coming from my heart. This endeavor I knew most definitely came from my heart. I also found it interesting that the class was scheduled to start on the anniversary of Brendan's death.

My life changed in the six months of my first One Light Healing Touch Basic class. The most profound shift came in my newfound ability to be fully present here on this earth whatever situation I was in. Previously I could not do that. Through all the spiritual work I had done to that point, the best it had gotten me in this arena was the ability to recognize when I wasn't fully there, when my feet were not on the ground. At our wedding I was aware a large part of me was not standing in front of the minister, holding the hand of my beloved. It (I) was off worried about what course Brendan's illness would take, even a little disappointed that this was not the wedding I had dreamed of. I could not bring myself fully to the gift I had been given.

The same thing was true with my ordination and graduation from seminary. The whole Intensive weekend prior to these celebrations had been such a spiritual uplifting I was completely unable to remember the part of being a human being having a spiritual experience; I was only focused on the spiritual experience. I was vaguely aware this wasn't ideal—that since I am in a human body I should probably be present in this form—but, again, no clue *how* to do that.

Learning how to get present in my body and on this earth was probably the greatest blessing my OLHT training offered me. There was a great deal of focus put on this as the foundation of all healing work, perhaps even of all genuine spiritual work. Every class day at least twice we did OLHT's six-position grounding meditation. We were also strongly encouraged to start every day with it, and reminded how necessary it was for a healer to do it before each healing and to clear out afterwards. The essence of this profound exercise is to release any energy that is not authentically and inherently our own, and to reconnect more fully to our own energy, fed by the sources of Mother Earth and Father Sun. The strength of the magnetic and solar energies allows the body to be revitalized and connected to its earthly experience. Since then, I have also come to realize the true blessing of my physical body – of all of our physical bodies – being the link between the Earth and the spiritual realm.

Shortly after I completed the OLHT class, I was given the perfect opportunity to see the huge impact it had in my life. I had just received news that round two of some legal proceedings was right around the corner. The first time through, I was bitter and angry, yet somehow didn't really feel as though I had the right to be there. Either family or friends sat with me during the entire process, yet I felt so alone. This time I used all the tools I had learned in the school: the grounding, the releasing of energy not my own and not serving me, the calling in of light, and many, many others forms of spiritual practice. It worked! This round saw me completely present and open to what was going on in the courtroom. It also allowed me to feel the energy, presence, and support of many who loved me, even though I sat alone. Plus it seemed my attitude can indeed affect the outcome of a situation—and did here. My case was resolved justly and in such a way that I found peace.

Another huge gift of my healing class was the awareness it brought me as to what had been the patterns of my life. Unbeknownst to me, the second class is particularly focused on this, so not surprisingly, I was having huge emotions coming up as the class approached that weekend. The first day of the three-day weekend I was torn between very much wanting to delve into whatever was there to work with and at the same time, great resistance to going there. That evening, after our day in class, I had an epiphany as to how much I placed others' needs before my own. This had started as a child where being the youngest of five and a girl in my family left me little choice but to do that. It continued through my advertising career and into all my relationships, most notably the one with Brendan. At this point in my life, it was taking the form of taking care of friends, employees, the community, family members, and customers, placing all of these people before me. The rage within me when I realized the depth of this reality was palpable.

It was in this frame of mind I showed up for the Saturday class that weekend. Our class was small, only three other students, but I still found myself trying to shift this pattern—trying to take care of my own needs without worrying what that looked like to others. As often happens, the form was dramatic.

As we started the six-position meditation and I tuned in more fully to the energy in my body, I knew it needed more release than the movement alone was going to allow for. While moving through the third position, that of engaging with each of the chakras, I felt a strong impulse to let out a big, long yell. I left the room in which we were doing the grounding, headed upstairs to the healing room, shut the door, and just let it all go. I screamed for a good three minutes, letting out as much of the pent-up frustration of years of self-neglect that would come at that time, and went back downstairs to join the rest of the group to finish the grounding.

It turned out my release was not welcomed by all. Just as Nancy was noting the big shift of energy that happened in the room by my actions, one of my classmates registered her offense to them. This woman had already portrayed herself as very sensitive to all forms of energy—food, electromagnetic waves, scent, other people. She complained about my actions, "I didn't come here to have other people getting in my face with their outbursts."

Nancy spent a great deal of time exploring her statement, inquiring as to whether she could think of other times in her life when she had felt the same violation. I participated in some of this exploration, as the other party involved in the interaction, but most of it was focused on this other woman's feelings about the situation. As we were wrapping up, as part of my no longer making others' needs more important than my own, it became very important I speak up and negate the proclamation I had gotten in anyone's face. I reminded everyone I had done whatever possible to minimize the impact on their experience while still fully embracing my own. Today I still view that whole sequence of events as critical to opening to my life and who I am.

Many other exercises throughout the class reinforced that notion and/or revealed more. Meditations on past lives, learning to connect with guides, and consciously working to enhance our clairvoyant and clairsentient abilities continued to open me. The healings we experienced every class peeled away layer after layer of old stuff that wasn't serving me—grief, hurts, resentments, instances of not feeling as though I was enough in life. All these came to the surface to be released. Each weekend I felt lighter, more available to what life was bringing me in that moment, not what it had brought me up until then.

Other than the release I just described during the second weekend, the fourth class also allowed me to let go of energy that was not my own, particularly energy I still held onto from people who had already left this world. Known in OLHT classes as "the male / female weekend," the healings focus on energy we have taken on from our mother, our father, and other significant males and females in our life. As the healing proceeds, we are invited to become aware of such energy in our body and to release it.

Starting the exercise, I felt as though I had already let go of all the energy I had picked up from others throughout my life. Not so; not so at all. In the healing, I became aware of how much I still held of my mother's energy—energy from her telling me men were not to be trusted, from her own unhappiness with her life, and of being told incessantly to "thank God you're breathing" (short form for don't expect anything else in life). This energy was lodged primarily in my back, my abdomen, and my head. I thrashed about and screamed to get it out of me once and for all. I knew it was not supportive of the life I want to live and the person I want to be.

As the session continued, I felt mixed emotions of releasing energy related to Brendan. There was not much I was holding onto—but there was an ache in my heart. I breathed with that ache until it released and I became free of it. I trusted that would allow my heart to become more available to today.

That weekend also included releasing feelings that were linked to our male / female energy. These emotions included grief, fear, unworthiness, jealousy, and people-pleasing, to name just a few.

Again becoming aware of where I held them in my body, I vowed to release them to the Universe through my focus and the skillful hands of my healer partner. By the end of the weekend, I was completely drained but in a good way. I was drained of so much blocked energy I had carried around in my body pretty much my whole life. There was a new freedom to life for me.

The following month's class was not nearly as exhausting but was equally profound in a very different way. That weekend we worked with the energies of the four archangels in doing healing work. As a precursor to doing healings with them, we were invited to go into meditation to connect with each, one at a time, note our impressions, and ultimately choose one to be our primary partner in archangelic healings.

It was Gabriel who captured my heart with a very simple message. (Appropriate since Gabriel is known as the Messenger of God.) I was lying on a yoga mat as we went through the full meditation. The first one was Michael, who I did not connect with at all; he seemed much too stern for me. Next was Uriel, the Light of God. I began to relax and trust the power of this group with the gentle energy brought forth with this angel. Third up was Gabriel, who the moment Nancy called him forth, I had a sense of his taking my hand and saying "Come. Let me introduce you to God." The last was Rafael, who was also a powerful guide for me but I had already pledged my allegiance to Gabriel in honor of the journey he was willing to take me on.

Some of the changes from that work happened between classes as I did my practice and shared healings with others. As I sat in meditation at my home one day, I was confronted by who I was in the fucked-up, confused, tumultuous drinking days of my 20's and early 30's. I was overcome with this young woman's confusion, her emptiness, her sadness. I didn't judge her for what she didn't know or what mattered to her. I was able to see her (my) brokenness, the brokenness she (I) desperately hid from everyone. I was able to find compassion for this younger version of me, the one who was trying to live by the rules. The one who didn't know who she was. The one who didn't know Spirit. The one who simply didn't know. I could forgive her at last. I could forgive *myself* at last.

So much opened up for me in that first time through the Basic, as soon as it was over, I signed up to take it again. I was aware this first time through I had been focused mostly on my own healing, but I knew this was work I wanted to offer in the world. Taking the class again would allow me to continue and deepen my own healing, but it would also allow me to become more familiar with the over thirty healing techniques that had been introduced in the class so I could use them more comfortably with clients.

It would also allow me to continue to strengthen my connection with Spirit. I had explained to a friend that One Spirit and One Light Healing Touch had been the two most transformative educational experiences of my life. One Spirit had introduced me to a more expansive and loving God than I had previously thought possible. One Light was now helping me to open to the possibility of a true partnership with that God, one where I could truly be used as a channel for Her power.

It was in my second experience of the OLHT basic that a new version of "Stories of my Heart" was written. As we did healing technique after healing technique, I more clearly saw all that had blocked my heart from being open, aware that residue had built up layer upon layer. As I clearly saw a physical representation of all these layers being removed, the following poem came to me:

My heart has been
buried under layers &
layers of armor for years.

First to go was the full-body protection
of a rusted steel suit—
impenetrable but also stifling.

Then I discovered the heavily padlocked concrete bar
blocking access to my heart.
With love & light, it too fell by the wayside.

Recently layers of heavy mud were hauled away.
These days a light clay coating still keeps
my heart from the sun—
but it is light enough that the flowers
are starting to break through

I look forward
to the
garden.

CHAPTER 43

D espite the deep healing and occasional glimpse of bliss my energy healing classes brought me, life itself continued to bring challenges. Financially "the wolves were at the door" (to borrow a friend's analogy). I had put my house in Hillsdale on the market as soon as all the renovation was done, but that unfortunately coincided with a major downturn in the real estate market, so the house sat. As it sat, I knew one thing I needed to deal with in that decision was that Brendan's ashes had been buried there.

Expecting the day to come where the house would sell, I did not want to add the heart-wrenching task of digging up his ashes when I was already in the very difficult process of selling the house he and I had bought together. So, with much trepidation, I plunged into the hard task of digging them up and relocating them to the basement of the store. They sat there for a few months, since I was absolutely clueless as to where I would end up living long-term.

Finally, one day as I took my winter stroll along Coumeau Trail in Woodstock, I realized Brendan's request that I keep him with me no longer felt as true. It felt like it was time for him to join Mother Earth once again. I knew this was the right place. It was where I went for peace and solace when life got too hectic so I wished to offer him its eternal peace and solace. Admittedly, it was also perfect that it was in Woodstock, an appropriate resting place for the rock star wannabe.

On my next visit to the trail, mid-afternoon on a wintry day, I took his urn with me. Carefully looking around me as I did not want to share this moment with anyone, I strolled onto my favorite rock in the middle of the stream, said a prayer, said "I love you" and scattered half the ashes in the flowing water. Wiping a freezing tear from my cheek, I then hiked back to land, sat on a large dead tree that now served as a perfect sitting place, and emptied the rest of the remains onto the ground. I was surprised to see the ashes recognizable even months later as I took my strolls.

While this was a choice that gave me freedom, and I believe gave Brendan's Spirit freedom as well, in retrospect it was a choice that didn't thrill his family. Gail, Brendan's mother, borrowed the explanation of her oldest son, who had commented he wanted a place where he could go visit Brendan. Although he never had visited Brendan's resting place when it was on our house grounds, I do understand the comfort that can offer people. That belief is just counter to mine, which is that we can visit our deceased loved ones anytime, anywhere by merely calling them forth. I chose the freedom.

Several months afterward, I realized there was another area in my life that needed freedom as well. It was time to close Inspired! With the house not selling, I had moved into it and rented the apartment above the store in an attempt to stop the financial bleeding. That meant I was living an hour's drive from my store that had never been anywhere close to breaking even financially. As much as I loved my store and what it offered me from a heart and spiritual perspective, practically it was draining me on many levels. That had to change.

On another front, a line in Stephen Levine's book, *Unattended Sorrow*, struck me deeply. It read, "We need to forgive ourselves

for occasionally being more desirous of love than able to offer it."
I knew that was the perfect description for how I had dealt with
any close relationship—family or romantic—until I got sober
and met Brendan. I was determined not to return to that same
modus operandi, regardless of whatever fear was coming forth.
I increasingly longed for deep connection with the people in
my life and I promised myself I will not settle for less—but that
doesn't mean it's easy.

I had dated a few men since Brendan's death and was most
definitely becoming more available to the connection and intimacy
a relationship could offer. When I had moved back to Brooklyn
from North Carolina, I finally let my heart open (even before
taking any healing classes, surprisingly enough). Pete, who I had
known from living in the Slope previously, was consistent in his
pursuit, despite my apparent fear. Our relationship only lasted three
months due to Pete's other commitments, mostly taking the form
of four children from two previous relationships, but I knew a shift
had taken place in my life. Pete remains in my heart to this day, even
though he, too, has left this world due to a massive heart attack.

My next significant relationship was with Blair. He and I had
been friendly but I was still surprised when he came by the store
one Friday evening to invite me over for a specially prepared
home-cooked dinner. That dinner turned into nearly a year of
dating, including a lovely vacation to Mexico. Although our time
together was easy, comfortable, and sweet, it became clear that this
relationship too had its limitations. We split between Christmas
and New Year's. As we were hanging out at his apartment, I
offered hesitatingly, "You know, I have this sense that, even
though we don't have a failed relationship now, we will before
long if we stay together." He sadly understood and agreed, but
remains a very close friend to this day.

The next man I dated proved to be my biggest romantic
mistake since my engagement to Ed back in my alcohol-drenched

life. The whole experience reminded me how easily I could still get off track if I didn't take my time, listen to my intuition, and check in honestly with people I respect. A few months after breaking up with Blair and moving full-time back to Hillsdale, I met an attractive man who came on very strongly. I was in a very vulnerable place, living in a new area where I knew very few people, and running a failing business. I was "ripe for the picking" so if this guy was going to pledge everlasting, undying love to me, even if it was ridiculously and inappropriately early in our relationship, that was fine by me.

It didn't take long for me to realize this was not meant to be. He fought with me over many decisions in my life, instead of supporting me. Even more important was that he wanted me to deny big chunks of who I was and what I believed. The ending took the form of a phone conversation when I said to him, "You know. I just feel like I need to speak some things here. I am an Interfaith minister. I am an energy healer. I am a woman who is involved with politics and social issues, and I am a person who will engage with our judicial system when I feel like that's the best way to resolve a dispute." As I finished "speaking my truth" (to borrow his own words), he got angry at what I had said, stated he wasn't going to try to keep up with that, and hung up the phone. We did the obligatory exchange of personal effects a couple weeks down the road, but the relationship was definitely over with that conversation. It was replaced by my discovering the song "I Am What I Am" from *La Cage aux Folles*. I spent most of the summer blaring that tune, singing along and reminding myself of my passionate desire to live true to my soul.

Just as had been the case with my relationship with Ed and the resulting break-up, this relationship made it clear that, given what was going on in my life, I was not in an emotional state to be part of a couple. I took some time off from dating.

CHAPTER 44

During the time off from dating, life presented me with the opportunity to focus on family relationships instead. Having caught up with one of my cousins on Mom's side of the family, Dan and I talked about the last time most of the family was together, almost twenty years earlier at Grandma Karpen's funeral. Since I hadn't attended that, due to Ed's insistence we couldn't afford for me to go, it had been even longer since I had seen most of my Karpen relatives. We talked about how nice it would be for everyone to get together again.

Instead of letting the talk stop there, I arranged a conference call with a few other cousins, especially those in the Jefferson, South Dakota area since we would hold it in the home base. My cousin, Doyle, and his wife were all over this idea, as were several others. After a series of conference calls where we collected everyone's email addresses, assigned tasks, and secured the location, the reunion was definitely on. In July 2009 we had an amazing gathering with Mom's three remaining Karpen siblings, ranging in age from 88 to 94, all looking amazingly sprightly, and approximately seventy-five of their descendants now spread over three more generations.

I was so touched by the gratitude of Mom's brother and sisters especially, but of many that attended. It was gratifying to have worked with cousins I hadn't seen in years to put together a reunion where cousins shared memories, distant cousins played together for the first time, and aunts saw the children they had often unofficially helped to raise as adults getting on in their own years.

That amazing family experience was followed just a week later by a trip to France with Brendan's family for the wedding of Julia, the oldest niece. Since Vero, Julia's mother, was originally from France and their family visited every summer at her maternal grandmother's house, Julia and Kurt had opted to have their wedding there. My mother-in-law, Gail, had graciously given all the kids, spouses, and grandkids (me included) their flight over as our gift for the previous Christmas. I was touched and a bit surprised to be included to that extent. When I had first heard of the engagement, I figured I would get an invitation but didn't expect what I got—at any level.

It was indeed time for me to finally understand I was fully a part of Brendan's family, even years after his death. This was driven home beautifully at the welcoming party the first evening everyone had arrived at her grandma's estate. A lovely barbecue dinner was held with people joyously mingling around greeting old friends and making new ones. In speaking with one of Julia's friends from college, she asked me how I was connected to this group. I hesitated, repeating the question to buy some time. I didn't want to get into the full explanation of Julia's Uncle Brendan and possibly bring down the joy that was all around but I didn't know what else to say. Fortunately Julia herself was in earshot of the question and very simply and joyously offered the answer, "She's my aunt", to which I replied, "Yep. I'm her aunt." It turned out nothing more needed to be said.

Now that I had finally gotten it through my thick head that Brendan's family was indeed my family, I felt more comfortable inviting them to join me in a tenth anniversary celebration of Brendan's and my wedding. Understandably there was some discomfort with that until I explained where I was coming from in an awkward but sentimental toast to all of them. I said, "I realize it is a strange thing to celebrate an anniversary when half that couple has been dead for several years, but really an anniversary celebration is about the journey. That's why I wanted to honor this day with all of you that have so graciously shared that journey with me over these last ten years." While choking back tears, I then went on to admit it had taken until just the year prior before I finally allowed myself to consider them family and me a part of it. I explained, "It was not until Julia's wedding shower, as I watched photos being taken of Vero and the four girls, and thought about all we had shared in the time I had known you all, that I really understood that we are all family." I then added the story about Julia's simple acknowledgement of me as her aunt at the wedding and how much that meant to me.

They were all words I meant with my heart and soul; indeed saying those words to them was the sole (and soul) purpose of honoring the tenth anniversary of our wedding. Those words now carried new depth to them, since just two days before I had gotten a call from Gail, my mother-in-law, that she was very ill. After having dealt with bouts of exhaustion for a few weeks, she had gone to the doctor who had diagnosed her with lung cancer. They were also concerned it had most likely spread to her brain already. She did not have all the information, but the prognosis did not look good.

I hung up from that phone call with another round of sobs in what felt like an already sob-filled life. In some ways, I loved Gail more deeply than my own mother. I had had nothing but love and support from her in the over ten years that I had known her. I had watched this woman go through so much in that time—burying all three of her siblings, her husband, and her son—with more faith and grace than any other human I knew. I had seen her blossom from a rather dependent wife, certainly second fiddle in their marriage, to a laughing, strong, independent woman. I had come to personally learn firsthand of a tribute that Brendan had paid her, that she was able to have a unique and special relationship with each and every one of her seven children, knowing and honoring each of them as the individual he/she was. This gift also encompassed her four daughters-in-law, two sons-in-law, and thirteen grandchildren as well. I expect it also encompassed each and every one of her friends, a few of whom she had been close with since grade school. This was a special woman the world was losing, that I was losing.

Even though I did get to say my piece at that Sunday gathering, Gail's news was a prominent backdrop to the day. She had requested it not be mentioned then since some of her grandchildren hadn't yet been told about her illness. It surprised me a little, therefore, when that day she openly—albeit discreetly—offered the comment that she had thought she was ready to go as soon as her beloved Joe died, but that she was seeing things in a new light now that she was actually face-to-face with her own likely demise. I just listened and held her hand. A little later in our conversation, she mentioned the song I had heard after Brendan died and asked me what the title of it was, noting she would like to hear it again. I answered, "The Other Side" and made a mental note to buy her a copy of the CD.

The next appointment with her doctor was, as expected, not good news. She started on a treatment of radiation and chemotherapy, with the expectation it was likely to be palliative and not curative. So she set about cleaning up her already beautiful life. She had a lunch at the Shore Club in New Rochelle for her friends and family, a lunch I did not attend because of healing class. The kids then arranged a Mother's Day celebration for her at her daughter, Sheila's house. It was there that I gave her my tribute—a card and letter thanking her for all she had done for both Brendan and me, as well as expressing my admiration for who she was and how she lived and loved. She told me later how much it meant to her, as well as her gift of "The Other Side." Next time I saw her was when I went to visit her at her apartment in Larchmont over Memorial Day. I couldn't help but remember it was that same weekend in the same apartment six years earlier I had said goodbye to my father-in-law. Gail herself was definitely looking more depleted all the time and acknowledged she was indeed starting to experience sensation and discomfort, still not pain, but a growing awareness of the tumors in her body.

It was another few weeks, during which I got updates about her decline including the details of her hospitalizations, before I saw her again. Even before Gail had been diagnosed, I had scheduled a trip out West for the end of June, first to attend a trade show promoting a small business I was trying to build, followed by a birthday celebration with friends who had moved to Santa Fe. I had intended to make the trip down to visit Gail on Wednesday, June 23, before leaving that Friday. When I called her home phone early Tuesday afternoon to confirm my visit and got no answer, I knew it was not good news. I called Eden to find out what was going on. Sure enough, they had taken her into Calvary Hospital for her final days, just as so many of her loved ones had seen theirs. Based on the conversation I had with Eden, I decided to cancel the two healing clients I had scheduled for that afternoon and immediately head down—and I am so glad I did. When I arrived, she was napping, but she soon came to and was fully present and fully conscious, in pain but most definitely the loving Gail I knew.

As I was getting ready to leave, I thanked her once again for who she was and all she had done for me, to which she graciously replied, "You were the best thing to happen to this family in a long time." Getting choked up, I retorted, "Yeah, you guys needed some sprucing up," knowing Gail would understand that as coming from love and the humor we so frequently shared. As I was heading out the door, Eden suggested I write down the phone number to the room so I could keep in touch during my travels. Very, very clearly after that suggestion, Gail said, "I'll be talking to you, Ann", which I knew meant even if not while in this world.

Two days later, the day before I was to leave on my trip to Denver and Santa Fe, I got a call from Joe, her oldest son, right around noon. I knew she had died. I knew it that morning when I woke up with a sense of peace and comfort coming from Gail's soul. It also didn't surprise me in the least when he said that she had died around 3:30 in the morning, for I had awoken at that time, not entirely certain she had passed but definitely aware of her soul.

I was sad I was not going to be present for her funeral, but I had invested time, effort, and money in this trip, and I knew Gail wouldn't want me to miss it. She had even told me so when I visited her at Calvary. I also trusted I would somehow be given a special opportunity to say my own goodbyes, and I was. During the trip to Santa Fe, my friends and I took a road trip to Taos. On the way there, Mario turned off the main road and said, "You've got to see this. We've only been here once ourselves, but it's an old adobe sanctuary that is incredibly special. People walk here every Good Friday from Albuquerque, which is an hour-and-a-half drive." As we got out of the car, I knew this was my chance to bid Gail "Adieu." It was a Catholic sanctuary—perfect given Gail's devout faith. The chapel and grounds were very simple, yet with exquisite mosaic tile statuary throughout. I chose one particular statue outside, a beautiful depiction of the Blessed Mary joyful and surrounded by birds, to say a prayer of good-bye and gratitude. I then went in to join my friends, comfortable in the way I had connected with Gail's soul.

CHAPTER 45

A couple weeks later, I was still feeling the heaviness of Gail's death when I went to the healing class I was currently taking, the Master's level course with OLHT. In this class, we were learning to work with energies and entities beyond those of our physical body and even beyond the physical realm. This class, taught by Ron Lavin, the founder of One Light Healing Touch, was opening me well beyond what the training I had had so far did.

Given this, it was no surprise to me I got a message from Gail during that weekend. After all, she did tell me she'd be speaking to me. Her message was I'd see her again, that I would know her two lifetimes from now as my best friend. I took great comfort in that thought, remembering the comfort Brendan and I took in realizing how intertwined our souls are with those we love most deeply. It would make sense that Gail's spirit and mine would connect again in another life.

There was, however, a surprise I did get during that Master's level class. On the first day, I was particularly intrigued to see a tall, cute young man of about 25 in with the group comprised mostly of middle-aged white women. I was glad to see Ryan break through the traditional boundaries of both age and gender in his spiritual quest, yet there was something about him that also made me a little uncomfortable. I did not know how to relate to him; I couldn't understand what had brought him there.

During a meditation in the third month of the class, I developed the sense that Ryan was Robbie incarnate. A tenderness came over me as I contemplated this possibility. With Robbie having been dead for over forty years, logistically it fit. Plus, Ryan had the same coloring as Robbie and a similar smirk as well. I realize similar appearances don't always happen across lifetimes—indeed it may be the exception rather than the rule— but in this case it added to my belief my classmate had been my cousin earlier in life. I decided to ask Ryan if this felt true to him, then brought in a picture that I had of Robbie for him to check out. Ryan had a sense this *might* be true, which was exactly my own perspective.

The following month as I encountered Ryan while entering class, I greeted him, "Hi, Robin." I was confused and a little embarrassed as to where this had come from, because I certainly knew his name. Why I had spaced on it and/or slipped up with it puzzled me. Then I realized what I had said and noticed the parallel between the names, that the name I had called him was actually a combination of Robbie and Ryan, his names over the past two lives. My sense of him as my long-lost cousin grew.

This possibility also opened my heart to Ryan more deeply than would have been the case if he was just another classmate— and that is always a good thing. It invited me to get to know this incarnation of a beautiful soul. In saying "yes" to that invitation, I was also given the honor of officiating at the wedding between Ryan and his soulmate, Ashling, in one of the sweetest, love-filled and joy-filled weddings I have ever witnessed.

Whether or not we will ever learn anything more to confirm Ryan as Robbie incarnate, I don't know. He may or may not be. What I do know is that having this possibility enter into my consciousness during spiritual practice has reminded me our loved ones are never really gone from our lives. We may not be able to play with them in the sandbox anymore, but they remain in our hearts and our souls remain connected to their souls throughout eternity. When the time is right, we will see them again; perhaps we will recognize them, perhaps not.

CHAPTER 46

One other thing I had shared with my mother-in-law, Gail, the last day I saw her was that I was dating a man, Mick, who had the same birthday as Brendan— October 15. It was in our first conversation he had off-handedly mentioned his birthday was in October. I immediately asked, "When?", having a very strong sense it was probably the day shared with my beloved on the other side. He responded, "Middle of the month. The 15th", causing me to take a deep breath and remind myself it might mean nothing. It did score him brownie points however. So did the fact that he was freaking hilarious, smart, and sexy. With a little distance between us, we only saw each other every few weeks but were speaking daily and dating exclusively. It was a good thing—not perfect, but good.

Until he dropped off the face of the earth Thanksgiving week as I traveled down to my brother's in North Carolina for the holiday. Each and every day I would dial the phone to check in, only to get his answering machine and no call back. By Wednesday, the day before Thanksgiving, I was livid and hurt; this behavior was completely inconsistent with what I had seen so far. Finally, the day after Thanksgiving it occurred to me something might have happened to him. Not knowing any of his friends or family members to call, I did a Google search using his name and town. Sure enough, a newspaper article from that week popped up. Reading the article, it was apparent his younger son had been killed in a car accident the previous Saturday morning.

I went downstairs to the kitchen where my brother and one of his daughters were having breakfast and told them what I had found out, adding I would be leaving immediately to get home in time for the service being held the next day.

I made it in plenty of time to get myself to an AA meeting before driving to the memorial service. The funeral home was overflowing with people of all ages—including dozens of Matt's compadres in their teens and early 20's. Many of them were sporting hoodies, with a picture of Matt and the phrase, "You will never be forgotten." I only spoke briefly to Mick, who was seated at the front next to his ex-wife, Matt's mother. He seemed happy to see me—as happy as could be anyhow—but I knew he was devastated beyond words. His sons had been the focus of his life since they were born. I had no expectations whatsoever as to what would become of us, knowing he was in the throes of the worst loss imaginable.

What I did not expect was I would be contacted by Matt's spirit, but that's exactly what happened. The second night after his memorial service, I was awakened by Matt's spirit, confused, disoriented. I had often heard that people who have not found their spiritual connection often don't know they are dead. Matthew, loving soul that he was, had not yet found a path in life that fed him, that nourished him. He, like many of our young people—let me take that back, like I was at his age—was concerned with doing what he wanted to do in the moment. Yes, that often included generous gestures such as being available to his friends, but it still seemed to lack God. So it's not surprising he did not know what was going on or where he was. Drawing upon my healing work, I called forth a column of Light and invited him into it. I did that the next morning after his appearance, and every day for the next week until I had a sense he was getting comfortable with where he was. I then used a more advanced healing technique to open the path to the souls who live on the other side, where he was now to live. Following in the Buddhist tradition that it takes a soul fifty days to make a full transition to the spirit world, I continued this work for that time period. The whole process reminds me of an invitation Elizabeth Lesser offers in *The Seeker's Guide*, that of ushering a soul to the spiritual realm when it is their time.

This work with Matt allowed me to remember Brendan's passing and the certainty it offered me that there is something on the other side. Now, through the healing work I do, I am able to have a more complete experience of what is there through my connection with Spirit—Divine Spirit as well as the individual Spirit of one who has died.

The other thing Matt's death reminded me is that people grieve in different ways. While I needed the support and love of family, friends, and community, Mick went into a cave to deal with his loss. While I was comforted by my spiritual beliefs, the loss of Matt had caused Mick to doubt that connection. I have learned that my way of being there for him had to be through sending light and healing and holding him in prayers, and trust that these are all getting through on the spiritual level. I must admit to being relieved that Mick shared with me a story about the accident that proves he was aware of Spirit's presence. We have spoken of this many times, and I know he is open and available to the spiritual world; I found hope in recognizing this perspective was present even in his horrible, painful time of grief.

Today Mick is making progress in rebuilding his life. He has done his own seeking, including making contact with Matt's soul through a medium. It took a full year after the tragedy of his loss before I felt it was right to give him the few pages I had written to document my journey with Matt. He remains a dear friend, albeit not one I speak with often. I have sometimes wondered if the reason Mick and I came into each other's lives was so I would be available to Matt when his time came. One never knows.

CHAPTER 47

W hat I do know is that grieving is a road we must travel. It is a journey, a journey that unfolded for me with little guidance and not a lot of support in my early experiences of loss. I had to piece together the process, so I would like to offer here what I have learned to be the core of healing from grief. Those things are:

- Get clear the unresolved grief you are carrying and the impact it's having on your life.

  So frequently grief is dismissed. We tell ourselves we weren't close enough to someone to grieve their loss, when in reality that person was part of our life for many years. We diminish our pain because of mixed emotions we had towards the deceased. We think our loss happened too long ago to still be having an impact on our life. These things are not necessarily true.

  When you feel stuck and unable to move forward, go back and look at the losses in your life and how you got through them. See if maybe there is more work, more healing, to do around them. This may even entail making a timeline of all the major losses and transitions in your life, as recommended by some grief experts. Be willing to do the work and delve deeply. As Ralph Waldo Emerson invites, "Be not the slave of your own past. Plunge into the sublime seas, dive deep and swim far, so you shall come back with self-respect, with new power, with an advanced experience that shall explain and overlook the old."

- Make a commitment to your healing; ideally, make it a central focus of your life.

There are responsibilities and tasks we face each and every day and there always will be—but these do not need to overtake our life and define us fully. Stephen Covey writes about how often we let the urgent (or what is perceived to be urgent) overtake what is important. Remember that at the end of our own lives, nothing is likely to be more important than the time and effort we put into the healing of our soul.

Make time every day to tune into this journey and how it is calling to you right now. Carve out larger chunks of time when it is clear what the next level of deeper work is for you. Acknowledge that your journey may indeed go beyond what is traditionally called "grief" but do not use that as an excuse to avoid or diminish the healing that needs to happen around the losses you have experienced.

- Build / strengthen a support network.

This is hard, deep work. Surround yourself with people that will support you in these efforts—both professionals and friends. Similarly, try to minimize time with people that will negate or diminish your feelings and what you are going through.

Be honest with yourself about the help you need. If you need help with the most basic tasks of life, give yourself permission to ask for that. It's all part of the process. Trust that by giving yourself this gift now, you will be able to be available to others when they need your support for the same reason.

• Develop faith in something outside of yourself to see you through this.

A lot of people get tripped up here, thinking it needs to be God with the capital 'G'. It doesn't. That was a part of my process, but I know plenty of other choices people have made. There are those who have been nourished by developing a closer relationship to nature and an awe and trust in its cycles. Others have developed spiritual (not religious) practices that served them.

It doesn't matter what you choose, but it is important to allow yourself the comfort of something outside yourself that can offer the possibility that—maybe, just maybe— things are unfolding as they should, even when your heart and mind is screaming that you shouldn't be having to go through this, that it's not fair. Something that invites you to take a breath, to remember that more is happening than meets the eye in any given moment.

• Go through the process.

Needless to say, there are many points to be made under this very broad category of "going through the process". I am going to keep this as simple as possible with what I consider the three main considerations here.

The first is to recognize the impact grief has on all aspects of your life—physical, mental, emotional, and spiritual—and therefore the need to bring focus to all of them. Be aware that your body and energy have taken a hit every bit as much as your emotions and psyche, so make sure that your healing is not one-dimensional.

In recognition that your entire being has been impacted by loss, be very, very gentle with yourself during this process. You may at times be forgetful, even on the most basic, simple things in life. You may be so out of touch with your physical being that you do not recognize when you are hungry or tired. Those are completely normal byproducts of grief so do not judge yourself for them. At the same time, it is also equally important to heed the nudges of loved ones when you do need to face things—whether that is life circumstances or how you are holding your relationship with the deceased. Allow yourself to open to the guidance of your compassionate, loving network as you move through the stages of grief and healing.

The last part of going through the process is developing a new relationship with the deceased. Yes, physically they are gone and you need to come to terms with that. Still you have an emotional and spiritual connection to your loved one. Learn to develop, honor, and cherish this new connection. Reach out to them when you need to feel their presence. Honor when you need to take a little space. Recognize you have a right to consciously choose how you relate to them, but don't just slam the door on your connection. It's too much of a gift. While this new way of connecting with your beloved may not be comfortable all the time, it is important to moving on in a healthy, available way.

- Enjoy the blessings of your efforts.

As healing starts to happen, the joys of life will come back to you. You will find pleasure in old hobbies, perhaps develop new interests, and engage deeply in relationships. Laughter will come once again, and you will find blessings in the first spring buds. Allow yourself to enjoy all this.

At this time in our recovery, our mind might try to convince us we are being disloyal by moving on. We tell ourselves that our beloved no longer enjoys these pleasures; why should we? The reason we should is because we are still breathing, we are alive. It is our right to enjoy our life, even a tribute to the one no longer in our life to do so. So let yourself learn to revel in the blessings of life once again.

- Know—and accept—that healing is a process, not an event.

We do not wake up one day and find we never again have an ache from the passing of a loved one. Instead we begin to realize that weeks have started to go by where our memories are sweet rather than painful. Then seemingly out of nowhere, a dark day will take over; one that has us reliving those first days after the loss.

That's perfectly normal. It does not mean you are not recovering. It is simply that integration is a two steps forward—one step back process. Special dates, certain events, and memories will bring on those steps backwards—but rest assured the healing process is still intact. It just means it isn't completely over, at least not until we are the ones that take our last breath.

CHAPTER 48

I have buried my parents, my husband, my in-laws, young cousins, middle-aged friends, and many elderly relatives. I have been through long illnesses with people, and I have received that shocking phone call or visit that someone near and dear to me has unexpectedly left this earth. It seems whenever I feel as though I have faced death, loss, and grief in every way possible, I am shown this is not the case.

The challenge in writing a book on the process of grief is that the process never ends. Always life gives us more loss, more death to deal with. Just a month ago, I led a memorial service for a very dear friend of mine who lost a long-standing battle to his disease. A few months before that, my 52-year-old brother was diagnosed with terminal colon cancer already metastasized to his lung, liver, and stomach. Now, every other weekend, he wears a fanny pack that carries the chemo that drips into his veins, trying to give him as much time as possible with his wife and five children.

Yet, despite the ongoing presence of death, I know grief no longer owns me. It does not define my life. It does not constrict my relationships. My past, present, and future all show me this is true.

A creative project for a Spiritual Counseling class helped me see this in relation to my past. The assignment was to use a creative medium to illustrate where we are today in our spiritual / life journey. Instantly it came to me to do a lifetime photographic retrospective set to the tune "Return to Innocence" by Enigma. As I assembled all the photos, I could look at all of them with equanimity and compassion—and, most important, own that they were indeed all me. The photo of Brendan and me on our wedding day brings a bittersweet tug to my heart, more sweet than bitter and certainly not the ache and pain of longing I experienced for years after his death. I hurt for, yet understand, the young woman I am in the Christmas picture taken right after Mom's death. She is (I am) immaculately dressed and accessorized, yet holding a glass of wine with empty—and confused—eyes. As I go through all of the photos of my 51 years, finally I connect to them all and know I am the same person, the same soul, as the woman in the picture. That is something I could never say when burdened with unfelt and unhealed grief.

The movie *The Bucket List* proves to me my future also is not restricted by grief. When I first saw the film where Morgan Freeman and Jack Nicholson play two older men in their final days of life who decide to list and then pursue all the activities they think will make their life complete, I loved the notion of that clarity and purpose to the days of life. But I couldn't get myself to commit to what those activities would be. I couldn't even get myself to commit to really *thinking* about what those activities would be. Now, on the list I have to set foot on all seven continents, drive cross-country (visiting all fifty states) by myself, watch a baby being born, and become a published author. All those things are slowly but surely being checked off—and I am bringing a level of presence and excitement to them I didn't have access to earlier in my life.

As far as today goes, I love each and every day of my life. I treasure the simple pleasure of taking the dogs for their morning walk, appreciating the beauty of the hills in the distance and the design of my neighbors' lawns and gardens. After spending years in an office trying to convince people to buy things they didn't need, I am in awe that clients share their journeys and their hearts with me, whether in a healing session or a spiritual counseling discussion. Even more, I am starting to teach the One Light Healing Touch work to others so they too can experience profound healing and know the honor of offering that to their friends, family, and acquaintances. My creative life continues to blossom with my writing, photography, and word prints. I have already seen more of this world than I would ever have dared dream of as I grew up on my suburban street—and my renewed passport just got here a few weeks ago.

Today I choose to live my life fully, to be open to whatever life brings, not to be haunted or bound by unexpressed, unhealed grief. As I wrote that sentence, my mind challenged me with the thought, "Yeah? How do you know you're fully living your life?" It's actually a very good question. I need to check in with the following questions: What is the condition of my spiritual life? Am I doing what I need to do to stay sober? Beyond that, am I doing what will allow me to learn, heal, and deepen my connection to Spirit? Am I following the nudges guiding my life? Am I pursuing my dreams? Do I even know what they are? Am I living authentically, saying what is true for me and not being driven by people-pleasing or putting on a show? Are my days being spent in a way that is consistent with my personal mission of offering healing and inspiration to individuals so they may more fully step into lives of purpose, consciousness, and joy? Am I grateful for every experience life gives me, even the painful ones? Most days I can answer those questions with an honest "yes."

At the core of all of this is a deep understanding that the only path on the journey from grief to joy is indeed *through* grief, and an equally deep trust it is possible to get to the other side. The path may not be pristine and well-trimmed with light shining down, illuminating the way. There are areas of thick, dark, mud—quicksand-like in that they seem able to swallow us whole if we just stand one second too long or take a step in the wrong direction.

It's no wonder so many of us are reluctant to tread this path. Nor are we usually encouraged to do so either. Well-meaning friends and relatives will tell us to "keep busy," to not venture too fully into our grief. Even those who acknowledge we need to go there, we often find calling out to us impatiently, figuratively tapping their foot or wristwatch, warning us—subtly or not—that time is up. It is no longer beneficial for us to walk this path…Correction. They feel it is no longer beneficial for us to walk this path.

Grief takes what it takes. It takes the tears. It takes the days, weeks, months even, of feeling spaced out, unable to connect with life at all.

I have been deeply blessed and honored to finally learn tools to get through this process. I now recognize Great Spirit is always available to me, even when it does not seem so. It may take a little more effort for me to reach out. I may even need to remind myself that I do have faith and trust in God. I have delved into many spiritual paths to better understand the cycle of life and death and have come to accept it as a never-ending journey. Plus I have experienced the true healing power of releasing energy from my body, energy that merely traps the loss, never allowing regeneration.

By trudging the path of grief every time we are faced with a loss that tears at our soul, we do get to venture onto the path of joy during this lifetime. Eventually, we get to travel that Divinely manicured road with the sun shining down on our faces. We do get to know our own version of "Paradise on Earth" that seemed so elusive when I first heard the prayer for it during my early days at Johrei.

I am grateful for each and every painful loss I have had to go through, for it has only been because of the love and the connection I had with each person that the sorrow ran so deep. I know that virtually all of the blessings of my life today have come from what I shared with the loved ones who are now gone from my life, especially Brendan. I honor the omnipresence of the spiritual realm, guiding me through the darkness of grief so I now can say, "I have grieved"—and I have a beautiful life as a result.

Still, I know this journey of needing to open to grief, to release the pain of loss, to do the work necessary to heal, will continue for as long as I breathe. But no matter how many losses I have in life, no matter how many opportunities for grief to overtake my soul, joy is still my birthright...just as it is for each and every one of us.

My wish is that everyone who reads these words finds their own path of healing, Light, and courage so they may know this peace.

CPSIA information can be obtained at www.ICGtesting.com
Printed in the USA
BVOW081456300613

324665BV00001B/1/P